Tragic to Magic

Beyond Suffering with the Akashic Records

Tragic to Magic

Beyond Suffering with the Akashic Records

Chris Wilson

Contents

Intention

My intention is to help people to open up to a bigger picture of life:

- To connect with their souls through the Akashic Records.

- To become empowered in their own right so they can take responsibility for every aspect of their life, in this lifetime and other lifetimes.

- To see and understand the truth of the human story - of where we have been, where we are now and where we are going.

- To learn to love themselves fully and utterly...

- To help move humanity beyond suffering forever.

Dedication

To my mother Helen Binns who carries the Codes of Light. Her life has been one of self-sacrifice and of giving to others. She has lightened the lives of many with her kindness, concern and sense of humour. Her love and devotion to her five daughters has made it possible for us to be of service to many people. This family legacy is now being passed down to her grandchildren and great-grandchildren.

Acknowledgements

Thank you to all those who have given me permission to share their soul information and stories.

To Stella Carruthers, my editor who reviewed this book and gave me many helpful suggestions.

To my husband, Martin Wilson who supported me in many ways as I wrote this book.

To Donna Falconer for her stunning cover photograph.

To Gail MacKenzie for proof reading help.

To Sue Davis, Jennifer Binns and Caroline Anson who provided me with peaceful writing spaces.

Introduction

Some of what I have written may be controversial. While there is increasing scientific evidence for many of the energy changes I write about, scientific method and research takes time and the proof usually lags behind what many of us know to be true. For some of my material the only validation currently available is from channelled entities or from Akashic information I have received. When I taught a new approach to parenting in my conscious parenting courses from 1999–2013, some of the ideas were considered questionable. These concepts are now mainstream and this has taught me to trust in my thoughts and in the information that I bring through. That being said, there is much I don't know and more yet to be discovered. This book is a reflection of my understanding and truth at the time of writing. It is important that you are discerning as you read. Take these words into your heart and find your own truth.

This book contains the energy of the magic of the Akashic Records. It is quantum. As I wrote it, I realised that I am becoming quantum too. Parts of it have come through at different times. It has not been a linear process. I am not an expert on the Akashic Records. I have purposely not read much about them because I wanted to come to them fresh. Some of what was written in the past reflects the old energy. Now that the energy on Earth is different, the Akashic Records are different. Everyone's take on them is unique and we all work with this multidimensional 'library' in the way that is perfect for us. What I have learned has been through being and working in their energy, on an almost daily basis, over the last ten years. I have received new information in a piecemeal fashion when I have been ready for it and I know there is more to come. I have had a glimpse into a different world of non-linear time and multidimensionality. I know that this learning will be an ongoing process for all of us in this life, in the next and probably in the one after that. We will never know all the answers. This is what makes life exciting!

This book has taken longer than anticipated. There have been some 'tragic' moments but it has mostly been a magical journey. As I near my destination I realise I have become a different person. In the process of writing this book I have been reborn. I have travelled from my own personal darkness into the light. It is my heartfelt wish that this book does the same for you. As you read it, I hope you have a magic moment (or two) and feel inspired to utilise the wisdom and life-changing energy of the Records to transport you to a higher consciousness and understanding.

Note:

- At the back of the book there is an alphabetical Glossary of words which may require extra explanation. They are marked in **bold** the first time they appear in the text.

- I have referred to the Third and the Fifth Dimensions repeatedly throughout the book. Sometimes they have been written out in full e.g. Third Dimension and Fifth Dimension and in others as 3D and 5D. These mean the same thing. Definitions can be found in the glossary.

- In some cases I have used a descriptor that is valid in its past life context but not acceptable now e.g. The use of 'gypsy' instead of Roma or Romany people.

- When I am sharing clients' past life stories I have placed quotation marks around their current name to indicate that I am talking about them in their past life context e.g. 'Chris' was filled with horror at what she had witnessed.

- I am grateful for the permission from clients and friends to share their soul information and stories. In most cases names have been changed to protect identities.

Chris Wilson, 2021

Chapter 1

Beyond Suffering

Nothing is as it seems. A magical transformation is happening on this planet. What appears on the surface to be chaos and mayhem is preparing the way for something better. As I write this, the world is at the mercy of Covid-19. Fear is raging and the uncertainty of the future is difficult to cope with. The pandemic has brought our planet to its knees and is forcing change on us at a rapidly accelerating pace. Today is not the same as yesterday. Tomorrow will be different again. The predictability of the past has gone forever. We are in a new normal.

For the **Old Souls** of Earth, change has not been good. Those of us who have lived many human lifetimes, hold the memories of some difficult experiences. Suffering has been our hallmark. On a deep level we know what has gone before and wonder why this should be any different. Our residual fear is bolstered and amplified by the society we live in. Fear and anxiety are everywhere, propagated by the media and exploding in the younger generation, many of whom have lost touch with the vital connections that have sustained us throughout the ages. At this crisis point, this crossroads, it is crucial that we remain resolute and calm in the knowledge that things can and will improve.

I have been working and immersing myself in the energy of the Akashic Records for ten years now. The main thing they have taught me is that the worst experiences of our lives can be our greatest gifts. As I said in *The Magic of the Akashic Records*, it was my grief, triggered by the life-threatening mental illness of my eldest child, that led me to the Akashic Records. They were a portal to the healing energy I craved and helped me to see the dramatic situation from a higher perspective. They gave me a new career which I love, more meaning to my life and are helping me to fulfil the deep desire I have had since birth to make a difference.

During this challenging and confronting time, new seeds were planted which are now bearing fruit. This low point in my life was the catalyst for new growth which has led to something so much better. I now live and breathe a higher purpose. I am able to look back on the heartache and pain of my daughter's illness with gratitude. I am grateful to my beautiful daughter, Alice, who is going from strength to strength and I am grateful for everything that has happened to me. My life has gone from tragic to magic.

The Akashic Records hold the energetic imprints of every thought, feeling and experience we have ever had in our lives on Earth. They can help us see and understand the bigger picture of our soul choices and human predicaments. Many of us have faced huge challenges in our current lifetimes. We are at the end of a cycle, moving from an energy of lower vibration (**Third Dimension**) into the Fifth and there are many loose ends to tie up. All that does not resonate with this new and higher frequency has to go. On a soul level many of us have chosen to be in close proximity to those we have unfinished business with. We have past life enemies in our families, our work places and even in our beds. We have set things up so we can let go of the old and bring in the new. We have planned our current life circumstances so we can release all that no longer serves us from incarnations in a lower consciousness. This is not an easy task. It has made for some difficult experiences, especially for the Old Souls who have many lifetimes under their belts.

Things often have to get worse before they get better. The unrelenting challenges and bombardment of energy have been testing in the extreme. This process has had its own timing and direction for us individually. No one has been spared and now the entire planet is experiencing it at the same time. It is important that we keep the faith, because just as society and life as we know it, is falling apart ... help is coming... the old structures are being dismantled and replaced by new, improved versions.

Just over the horizon is a new world of glistening possibilities. As humanity experiences this collective dark night of the soul it is important to remember that light is stronger than darkness, that the sun always rises in the morning and that soon it will be shining on a world of greater love, unity and joy.

As **lightworkers** it is our job to hold the space for this and the Akashic Records are the perfect tool for these changing times. They carry memories of the suffering we have experienced in our lifetimes on Earth but they also hold the potentials for the future. Where the soul is concerned there is always a bigger picture and a different agenda from the obvious. Working with the new energy it is easy to access the Records and find the answers to our deeper questions. This information can help us put a positive spin on the challenges and dramas we face.

The Akashic Records, the ancient library of the soul, is getting a twenty-first century make over. It is much more than a storehouse of past life information. It is a source of healing and high vibrational energy that we can use to transform every aspect of our lives. Within the Records, the possibilities are huge.

❋

For millennia the human race has suffered. Suffering has been our trade mark. It is what we have come to expect. According to Christian belief, from the moment Adam and Eve took a bite from the apple, we were condemned. We committed a sin and have been paying for it ever since. For centuries we have competed with and hurt and killed each other. We have been driven by greed, a lust for power and feelings of inadequacy. It has been estimated that 70–85 million people died in the two world wars of the twentieth century. From the lice, mud and trauma of the trenches in World War I, to the battle fields, genocide, civilian bombings and nuclear destruction of World War II, the suffering was immense. What did all this achieve? Was it necessary?

There were other wars in the twentieth century and there are still many hot spots on this planet of ours. We are still hurting and killing each other but there is change in the air. After centuries of murder and destruction, it has taken two global conflicts and we are not there yet: thousands of years of slaughter and competition to be more and to have more. Driven by the egos of mostly male leaders with psychological wounds, the senseless killings of millions of mother's sons and many innocent civilians has continued unabated. Suffering has become our signature and drama our birth right. It was almost as if humanity had to go through this monstrous blood-letting to rise above it.

In the past when human beings have come together to face a common enemy we have been fighting against each other. Corona-virus is a foreign invader of a different kind. It is transcending all barriers of race, religion and language and affecting every single person on Earth.

We all have our stories of suffering to share. On a personal level my pain has been witnessing the agony of my much-loved eldest daughter and feeling powerless to help. Following a sexual assault, at the age of eighteen Alice was pulled into a vortex of severe depression. For several years she became an unreachable stranger and was confined in a secure Mental Health Unit. Life was so painful for her, her emotions so intense, that it became unbearable and suicide (the most extreme badge of human suffering), seemed the only way out. Luckily she has survived her many attempts to leave this world. Fourteen years on she is (miraculously) still here, and still struggling at times, but the magic has started to kick in and she is courageously winning the battle in her own journey beyond suffering.

As battles go, the World Wars and their build-up and aftermath monopolised the twentieth century. Towards the end there were positive signs. In 1991 the U.S.S.R's communist strangle-hold in Europe was suddenly overturned and a new political and economic landscape appeared, not just in Europe, but globally. The 'Cold War' between East and West thawed and the prospect of nuclear conflict, significantly diminished. Soon afterwards, China opened up to a free market economy and the communist threat (as we knew it) was gone.

Now in the twenty-first century, a new era is dawning. Despite being in the midst of a pandemic and maybe because of it, there is more kindness and compassion in the air. The Covid restrictions have ironically allowed many individuals to find their voice and unique expression. They are sparking a transfer of power from the ruling elite to the masses, which is long overdue. The world around us is created by our thoughts and our **collective consciousness**, so nothing is certain but for many there is a new feeling of optimism on the planet. At long last it is time for us to move 'beyond suffering.'

Rare astrological configurations have ushered in these changes. In 1987 the **Harmonic Convergence** brought in and anchored a higher vibration energy. The momentous political events of the late 1980s/early 1990s in Eastern Europe and Asia were in response to this. There was another major surge of this energy in 2003, with what was called the **Harmonic Concordance**, but everything changed after the **Precession of the Equinoxes** on the 21st of December, 2012. Long predicted by the **Mayans** and other indigenous peoples, on this day Planet Earth lined up with the galactic core of the Milky Way, heralding an end to a 26,000 year planetary cycle and opening us up to the higher vibration of the **Fifth Dimension**. Since then, increasing influxes of this energy have streamed onto the planet. In the last few years they have been coming in strongly from the cluster of 22 galaxies that our Milky Way is part of, that some call the **Diamond Group**.

This high vibration energy is full of love and compassion. It is forcing us to shed the fear and barbarism of our Third Dimensional past and is helping us to move beyond suffering. Light is finally vanquishing the darkness and working to raise our consciousness and to alter the energy fields and magnetics of this planet. This high vibration Fifth Dimensional energy is the energy which is being called quantum. It is also the energy of the Akashic Records.

As a repository of soul memory, the Akashic Records hold the key to our past, present and future. I have been working in the Akashic Records since 2010 and they have shown me an expanded vision for humanity. All the information about our soul's journey on Earth and the potentials for our current lifetime (and sometimes beyond) are available in our Akashic Record. We can find out about our life plan, relationships, past lives and get valuable guidance on any issue. The answers to any questions we have (big and small) are in the Records.

As I write this it is over eight years since 2012 and the planetary change which is being called 'the shift' or '**Ascension**.' We are 'in amongst it,' as the saying goes and there is a lot to shift. We are recalibrating and adjusting to this energy both personally and collectively. We can't carry the dense energy of the Third Dimension into the Fifth. We must let go of beliefs, fears and patterns of behaviour that have become stuck and entrenched and which in the old energy, have been easily reactivated from lifetime to lifetime. We are being forced to live with integrity. Lower vibrational behaviours of competition, control, dishonesty and abuse cannot exist in this new frequency. Covid-19 has accelerated this process and is helping us to release all that no longer serves, on a mass, global level. There is no escape, but it will be worth it. It is time to move beyond the pain and suffering, to let go of all trauma: current-life, past life and intergenerational. It is time to leave behind anything that has created and perpetuated suffering and to break free of the holding pattern that has enslaved humanity for thousands of years. It is time to leave the paradigm of suffering behind forever.

In this new energy, the Akashic Records, are a powerhouse for transformation. They make healing possible on a soul level. In this Fifth Dimensional energy it is easier to connect with other dimensions and with aspects of our souls from past, parallel and future lives. With the help of the Akashic Records we can bridge this distance across time and space. Anything of a lower vibration is making its presence felt. So too are the magnificent soul and multidimensional aspects of ourselves which, unable to express themselves in the Third Dimension, have lain dormant. The Akashic Records are an easily accessible gateway to this energy and a safe place for soul healing and exploration to occur.

Many of my clients had past lives during World War II. They were part of the action in various ways and a common theme is of human potential being cut short by war. Coming into our current lives many of us, including myself, have been driven by a desire to complete what we were unable to last time and to co-create a different world. In our current lifetimes we have not only suffered collectively but many of us have chosen deep suffering on a personal level, to enable us to move beyond it once and for all.

Many of us are having intense experiences and the last fourteen years have been a roller coaster ride for me. Witnessing Alice's torment has been a bitter pill to swallow but it has helped me to shed layer after layer of personality, ego and pain, not just from this life but from many more. It has not been easy but I know that on a soul level I have chosen it. In this new energy the soul is making its presence felt. It is not an easy time to be on Earth but it is an extremely exciting one.

The thing that distinguishes human life is that we have freedom of choice. We can choose to follow the light or to follow the dark. As souls on Earth we have experienced both. I still have a way to go but I am grateful for the personal hell I have experienced. My husband and I have held the space for our daughter in the Psychiatric Ward, in ambulances, in ICU, in half-way houses and in our family and our home. We have never given up hope and now we are coming out the other side. We have been in the furnace and felt its heat. We have not let it destroy us and are emerging in a different form... transmuted, alchemised and enhanced. Our souls are driving this and it is helping us rise to a new level where we can fulfil our highest potential at this critical time on the planet.

I have found my purpose. My younger children, Hugh and Mary are open-hearted and compassionate leaders. We are all very strong but the strongest member of our family is Alice. We have been experiencing hell from the side lines. She has been living it. The fact she is still alive is testament to her courage and fortitude and also to incredible luck.

I struggled with low self-esteem when I was younger. From a very young age Alice also suffered from feelings of unworthiness. Aware of this and believing that loving ourselves is central to a happy and fulfilling life, I developed a conscious parenting course called *The Heart to Heart Course for Parents*. The best parents, I felt, were those who had a strong foundation of self-awareness and self-love. The aim of this programme was to give parents tools that would build up their children's self-worth and their own as well. I read every parenting book I could find and did my best to live and breathe my passion. I taught hundreds of parents these techniques.

Deep down I knew there was a new generation of children who had to be parented differently. Many of my age group had been parented from fear; fear of what could go wrong and fear of the judgement of others. This had disempowered us. I knew intuitively that it was vitally important that this didn't happen to these children. Now, with my greater understanding of the contribution the **Millennials** and **The Children** are here to make, in anchoring a higher consciousness on Earth, I can see why I was so driven. In order to fulfil their missions these children needed to be opened up to their individual talents and potentials, not shut down. I taught conscious, love-based parenting: a style of parenting that kept the souls of our children burning bright but encouraged strong boundaries and supported them to take responsibility for their lives. I taught these classes from 1999-2013 and they helped me learn to love and respect myself but did nothing to build up my daughter Alice's self-esteem.

In the late 1990s before beginning my parenting courses, I had opened up spiritually. I read widely and always had a fascination for the Akashic Records. When Alice became unwell, the Akashic Records and the soul kept coming to mind and I became convinced that her struggles went beyond this lifetime. Deep down I knew that in the Akashic Records I would find the answers I needed. I found a way to open the Records and discovered that Alice was attempting to release deep soul trauma from her most recent past life and from many challenging Earth lives prior to that. She had returned, very reluctantly, to do this work at the same time as Planet Earth was releasing the energetic imprints of suffering, which have characterised our Third Dimensional existence.

The Fifth Dimensional energy we are moving into is lighter and more loving. It cannot sustain the heavy vibration of fear and suffering that has been our human reality for thousands of years. It is time for us to offload the baggage we have accumulated in the density of 3D. The new energy that has been pouring into the planet is accelerating this process. The electromagnetic field that surrounds Earth holds the vibration of our consciousness and it is changing fast. As the planet has been transforming so has every single human being, whether we have been aware of it or not.

According to channelled sources and to spiritual teachers such as Diana Cooper (www.dianacooper.com), this process is expected to last until approximately 2030–32, when our planet will be fully Fifth Dimensional. I had been asking myself how we could create such momentous change in such a short time. The advent of Covid-19 has answered that question. Political, social and economic chaos is all around us. The higher vibration energy is the energy of truth and transparency. Anything that is not aligned with that frequency is being revealed. The light is winning and the dark has nowhere to hide. Any ways that we are living that are out of integrity, both personally and collectively, are being exposed. The planet is in turmoil, and so are many of us as we are forced to release the old and let go of the behaviours, beliefs and habits that have sustained us in the past.

The prophecy of the ancient Mayans and others, that the world would end on the 21st of December, 2012 is well-known. None of these ancient forecasts about the 'end times' went beyond 2012. The Mayans were right. We are facing the end of the world but it is not total extinction, just the end of the world as we know it. We are moving into a new energy and a new era that is unprecedented. Before 2020 there was a grey area where the dimensions over-lapped but now the 3D and 5D timelines are separating out. There are two distinct pathways in front of us. One is the well-trodden path we have followed for thousands of years. On this route we know every bend in the road and are all too familiar with the challenging terrain ahead. The other is a path we have not walked before. What road we take is our choice. Stepping into an unknown future will take courage and a leap of faith. It will involve letting go of all that is familiar and a change in identity. We are reinventing ourselves individually and collectively at this time but the rewards will be great.

The Akashic Records are giving me strength and support as I step into uncharted territory and get to know the new me. My challenges have been triggers for the release of much that has limited and slowed me down in this life and in others. Letting go of all that has kept us small and stuck has been a constant theme in recent years. This has involved physical and emotional healing to bring our bodies back into balance and their natural state of perfection. On an energetic level many of the distorted beliefs and the memories of our human suffering have been carried from lifetime to lifetime in the cells of our bodies and in our energy fields. We have been releasing these so they no longer hold us back.

As I described in *The Magic of the Akashic Records*, the energy of the Records with its soul connection is the perfect place for the clearing and releasing of past life trauma. There are some special souls that have agreed to do this work on behalf of others. I believe that Alice is one of these. Every time she sheds a layer of pain for herself, she is helping the entire human race to release the cumulative imprints of suffering. This is not an easy path.

As **Kryon**, a collective and enlightened wisdom from beyond this planet, channelled by Lee Carroll, says, towards the end of the twentieth century, human (nuclear) annihilation was a strong potential. Rapidly expanding awareness in the late 1980s and the 1990s changed this and against all odds we made it to 2012.

Since 2012 the new energy has been working its magic. Kryon says that human beings have destroyed themselves four times before and that in the late twentieth century we were headed in the same direction. The sudden burst of high vibration energy in 1987, lifted the consciousness of the planet to a degree that changed everything. The 'wildcard' collapse of communism in the U.S.S.R occurred and despite the dire 'Armageddon' predictions we crossed the line into the twenty-first century. We made it through to 2012 and into a new part of our solar system with energy unlike anything we have previously experienced. This energy is pure light. It can easily be shaped by our thoughts and intentions and is shaking up our world. The same as the energy of the Akashic Records, it is sending Planet Earth a lifeline that will take us beyond suffering forever. For the first time as Kryon says 'We have the wind at our back.' There has been a backlash from those who are desperate to retain the status quo, but after many years of **darkness** ruling and claiming victory in battle after battle, they will not win this one.

❀

In late 2018, Alice returned briefly to the Psych Ward for a short admission which was the result of an incident which reopened old wounds. As my husband and I sat around the table with Alice, her psychiatrist and several Social Workers, I reflected on how much things had changed. The way our local mental health facility is transforming is a prime example of the new energy at work. When I suggested I come for a visit, Alice said that with inpatient Art and Yoga Classes, meditation and other activities, she was too busy to fit me in.

In stark contrast, the day that Alice was admitted to the adult Psych Ward in 2008 was one of the worst days of my life. In the centre of the ward there was a work station for staff that was straight out of the movie *One Flew Over the Cuckoo's Nest*. Screened behind glass, the nurses were unapproachable and distant. Patients stood in line waiting for medication or for someone to listen to them. From my perspective, parents were seen as the enemy and treated with suspicion. Ten years on, the Psych Ward was a completely different place, the 'gold fish' bowl and cell-like bedrooms had been replaced by a much more homely environment. There was a shared kitchen, landscaped gardens and even a visiting cat. Parents were welcome. Compassion was in the air.

There is still huge suffering in the world. It is everywhere and with the media's penchant for human angst, impossible to avoid. Humanity is going through a period of rapid transition. Wired into us from our previous human experiences is a belief that change cannot come without suffering. We are feeling the new energy but most of us can't explain or understand it and it is scary. Resisting and fearing it will only make it worse. What we don't understand is that this energy is different. If we go with the flow and trust that it is a benevolent force working for our highest good, our experience will also be different.

This energy is forcing us to wake up. We are being challenged to address dysfunctional behaviours and habits as well as cultural constructs that are no longer sustainable: inequality, abuse and imbalance in all forms. The good news is that despite outward appearances, things are getting better and they will continue to improve. The process of Planetary Ascension from the Third Dimension to the Fifth is well underway. A huge purging and cleansing has begun. The elemental forces of Earth, Fire, Water and Air and now the advent of a global pandemic are assisting in this process. **Climate Change** is a scientific reality. The earthquakes, fires, floods and hurricanes we are hearing about on a daily basis are mirroring the healing process that we are all going through. Our energy is rising all the time. As our consciousness lifts so too does our vibration and the vibration of the planet. As the energy around us is upgraded it works with our thoughts and feelings in a symbiotic way so they become more positive.

This book is about healing and transformation. In the last fourteen years I have witnessed huge transformation in my personal life, in the lives of my clients and on this planet. As I reflect on the changes in me since 2007, I know they would not have been possible without the Akashic Records. Alice and her trials as well as the Records have been a primary catalyst in my metamorphosis. My experiences have helped me change from a heartbroken parent, powerless and buffeted by forces beyond my control to a more humble and thankful version of myself. I am still a mother, a wife, a sister and a friend but I now know I am so much more than that.

Thanks to the Akashic Records I have a constant and close connection with my soul. I have information and insight about the roles I have played in other lifetimes. I have a tool I can use to clear cellular programming that has held me back for aeons. The Records have helped me to improve my physical health and wellbeing and to create a force-field from which to manifest my greatest dreams and desires. From the familiar comfort of the present, I have been able to link in with talents and lifetimes from my past and future human expressions and bring them in to help me now.

When I began my work in the Akashic Records I was crushed and defeated and ruled by fear. I used them to access my own guidance at first and then for others. After several months of being in the Records regularly, I noticed a change. The energy of the Records was like a warm and loving embrace. I felt supported and calm. They helped me to rise above the torment that was my life and to cope with the challenges I faced. I have accessed the Records on an almost daily basis and they have transformed my life. If they can do this for me they can do it for anyone.

The Akashic Records can help us move beyond suffering in many ways. We can see the painful events we experience from the vantage point of the soul. We can clean up the debris from the heavy energy of the Third Dimension on a personal, familial and collective level and leave it behind forever. The Records enable healing on a deep soul level that relieves our mental and physical suffering. They connect us to our authentic selves, to our intuition and to our magnificence. They are the key to our deepest truths. They hold the secrets of our past and the potentials for our future. They are a wellspring of miracles that can take us from tragic to magic!

Chapter 2

My work in the Records

I have been working in the Akashic Records since 2011. I taught myself how to access them in 2010 using Linda Howe's method (see bibliography) and sensed and became increasingly fascinated by their potential for healing. The next year I was about to register for an expensive soul healing retreat. My counsellor and friend Terri Morehu, helped me realise that I didn't need to go because I already knew what to do.

The timing must have been right because once I committed to it everything happened very fast. After practising with some volunteers, I emailed every spiritually inclined person I knew, offering them readings at a low price. My friend Donna created a website for me and promised to help me at an upcoming spiritual fair. After that things rapidly gained momentum. Word of mouth has been my best marketing tool.

Early on, I started doing basic healing to remove the imprints of feelings, beliefs, fears and patterns that I could see were holding clients back. Since then I have expanded my healing in many wondrous ways. I am always learning something new and my clients are my teachers.

In 2013, I started running my Soul History Workshops. Level 1 taught participants how to read the Akashic Records for themselves and others. Level 2 (from 2015) taught simple healing techniques and how to use the Records for **manifestation**. At my Level 3

Residential Retreats, I share and demonstrate many of my healing methods to those who are interested in becoming practitioners in the Records. I now teach these workshops online to individuals and groups. I am enjoying every moment of this wonderful journey.

It is a privilege to do this work. The splendour of my clients overwhelms me. As I open their Akashic Record I enter the private sanctuary of their soul and fall in love. When I see my clients as they really are - they sweep me off my feet. Within their Akashic Record I can feel their majesty and tune into their different soul expressions. A soul thread or theme usually runs through and I get an overview of the essence they have carried through many incarnations. It may be a dogged determination, leadership abilities or a lightness of being that brings out the best in people. This was the case with a client called Clare who had carried similar personal attributes and abilities from one life to the next.

Just before I began Clare's session, the words 'She leaves a trail of light wherever she goes,' popped into my head. As soon as I opened her Akashic Record I saw that she had been a positive influence for many people in her 69 years and that now she had a mission to share her wisdom and gifts more widely. She told me that before her retirement she had worked for a doctor as a receptionist.

When I tuned into her family energy there wasn't the trauma that many of my clients carry. I saw that Clare had chosen two beautiful and advanced souls as her parents. I was not surprised when she told me her father had been a lighthouse keeper, exempt from fighting in World War II because he provided an 'essential' service. He had kept the light burning brightly, through some very dark times.

In her most recent past life Clare, had lived during those times. An American woman in France, she had worked tirelessly to get people to safety as the Nazi war machine 'snapped at their heels.' The German armies had advanced much faster than expected, engulfing France before 'Clare' (as she was then) could honour her commitment to rescue people. Although she helped many, I saw that she had been upset about those she had been unable to save.

The occupying Germans knew her history and kept her under close surveillance. When the war broke out, her husband was in the US. She had two young children to care for and protect so she felt that joining **the resistance** wasn't an option. She was keen to fight back and didn't lack courage but as most mothers would she put her children's needs first. Eventually she got passage for the three of them on a commercial ship going to the US. It was torpedoed and they lost their lives. As the ship went down she berated herself for not doing what she knew was right and continuing her work of helping people to freedom. As she and her children were going to die anyway, she reasoned, she may as well have died fighting.

Clare asked about other past lives. I went back to the three before her recent one in World War II and could see a progression from one life to the next. In France she had worked hard to arrange immigration for people under threat. In the lifetime before that she had also helped many immigrants. She was again, an American, a family man working as the foreman in a factory that employed new migrants. In the same way as Clare had held the space in a doctor's surgery in this life, this man had been humble and had quietly done his best to help those around him. In the life prior to that she had been a priest, who with the same honest and open heart, had tended to his congregation.

In the lifetime before that, I saw Clare as a soldier in Napoleon's army who had been singled out and mistreated for challenging his superiors. In that life 'Clare' could see the potential for improved systems that would make the soldiers' lives easier. His suggestions for change were not appreciated by those of higher rank and he became a target for bullying

> and abuse. At that point he decided it was not a good idea to 'stick his neck out' and draw attention to himself and that he must 'play it safe.'
>
> In her subsequent three lifetimes 'Clare' had followed this mantra, working courageously, but as inconspicuously as possible, to help those around her. In her most recent past life she had designed and created efficient systems to get others to safety. She had also utilised her organisational skills in her receptionist job in this lifetime.
>
> I helped Clare to let go of fear so she could take her work to the next level and assisted her to release the belief, 'I can only help people in a way that doesn't upset those in authority.'

Clare will continue to spread her light and will now be able to use her integrity, humanity and wisdom in an even bigger way to help those on this planet.

Seeing people at their best and reflecting back their highest potential is what I love most about my work. Through linking in with the positive and heroic lifetimes they have lived, I help clients see beyond the person they think they are. The reflection of their soul which I provide can be life-changing. The Akashic Records not only carry the imprints of programming that is no longer serving us but of positive memories and gifts and abilities we have possessed in other lives. Kryon calls this 'Mining the **Akash**' and it is possible to reconnect with and to work with the gold in our soul timelines as well as the dross. Being in the energy of our open Akashic Record is transformative in itself. The energy is soothing, healing and affirming and I love seeing clients finish a session lighter, with a spring in their step and a smile on their face.

The Akashic Records I work with are those of this planet. They contain the information about every lifetime that each soul has had on Earth. They are an energetic which exists in the following places:

The Hall of Records

A large library on the 'other side of the veil,' (known to many as heaven), presided over by the Lords or Keepers of the Records.

In the cells of our bodies

Our Akashic Record is in every cell of our bodies. It is Layer Eight of our so-called 'junk' DNA. These are twelve layers of multidimensional, quantum DNA that is coming to life as Fifth Dimensional energy streams into Earth. (I will write more about this later).

In our Merkabah or energy field

Our Akashic Record is in the auric field around our bodies. It holds the energy of past life experiences especially as it relates to our physical and emotional state.

The Crystalline Grid

A band of energy that surrounds the Earth that reflects the consciousness on the planet (what we think, feel and do). It holds the energy and the memories of what has happened in each place throughout time. It contains Akashic information for Planet Earth. This is also carried on a cellular level by the cetaceans or whales and dolphins of this planet.

The Cave of Creation

Kryon introduced me to the Cave of Creation. It is not a physical place but is a part of the crystalline grid that holds our personal memories. We each have a crystal in the cave. Kryon says that at birth and death our soul passes through and connects us with our crystal which holds the energy of our Higher Self and the essence of our Akash (Akashic Record). There are stripes on our crystal for every human lifetime we have had.

The Halls of Amenti

These contain an energetic record of our Fifth Dimensional (and higher) soul experiences. This includes the information from what some call 'the cosmic moment,' the 21st of December, 2012 and also of our soul experiences prior to entering the Third Dimensional vibration of Earth. In these halls it is possible to connect with expressions of our soul that exist in other dimensions, time frames and galaxies from lifetimes before we came to this planet.

The Akashic Records are helping me to transition from fear to love and will be invaluable to humanity as we navigate the shift from the old to the new. As with the Halls of Amenti, until relatively recently the Akashic Records have been the preserve of a few. Now they are being opened up and offered more widely to those who are drawn to them and have purity of intent.

It is, I believe, my mission to teach as many people as possible how to use these simple but transformational tools. It delights me that there is a growing group of my students doing powerful work in the Records. As I teach, I encourage them to think about specific ways they can use the Akashic Records to help themselves and others. There are some guidelines for working in the Records, and there are good reasons for these, but few hard and fast rules. I teach my students what I know but encourage them to put their own spin on things. I stress their capacity to adapt them to their current lives and lightwork and to make them their own. We all have a different filter and how we express ourselves through the Akashic Records is unique.

I demonstrate the healing methods I have developed but know that what I do is the 'tip of the iceberg.' My joy is in giving others the freedom to adapt and use the Records in a way that works for them. I love it that my students are combining other modalities and incorporating their individual skill-set into their work in the Records. I tell them that as long as the Akashic Record of whoever they are helping is open and they state an intention for the healing they would like to occur, they can do anything else they feel guided to. At my first Level 3 Retreat weekend I was lucky enough to be on the receiving end of healing from my students. One used *Theta Healing* to assist me and the other *EFT* (the Emotional Freedom Technique). Others incorporated **Light Language, toning** and *Reiki* into their sessions. I love the flexibility of the Records and the way we can make them work for us.

One of the few rules I teach is that it is not possible to open someone's Akashic Record without their permission. Many of my students who work in healing occupations, open their own Akashic Record before client sessions. They say this takes their work to a new level. A counsellor who I taught online has clients with long-standing issues. He told me that he doesn't open their Record but has his open and asks them if he can do some spiritual work with them. He identifies a theme for each person e.g. abandonment, rejection, and then an associated belief. For a client who had been sexually assaulted several times, it was 'I don't deserve respect.' He then clears the energy of this belief by invoking Saint Germain's **Violet Flame** and then connects them to past lives where they didn't think this way. He says if their belief is part of a wider family pattern, he can clear it for the family line as well. Using this technique is enhancing his therapeutic work and shows that opening up a client's Akashic Record is not necessary when facilitating healing. People who seek out mainstream healing professions may not understand or might feel a bit threatened by the Akashic Records so this combined approach is perfect.

This method also worked for Lynnette, a friend who was working with an eleven year old, who suffered from stress and anxiety. Lynnette uses *Heartmath* techniques to relieve the anxiety of her clients. She told me that since coming to my Level 3 workshop she has been working with her Akashic Record open. She was able to bring in the Higher Self of her client and to also incorporate **unicorns** and **dragons** which helped the young girl to shift a deeper layer of fear.

One of my guidelines is not to open the Akashic Records of anyone under the age of eighteen. At times I have made an exception but have needed to talk to the young person to make sure they understand what the process entails. In general, it is thought that getting information about your life path or past lives at a young age could be confusing and limiting in the future. I use my discretion and once taught my workshop to a twelve year old who was very interested in and already knowledgeable about the Records. I learned a lot that day.

❈

The information in the Akashic Records for most of us is vast. The technique I teach connects us to information relevant to our Earth lifetimes. If we are Old Souls on the planet the details in our Record are immense. When we access the Akashic Records we can't sit and wait for the information to come to us. We must go in with a specific intention or purpose. For this it is helpful to ask questions. When I give readings for others I always go in with the question, 'What is it helpful for xxx to know?' It is an interactive process. We are working with a different level of energy and we have to get that energy moving. We can do this by starting to talk or write as soon as we open the Records, even if we have no idea what we are going to say. Once we set the energy in motion the answers come. It is best to ask questions that don't have a yes or no answer. Questions beginning with Why? How? or What? work well. It pays to be careful with what we ask as we will only get the exact answer to our question.

The Akashic Records are a quick and reliable way to gain clarity on the day-to-day issues we have as well as the dilemmas we face. I encourage a daily practice of writing with your Record open. It is a form of journaling and a way to access a higher wisdom that can give us immediate relief. I have found this information extremely helpful over the years. The Akashic Records are the easiest way I know to get our own answers. They are perfect for this new energy which is all about taking responsibility for ourselves and not relying on others.

When I open someone's Record I get an overview of why they are here and what they are trying to achieve. I ask to see their highest potential and get information about their life purpose. Every reading is different and tailored to the needs of the individual at the time. I can give someone two readings, a year apart, and there can be significant differences. I connect to their Akashic Record but their future potentials are affected by the energy that surrounds them. This energy changes with the thoughts and consciousness of the individual. It is these thoughts that create their reality.

We all come into each lifetime with a rough plan and an idea of our goals and aims. The choices we make determine how our life unfolds. We can stick to the plan, deviate from the plan or go way beyond it and create a new one. It is all possible and more so now with the intense upgrade of energy on this planet and the rapid evolution and transformation it has activated for humanity.

Giving readings has been a necessary part of my path. It has helped me to hone and develop my abilities and I learn so much from them. I am sometimes in awe of the words that come out of my mouth as a forgotten truth or an interesting gem of soul information emerges. I often give several readings in a row that have a similar theme, which enlarges my understanding of a period in history or a cataclysmic event. My clients have taught me so much and have helped me develop ways of facilitating emotional and physical healing and empowerment, but I would rather teach them how to do this for themselves. Relying on others to chart our lives or to tell us what to do does not sit comfortably in the Fifth Dimensional vibration. The thing I love most about the Akashic Records is that anyone coming from the right place can access them to help themselves. They can be used in a myriad of ways to ease our human suffering and to help us navigate our way through the accelerating change on this planet.

One thing most of my clients say, is I give them confirmation. Confirmation that they can trust their inner voice, that the intuitive hunches they have are correct and that their thoughts about their future path are accurate. I think it is strange that we place more importance on the words of someone else than our own inner wisdom. It amazes me how people can pay a stranger (me) who they have never met, to tell them what to do with their lives. This aspect of my work makes me a bit uneasy and I ask my clients to be discerning with the information and to only go with what resonates.

We need reassurance from outside of ourselves because most of us, including myself at times, are riddled with self-doubt. Self-doubt is linked to fear and is the aspect of being human that limits us the most. If we are Old Souls this has been reinforced through many lifetimes of being different and suffering for it. If we are newer souls to Earth it comes from the feelings of insecurity and discomfort of being far away from home and not feeling as if we truly belong. It has been an intrinsic part of the human condition and one of the most destructive.

If my clients could see what I see when I open their Akashic Records, they would never doubt themselves again. The people that come to me for readings have, without exception, noble soul lineages and many talents and abilities. Resplendent in all of their human brilliance and multidimensional grandeur, they take my breath away. I help my clients to see themselves as they really are: majestic, magical and marvellous. They are not who they think or have been told they are - they are so much more. The best part of my job is opening my client's eyes to their true potential and helping them to believe in themselves so they can leave fear and suffering behind forever.

I see the sparkling potential of each soul but I don't get a human time frame. I can't see whether what I pick up will happen next week, next year or in the distant future. The Akashic Records are not bound by the constraints of linear time. Within the Akashic Records anything is possible and we are able to create whatever we focus our intention on. This means that for all of us, our dreams are out there. They are an energy that will bear fruit when we are ready on all levels of our being. We can't rush or force this process and for those of us with big dreams it can often take longer.

When I trained as a coach with 'Coach U' in the late 1990s they stressed the importance of having a 'Personal Foundation.' Just as the foundations of a house have to be able to support the structure above, we have to be able to cope with our success. We must have the energy, the knowledge and most importantly the self-belief to not only make our dreams a reality but to live with them once they are realised. In the meantime we must be patient and learn to trust. We are not alone. We have many helpers in Spirit and more help is available if we ask for it. The higher vibration energy we are moving into is powerful energy for manifestation. When the time is right and everything is in alignment things can move very quickly.

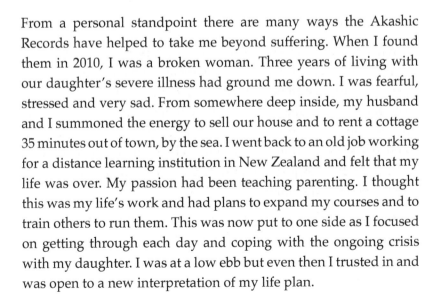

From a personal standpoint there are many ways the Akashic Records have helped to take me beyond suffering. When I found them in 2010, I was a broken woman. Three years of living with our daughter's severe illness had ground me down. I was fearful, stressed and very sad. From somewhere deep inside, my husband and I summoned the energy to sell our house and to rent a cottage 35 minutes out of town, by the sea. I went back to an old job working for a distance learning institution in New Zealand and felt that my life was over. My passion had been teaching parenting. I thought this was my life's work and had plans to expand my courses and to train others to run them. This was now put to one side as I focused on getting through each day and coping with the ongoing crisis with my daughter. I was at a low ebb but even then I trusted in and was open to a new interpretation of my life plan.

Moving to the seaside was the perfect step for us all. We had a month between houses and rented an apartment in one of our city's most prestigious streets. It had beautiful harbour views but very bad energy. Our cat, Cobweb, hated it there, refusing to go outside for the whole four weeks. Within an hour of arriving at our cottage in the coastal village of Paekakariki, she was out chasing rabbits. She noticed the different in vibration and so did we. We were exactly where we needed to be to re-group and to heal.

In this beautiful place we had time to breathe and the daily walks along the beach were calming and invigorating. Into this void, just when I thought my life-long dream of helping humanity had gone forever, stepped the Akashic Records. They came in quietly without fuss or fanfare. The first time I opened my Akashic Record I felt very little. There were no fireworks, no 21 gun salute, just a subtle change in energy. By the following year, when we were back in town and I was in the Akashic Records regularly, I was happier and more energized. The fear and sadness that had gripped me for four years had lifted. Everything about my life had improved. The Akashic Records had given me the strength and the greater understanding to move forward. They pulled me out of a dark place and for that I will always be grateful.

When I teach others how to access the Akashic Records I always tell them that even if they never use them to give readings, if they open them up just to be in their energy, they will transform their lives. It is best to build up the time spent in the Records slowly, but once we do the energy is there to help us in our everyday lives. These energies can transport us out of chaos and despair and help us to cope. It takes just one minute to open your Akashic Record and the benefits are immense.

The more I was exposed to this beautiful Fifth Dimensional frequency, the better I felt. The Records lifted me out of the darkness and helped me to deal with life's challenges. I gave myself readings to make sense of what was happening and spent as much time in their calming and compassionate energy as I could.

With the help of the Akashic Records, my life has changed for the better and so have I. They have helped me to connect with the sanctity of my soul. When you are constantly in this energy you have to be true to yourself. It is impossible to lie, feels uncomfortable to gossip and judge and it is much easier to speak your truth. You have to walk your talk and drama in any shape or form becomes intolerable. It is easier to live in the moment and to trust, and your intuition expands exponentially.

The Akashic Records have shown me lifetimes I have lived as different expressions of my soul. They have helped me see that I am so much more than Chris Wilson, living in New Zealand, at the beginning of the twenty-first century. They have opened me up to parts of myself I didn't know existed and to wisdom and talents I didn't know I had. They have brought me closer to my Higher Self so that now we work in partnership, with my intuitive hunches and 'knowings' playing a greater role in my daily life. With the help of the Records I am letting go of the limited version of myself. They are also helping me let go of certainty and of allowing my conscious and rational mind to be in control. Letting go of ego is taking longer but the soul space created by the Akashic Records is assisting with this as well.

With the aid of the Akashic Records I am learning to live in a way that relieves stress and will become normal in the future; less head, more heart and totally in the moment. One of the main differences between 3 and 5D is that the Fifth Dimension has no linear time lines. Already many are noticing that time is not what it used to be. It seems to be moving faster but there are also times when we can slow it down at will. The Akashic Records are in this timeless energy and living in 5D will make it easier to be in the now. My husband teaches *Mindfulness* which is another perfect tool for this age.

Once we are completely in this new energy the only reality will be the now moment and our lives will be less complicated.

It is ironic that when I work with clients to access their soul histories from the so-called past, I am in the present moment. I never know what I am going to say. I ask them to come with some questions and issues to discuss and send them information to help them to prepare. I make sure I don't see these in advance so I haven't any preconceived ideas. I read a short intention statement to access their Record and open my mouth and out it comes.

The Akashic Records are a soul space. Our Higher Self, the aspect of our soul that has been with us in every human lifetime, can remember all that has happened in the past. It can also see the potentials for the future. In the process of planetary ascension as humanity steps up a gear or two, aspects of us that were shut down in the Third Dimension are returning. It is getting easier to connect with the multidimensional parts of ourselves, including our Higher Self. When I am working with clients and in the rest of my life I am increasingly letting my soul do the talking. It is a beautiful feeling. This Fifth Dimensional energy is giving me a taste of a human future where there will be no separation between our human and soul selves.

The Akashic Records have helped me to rise above the drudgery, despair and disappointments of everyday life to a higher view point. This expanded vision has made it easier to accept whatever life presents to me. The Records have taught me to go with the flow and to trust. They have shown me that there is a higher plan not just for us as individuals but for the planet. They have given me comfort in my pain and provided hope for the future. They have helped me to come to a place of peace, acceptance and joy.

Giving readings is an interesting job. On any given day I can be transported to **Atlantis**, Ancient Egypt, Communist China and the trenches of World War I. The confirmation that comes as I give a reading lets me know I am on the right track.

When a client asked about his soul connection to a close friend. I told him that they had shared many lives and that I could see them together as soldiers, side by side, in the trenches in World War I. He gasped as he told me that his criteria for a good friend had always been, 'Someone I would happily stand next to in a trench.'

I saw another client's boyfriend as the US soldier who in her past life in World War II had rescued her from Russian soldiers. She told me that in this life he is a mimic and that one of his favourite accents is Russian.

Linking in with the life purpose of another client, I described her as 'a lighthouse beaming down on everyone to help them find their way out of the darkness.'

'I love lighthouses, I have lighthouse pictures all over my house,' she told me excitedly.

To my client, Rachel, I described a past life where she had run away to join Napoleon's army. In my mind's eye I could see her soldier self in a dark-coloured uniform with double-breasted brass buttons. When I noticed and commented on the jacket Rachel was wearing as she sat in front of me, we both laughed. It was almost an exact replica of what I was seeing in my mind.

In my line of work Google has become my 'friend.' After a session I often go online to check on information or an image that has come up in the reading. Sometimes my clients get in first.

I helped a woman to heal from the trauma of her death in a past life as a polish **partisan**. A young boy, she died as a 'sacrificial lamb' after being sent into a dangerous situation by older men who were also part of the Resistance. During our session she described her past life self as wearing a green uniform with a red arm band. I received this email from her shortly afterwards:

'I googled the WW II Polish partisan uniform and the colours were exactly the same as I saw in our session.'

When I opened Josie's Akashic Record I saw her as a 'gypsy' in two recent lifetimes. In one she was a beautiful and captivating young woman, a card reader who helped many people. Musical and a dancer, she spread joy wherever she went. In a more recent life she was a Romany boy with no father who felt huge responsibility for his mother, sisters and grandmother. After I shared this information with her she told me she had come to me because she felt the need to move on and was unsure if it was the right thing to do. One of her prepared questions was 'Why am I so nomadic?' In this life, as in others, she has a history of packing up and leaving without saying goodbye. Understanding where this urge came from was helpful to her in deciding what to do next.

A client, Renee, asked me to look at the deep divisions in her family. She told me her parents had been in conflict her whole life and that her six brothers and father were all carrying anger that they found difficult to express. In a past life I saw them together in what is now the Middle East. In that life Renee had the same father and siblings (brothers) as in this one. There was a drought in their village and they were very hungry.

Her mother, in her current life, was the village leader and wanted to stay put and ride it out. Her father wanted to leave in search of the legendary fertile valleys of Mesopotamia.

Her family decided to follow the majority decision which was to leave. It was a disaster. They never found the valley and starved to death, one by one. They became very angry at each other and turned on their father who was strangled by one of his sons.

Renee told me that in this life her mother had wanted to sit tight while her father had always been keen to move on.

In my country, New Zealand, there is a tiny village called Mesopotamia. Online it is described as an 'unspoiled piece of paradise'. Renee told me that her father had loved this place when she was growing up and always wanted to go there. I spoke to her recently and she told me that her father had just bought a lifestyle block on the outskirts of the town he lives in. 'He is still looking for greener pastures,' she laughed.

Very few of us have been famous people in other lives. When I give readings, it is unusual for me to find a past life connection with a well-known person from history. When this occasionally happens, I question it.

During a session I saw that my client had been a courageous young woman who had openly opposed the Nazi regime and had been tortured and killed as a result. The name Sophie Scholl came into my head. I had read about Sophie and her 'White Rose' movement but was still doubtful. Silently I asked for confirmation. It soon arrived. My client emailed me to say she had done some research on Sophie Scholl and that they were born on the same day. That was proof enough for me.

Being able to access the Akashic Records for others is such a gift. Seeing who they are on a soul level helps them to understand their human selves. I gave a reading to a friend's daughter, Anna. She had ruffled a few family feathers with her uncompromising stance on various issues, in particular her divorced parent's choice of new partners. She told me she loves her husband, but that their relationship is a bit volatile because she refuses to back down.

On opening Anna's Akashic Record I could see why she was not afraid to 'rock the boat.' I saw that in five recent lives she had been manipulated by others and had not managed to live and speak her truth.

On a soul level I could feel she deeply regretted it. I identified the lives that were affecting her:

1. A pampered daughter in a wealthy Italian family who was not only gay but a talented sculptor. The life she was expected to live was boring and unfulfilling in every respect. As a female her artistic talents were not encouraged and she was forced to live a lie.

2. A Chinese girl who was happy and carefree until the day she was held down while her feet were bound. This custom involved breaking and bandaging the feet of young girls to make them more desirable to males. It resulted in life-long pain and severely limited mobility.

3. A young Portuguese woman who was forced to marry a man her parents had chosen for her.

4. A young woman in England who was going to elope with the man she loved but decided against it at the last minute because, as the eldest daughter, she felt she had a duty to look after her parents.

5. In her most recent past life, I saw that she had managed to follow her heart and live her truth as a resistance fighter in World War II, but that outside circumstances had intervened and she was captured and killed before she could put her plans into action.

With each successive lifetime her frustration had built up and she had come into this one determined not to let anything or anyone stop her from living an authentic life.

As we discussed her life in China, we both saw the funny side when she told me that in this one she has size 10 feet. Our session also revealed that her parent's respective partners had held her back in these other lives and that her current husband was the man she had decided not to marry in her English life. She is an amazing soul who has lost time to make up. Her determination to follow her inner voice rather than those of the people around her does not surprise me at all. She is training to be a Social Worker and in years to come I am sure she will speak out to help her clients and inspire and empower them to be true to themselves.

In the light of the Records and our soul history the way people are always makes perfect sense.

❀

In this time of upheaval it is helpful to take a step back. The life we are living on Earth is like a theatrical performance we have agreed to take part in for our higher learning. When we incarnate, an aspect of our soul comes to Earth for a finite period to have experiences that will help us to learn and grow.

Before we are born we think carefully about the circumstances we need to maximise our learning potential in the life to come. For example, if we have had many lives with a soul who has been a thorn in our side, we might choose to have them in our family circle to support our soul evolution. If we have a pattern that has been repeated in many lifetimes such as 'self-sacrifice,' we may set up our lives so this behaviour is impossible to ignore; e.g. having people around us who are needy and unwilling to take responsibility for themselves.

It is not surprising that our lives can unfold like the very best of soap operas, especially at this time on Earth when we are being haunted by the past.

Before birth we agree to play roles in others' dramas to give us the chance to learn our chosen lessons and to evolve. Our life on Earth is just one of the many realities our soul exists in and according to channelled information I have received, the least real of all the dimensions. We are so much more than we think we are. Next time you are triggered by your father, sister, workmate or child, be grateful to them for doing their job and fulfilling their contract with you. When they hit your weak spot for the one-hundredth time, send them love and look at what they are here to teach you. Don't take them or life too seriously. Somewhere there is an aspect of your souls, in harmony, high-fiving each other for a job well done!

The Akashic Records are an energetic of loving wisdom. They are a precious gift that can help us detach from the daily intensity of our lives and to expand our vision. Seeing our circumstances and relationships in the light of many lifetimes and the potentials for the future helps us put our challenges into perspective and to stay upbeat. With the support of the Records we can be the 'bigger person' and see life as it really is, an experiment in another reality to help us understand ourselves and get closer to the 'God' within.

Chapter 3

Quantum Energy

The Akashic Records is not just a library of 'past life' experiences. To me the best thing about them is not the information they contain but their energy. It carries the uplifting and high vibration of the Fifth Dimension and is healing, loving and compassionate. When you are in the energy of your open Akashic Record you are bathed in light.

The energy is quantum energy. Carrying the frequency of magic and of miracles, its intertwined strands make healing and the alchemy of mind, body and spirit possible. It is energy that reflects our true soul nature. It doesn't fit a rigid construct, but is all over the place, just as we as multidimensional beings, existing throughout time, have been all over the place.

As I have mentioned previously, Quantum Energy first arrived in 1987 with the Harmonic Convergence. Since the 21st of December, 2012 it has been coming into this planet with increasing intensity. Found in many places, the energy of the Akashic Records is also the energy of:

- The Higher Self
- 'Junk' DNA and the 24th **Chromosome**
- The Innate (Cellular Wisdom)
- The Merkabah
- The Magnetic Grids

- Spirit
- The Angelic realms, Dragons and Unicorns
- The Stars

In the movie *The 1 Field,* released in mid-2020, anything quantum is referred to as 'the field.' The field exists everywhere and particularly in the places mentioned above. The movie looks at the ground breaking and miraculous attributes of this energy and at some of the scientific experiments that are proving its existence.

The Higher Self

The Higher Self is the soul part of us that has been present in all of our earthly incarnations. This aspect of us is all knowing and wise. It has an expansive view of not just our current but of all of our lifetimes. It sees the obstacles we have faced and overcome and how they have contributed to who we are now at this crucial time on Earth. It knows what we are trying to achieve and create. It knows our life purpose and wants to help us fulfil this. Our Higher Self is connected to our soul and is a part of, but not all of it. The soul is multidimensional and can exist in many places at once. (There is more about this in Chapter 10).

'Junk' DNA and the 24th Chromosome

'Junk' DNA is really quantum DNA. For thousands of years humanity has had twelve layers of DNA that have been unable to express themselves as the consciousness and vibration on this planet has been too low. Only the approximately 1.2% that carried our genetic code seemed to scientists to have a purpose, the rest they labelled 'junk'. With the boost of energy and heightened consciousness as we move from the Third Dimension to the Fifth, these energetic layers of our DNA have been activated and are making their presence felt. Many are now using the term, 'non-coding DNA' to describe them. (I will use this term from now on).

In the book *The Twelve Layers of DNA,* Kryon, channelled by Lee Carroll, says they were an energetic gift from our **Pleiadian** ancestors who seeded us 200,000 years ago. Darwin's theory is still the accepted scientific principle of evolution but as Gregg Braden, author of the book *Human by Design* says, the DNA in ancient human remains is different to that of modern-day humans. Science's increased ability to test fossilised DNA in the last decade has shown that Neanderthal humans and all other mammals have 24 chromosomes, while we only have 23.

'We 'shared the Earth with them but could not have descended from them,' he says.

In a talk at the online Kryon 'Science and Spirituality Conference' in 2020, Braden revealed that the **Anatomically Modern Human** (AMH) that appeared on Earth 200,000 years ago had different DNA from the **Cro-Magnon** man that preceded it. He said, 'We aren't the product of 'random mutation or adaptation over millions of years but a series of 'mysterious mutations, that happened around the same time 200,000 years ago.' These, he maintained, have given us extraordinary abilities and changed the nature of humanity. While we share 98% of our DNA with chimpanzees, we have a genetic twist in some of our chromosomes and there is a gene in Chromosome 2 that helps us to consciously regulate our emotions and our biology. This is, he continued, responsible for our rare capacity to feel both empathy and compassion. We are, stated Braden, the only species of life with this capability.

Others have spoken of the different structure of Chromosome 2. In a talk given in June 2021 on the virtual summit *Pleiadian Passport to Earth*, Dr John Ryan confirmed that in this chromosome there is a truncated **telomere** in the middle and two **centromeres**. This, Ryan says, suggests that two smaller chromosomes fused into one chromosome at some point in human history.

An article in the National Academy of Sciences Journal from October 1991 (Vol 88, pp 9051-9055) about the study of these chromosomes came up with this conclusion:

'We conclude that human Chromosome 2 is the relic of an ancient DNA fusion of two ancestral chromosomes.'

According to Braden, telomere fusion such as this does not occur in nature. He says that this is not suggestive of evolution but of 'intentional intervention.'

The beliefs and traditions of many indigenous peoples, the **Māori** people of New Zealand, included, supports the theory of a pleiadian connection. It is part of their creation story. **Matariki**, the Māori name for **the Pleiades**, will from 2022 be a mid-winter holiday in New Zealand, celebrating the Māori New Year which traditionally coincided with the rising of this star cluster.

According to the Kryon channellings **Lemuria,** (an ancient civilisation), existed in present day Hawaii from 50,000 to 15,000 years ago. As these islands started to sink the **lemurians**, who had learned the core truths of human life from pleiadian teachers, took to their canoes and resettled in distant islands bringing this wisdom with them. Some came to New Zealand. Māori legend has it that their ancestors came, by canoe, to New Zealand / **Aotearoa** from Hawaiki in Eastern Polynesia. Matariki, the Māori mid-winter festival is very similar in name to the Hawaiian equivalent, Makahiki.

The Twelve layers of DNA are not genetic but exist in a quantum form. In their book *The Twelve Layers of DNA*, Kryon and Lee Carroll discuss these layers in depth. One of these, Layer Eight, is our Akashic Record. Other layers are a healing layer presided over by **Saint Germain** and layers that connect us to our divinity, our lemurian and pleiadian heritage and the angelic realms. As we move into a higher vibration, they are coming alive with all of their special attributes.

The Innate (Cellular Wisdom)
The cellular intelligence within our bodies which Kryon calls the **innate** and is also known as our 'body wisdom' or 'smart body,' is also quantum. It listens and responds to every thought and statement

we make. It wants what is best for us and follows our commands. It is always balanced and can be worked with to restore our bodies to perfect health. It can be instructed to release blocks and to activate and anchor the divine cellular blueprint of health and perfection which exists for all of us in the etheric. Our innate responds to our thoughts, feelings and intentions and our physical reality is the result.

The Merkabah

The Merkabah is the quantum field that surrounds us. An energetic reflection of each human, it holds the essence of our Higher Self and of our soul experiences, as well as the imprints of our conscious and subconscious thoughts and beliefs. The energy from the other quantum aspects of our bodies, (Non-coding DNA and the Innate), is also carried in this field. Our Merkabah expands approximately eight metres around our body. This field is tapped into by healers who work with physical and emotional imbalances.

The Magnetic Grids

Three main grids have been identified in the Kryon channellings. They are all bands of energy that surround our planet. Interesting things have happened at the places on Earth where they overlap e.g. The Bermuda Triangle and in Ireland.

(a) The Magnetic Grid

This grid consists of the magnetic energy surrounding the planet that reflects consciousness. The 'Global Consciousness Initiative' run by the HeartMath Institute proved that there is an interrelationship between the two. In a talk he gave on the planetary grids, Lee Carroll said that in the wake of September 11, 2001, two National Oceanic and Atmospheric Administration space water satellites monitoring the Earth's geomagnetic field registered a significant increase at the time of the attack and in the days afterwards. This pattern has also been noticed at other times when emotion has been running high on Planet Earth.

Carroll also said that since 1993 the Magnetic Grid has moved more than in the previous 100 years. Consciousness is rapidly changing and expanding at this pivotal time and it is not surprising that the quantum magnetic field is registering this and being affected by it.

(b) The Crystalline Grid

The Merkabah is the quantum field that surrounds our bodies and the Crystalline Grid is a quantum energy band that circles the Earth. The Crystalline Grid is like an Akashic Record of people and places. It holds the energy of what has happened in each location. In parts of the world where there have been ancient civilisations, the energy of this grid can be intense. In countries that have been settled relatively recently, the energy of the Crystalline Grid is much lighter. Sensitives can feel this energy. When I went to Europe in 2017, I felt it when I visited the battle field of Culloden, Holyrood Castle and the Castle of Montsegur where 225 Cathars were burned at the stake in 1244.

I shared this information about the grid in a reading I gave to a man who in an earlier life came from the Pleiades to help set up the Crystalline Grid around the Earth.

This grid is energetic and reflects the consciousness of mankind. Much like a mineral crystal, it contains the memories and energy of everything that has occurred in that place. It reflects the degree of evolution of the planet and is a multidimensional record keeper of consciousness and events.

(c) The Gaia Grid

Kryon also talks of the **Gaia** or **Ancestral Grid**. This also acts as a record keeper and reservoir of quantum energy. The **Gaia Grid** holds the memory of Mother Earth and of all who have walked upon her. This energy field is intricately connected to the natural world, the **elementals** and the animal kingdom, and resonates strongly with their frequencies. It is sometimes called the Ancestral Grid as it holds an energetic that connects us directly to our ancestors and their wisdom and love.

Spirit

Spirit are beings attached to Earth that are non-physical and can include the deceased and the **Ascended Masters** e.g. Jesus, the Buddha. Those of a Fifth Dimensional Frequency or higher e.g. Ascended Masters and Archangels, are quantum.

The Angelic Realms, Dragons and Unicorns

The angelic realms hold a high and loving vibration. The most potent energy belongs to the Archangels and the Ascended Masters.

Dragons are etheric beings from the angelic realms who, like the unicorns, are finding it easier to connect with us as the planetary vibration increases. They can be invoked to breathe their fire through our bodies and energy fields to remove negative imprints from the past. They also have the power to bring in high vibration and positive energetic potentials for the future.

Unicorns carry much light which can be used to release, purify and alchemise trauma on a deep soul level. They also work to spread joy on the planet.

The Stars

The star systems in our galaxy and beyond and the beings that reside there also vibrate at the Fifth dimensional frequency (or higher) that is quantum e.g. Pleiadians, **Arcturians, Sirians.**

Quantum energy has many startling attributes but the most significant one is its ability to react to the consciousness that surrounds it. It responds directly to our thoughts, words, feelings, beliefs and most of all to our intention. This has exciting implications for both healing and transformation.

What we think we create. As John Kehoe says in his book *Quantum Warrior: The Future of the Mind,* with every thought, feeling and action we are 'weaving the web' and adding imprints to our Merkabah Field which then become our reality. Our conscious and subconscious minds have approximately 60,000 thoughts a day. Our subconscious mind is responsible for 95% of these thoughts which are mostly the reflection of fear-based patterns and beliefs from childhood and other lifetimes. Most of us are not aware of these subconscious beliefs or the power they have to keep us stuck. Many of the core beliefs that sabotage our progress have their origin in past life experiences.

Quantum Physics is the scientific study of the behaviour and attributes of quantum energy. This branch of science, birthed in the mid-1920s, differed from Newtonian physics in that it focused on energy not matter.

Scientific discovery has long been divided into the three disciplines of Physics, Biology and Chemistry. There is a growing understanding among the **New Scientists**, including Gregg Braden and Bruce Lipton, about the importance of energy to all of these 'separate' sciences. New scientific discoveries about the quantum elements in our bodies and in the 'field' around us are helping us see how this energy is connected.

This energy is also bringing Science and Spirituality together. There is increasing scientific proof of the energetic component that has long been at the centre of many spiritual traditions. Physics and metaphysics are no longer mutually exclusive. Ironically it is quantum energy that is demonstrating our connectedness and teaching us that there is no separation and that we are one.

The Fifth Dimensional energy streaming into the planet is activating the quantum fields within us, around us and of Planet Earth. Having a strong Merkabah Field optimises our capacity for healing, personal transformation and manifestation. Most spiritual practices help us to strengthen this field.

Anything that raises our vibration, purifies our body and re-inforces these positive energetics. Opening our Akashic Record is an easy way to connect with and unlock our quantum potential. The timelessness of the Akashic Records mirrors that of this energy which doesn't operate in a linear time frame but consists of waves which can exist in the past, present and future simultaneously. Within our Akashic Record we can travel to the 'past' and the 'future.' This time travel enables us to connect with experiences and attributes that can help us in the present and supports us to release the energy of anything that is keeping us stuck.

The quantum aspects within the cells of our bodies have their own intelligence and respond to our instructions. By engaging with the quantum energy field held at a cellular level in our non-coding DNA, we can clear emotional and physical blocks and heal ourselves on a deep soul level. We can work within the quantum field of the Akashic Records for personal transformation in the form of:

- emotional and physical healing
- manifestation and miracles.

The more our bodies resonate with the high vibration quantum energy, the easier it is for us to transform ourselves and to create our own heaven on Earth.

As I stated earlier, the most important attribute of this energy is the way it responds directly to our consciousness, and most significantly, to our intention. Within our Akashic Record, with the power of pure intention, we can release beliefs that are limiting us and use words to upgrade and re-programme our subconscious minds. Once these new linguistic imprints with all of their power and potential have been created in the etheric it is only a matter of time before they are transferred to our conscious mind and become our reality.

As well as its ability to react to the consciousness that surrounds it quantum energy has many other attributes.

Quantum energy is:

- high vibrational energy of the Fifth or higher dimensions
- not linear but multidimensional; it travels in waves or packets of light
- not limited by time and space; it can be in many places at once
- able to communicate with other quantum energy
- intelligent and sociable; it is drawn to other quantum energy
- Benevolent; it works with other quantum energy for our highest good.

Evidence of these attributes is starting to emerge. Scientific method and its research processes take time. Current scientific proof is not keeping up with what is becoming obvious to many... that there is a new field of energy on the planet.

Despite this, research, such as the often quoted 'Double-Slit' experiment have revealed the quantum attributes of this energy. In this experiment scientists fired tiny pieces of matter (photons and atomic-sized objects) at a screen with two small openings in it. When both slits were opened, an interference pattern emerged which showed that the energy travelled in waves. When the experiment was observed, the energy travelled separately through the openings, appearing as the two separate strips we, as linear thinkers, would expect. This suggested that the energy was affected by and responsive to the consciousness of the person conducting the experiment. This tendency has been noticed by other scientists and is called 'the observer effect.'

Other experiments are also suggesting that this new energy is affected by consciousness and that it is responding to the thoughts and feelings of those around it. In her Intention Experiments (more about this later), Lynne Mc Taggart, a New Scientist, teacher and author has worked with Russian physicist Konstantin Korotkov and his device called *Sputnik* to prove its existence. *Sputnik* is a sensor and attachment system which is able to pick up on changes in emotion. These changes then alter the surrounding electromagnetic field and result in a dramatic change in the atmospheric charge in the laboratory.

The amplitude of the electromagnetic waves that surround the planet is called the **Schumann Resonance**. Instruments assessing this activity suggest that consciousness can be measured and that the Schumann Resonance is a reflection of this. Noticeable upsurges in electromagnetic energy have been registered around the time of huge outpourings of emotion on the planet such as the Boxing Day Tsunami and when Princess Diana died. What is interesting is that these spikes in energy occurred before the event which suggests that something 'beyond linearity' is happening and that the band of quantum energy that circles the Earth can operate outside of time and space.

Other experiments are also proving this quantum ability to communicate at a distance. In one such experiment DNA, in the form of human tissue, was taken from a volunteer. The human 'guinea pig' was then shown stimulus that evoked strong feelings. When the volunteer experienced positive feelings their DNA tissue expanded and when they felt negative emotions, the DNA contracted. This not only demonstrated a clear connection between consciousness and matter but that separation made no difference to the outcome. The results were the same if the subject and their tissue sample were in the same room, or miles apart.

Other research is also revealing the existence of the most exciting attribute of this new energy, that our thoughts create our reality. In one experiment when a human tissue sample was placed in a vacuum, scientists noticed that the surrounding photons, atoms or molecules took on the shape of the sample. They concluded, that if our thoughts and feelings influence our DNA and our DNA is able to shape the world around us, that we are the creators of our experiences.

Entanglement is the scientific term for the attribute that quantum energy has to connect and work with other quantum energy. This phenomenon, where particles of matter that are separated react in a similar way, was first observed and studied in 1935 by Einstein and two others. Einstein called it 'spooky action at a distance.' These and subsequent experiments supported the view that quantum particles can communicate and work together at a distance.

Quantum energy has always existed but the dense energy of the Third Dimension was difficult to penetrate and transcend. Since December 2012 everything has changed. This energy is taking over our world and is affecting our reality. Quantum energy responds directly to our consciousness and as our consciousness changes so too is our human experience, moment by moment, thought by thought. There is an interdependence. What we think and feel goes out into the field and what is in the field affects what we think and feel.

Fifth Dimensional energy is attracted to anything else that is quantum whether it exists in the human body, on this planet or elsewhere. It is benevolent. It wants to help us and is ready to work with other quantum aspects to heal and transform our lives. In the words of Kryon, 'You need quantum energies to activate, energize and study other quantum energies. They will only wake up when exposed to other multidimensional energies.'

As a portal to quantum energy the potentials for healing in the Akashic Records are immense. It is easy to facilitate in this amplified Fifth Dimensional space where intention is key. I open the Akashic Records with a short statement I call 'The Access Intention.' I then create a healing intention statement with the help of whoever I am working with. If we are dealing with an emotional issue I get them to read it, if it is a physical issue I read it out.

Simple examples are:

- *It is my intention to completely release all feelings of unworthiness so I can find the peace, love and fulfilment I deserve.*

- *It is my intention to assist xxx so they are completely healed from their condition of sinusitis.*

Once the intention is out there in the quantum entry way of the Records, the aspects mentioned earlier rally around to effect the healing that is necessary. Sometimes it just involves talking to the innate and releasing and re-programming.

I am not able to open someone's Akashic Record without their permission but I can bring in the Higher Selves of others and call on the assistance of Spirit Guides, Archangels, Ascended Masters, Star Beings and elementals. I always work with the Ascended Master St Germain to remove the stuck energy of feelings and beliefs of limitation and in recent years have been bringing in energy from higher dimensional dragons and the unicorns to assist with the releasing process.

Manifestation Magic

The high vibration, quantum energy of the Records is perfect for manifesting. Responding directly to consciousness and intention, whatever we are thinking of becomes our reality.

As mentioned earlier, the Merkabah, which surrounds our body is the magnetic field which holds the energy of our consciousness. Within our Merkabah is our light body which is a Fifth Dimensional energetic version of our physical body.

Regularly being in the Records creates and strengthens the light body, activating lines of light that come out from the physical acupressure points in our **meridians**. These energetic points form a golden lattice around us which is a hothouse for manifestation and creation. It is through working with and within this field that we can transform our lives.

The energy flowing into and being activated on this planet is making it easier to create and design our lives at will. As the saying goes, we must be careful what we wish for. In the new energy we will attract what we focus on and much faster than ever before.

Teachers and visionaries, John Kehoe, Bruce Lipton and Joe Dispenza among others, have talked of the power of our subconscious mind. If our beliefs shape our reality and we are not aware of the origin and content of the majority of these, then it is hardly surprising that our lives rarely reflect our wishes and desires. The Akashic Records are a gateway to the subconscious. With their help we can find the root cause of a thought, fear, feeling or behaviour pattern. Working with St Germain and by talking to our bodies we can work to release and transmute this. Transmuting the energetic imprints that keep us stuck creates a space of high vibrational energy within and around our bodies that is perfect for manifesting. The vortex of energy can be used with conscious thought to magnetise into our reality what we think and dream of. This Akashic forcefield is a powerful tool for positive change.

Lynne Mc Taggart, who I mentioned earlier, has conducted what she calls 'intention experiments' all over the world. In these she demonstrates the power of group intention to influence outcomes and to create miracles. Her 'Power of Eight' groups, also operate globally. These groups of approximately eight people meet regularly online and create an intention for the healing of a member of the group or someone known to them. They concentrate on this statement for ten minutes. These focused group experiments have had miraculous results and many heart-warming spin-offs, not only for the 'Power of Eight' members, but for others in their lives.

Mc Taggart also facilitates global healing where thousands of people all over the planet connect physically and online to focus on specific outcomes such as 'To bring Peace to the Middle East.'

This was the intention for a healing she conducted in November, 2017.

Our intention is to lower violence and restore peace in Jerusalem by 20% or more.

In this experiment Lynne worked with the Russian, Korotkov. She showed participants a photograph of *Sputnik* and a container of water nearby. She asked them to focus on the intention and the water. At the end of ten minutes the water was brighter and more harmonious. Lynne reported that these characteristics were even more noticeable later when the participants were speaking from the heart about their experiences.

Water is not quantum as such, but as **Masuru Emoto** proved, it is programmable, and able to carry and reflect the consciousness around it. After the group meditation, the higher frequency readings on *Sputnik* reflected a more enlightened consciousness. Some time later Lynne received notification from the Israeli police that there had been significant decreases in violence in the old city of Jerusalem between the end of 2017 and the beginning of 2018. After this experiment and others with a similar focus, many participants reported that their relationships improved and their lives became more peaceful. Lynne's findings are reflecting this trend of the altruism of participants being rewarded. Those who give receive many blessings in return. This is how quantum energy works and to my mind is the core of its beauty.

As a teacher I have had first-hand experience of the power of group energy. There is no comparison between the vibration at the beginning of a workshop and by the end. The energy of the group synchronises and harmonises itself to the highest level in the room. By the end of a weekend the close energetic connection is palpable. A state of coherence has been created.

The *HeartMath Institute* teaches techniques for creating internal coherence between the heart and the brain. The heart has a magnetic field around it which is 100 times stronger than the magnetic field of the brain. Linking in to these fields makes it easier to connect with and utilise the energy of the wider 'field' and its healing potentials. Experiments have shown that this state of heart/brain alignment has many physical benefits among them hormonal balance and reduced blood pressure. Being in the Fifth Dimensional energy of the Records, I believe, promotes coherence and other feelings of wellbeing. The bubble of quantum energy that forms around us when we are in the Records helps us to link in with other reservoirs of this energy and to the larger quantum field. Writers, such as Ervin Laszlo and Kingsley Dennis are even calling this matrix 'the Akashic Field.'

As I touched on earlier, we have a two-way, push-pull connection with this soup of energy. The thoughts and feelings we are putting out become imprinted in the field and we can also pull information in from it and anything else we desire. This field is like the world wide web, an energetic version of Google. Like Google it is best to go in with a specific question or purpose. The answers to our questions are in our Akashic Record, but increasingly everything we want to know is out there in the quantum matrix, which reflects the collective consciousness.

Being in the Akashic Records makes it easier to access this field. From this place it is also easier to create. The golden web around us acts as a 5D transmitter which broadcasts our feelings, beliefs and dreams out to the universe to be picked up and acted on by quantum elements. Again, intention is the key. We have to be careful what signals we send out and we also need to be specific. Just as what we think, feel and believe as individuals is imprinted in our Merkabah and creates our reality, our group consciousness is also etched into and carried by the web of quantum energy loosely referred to as 'the field.' This energy works with other quantum energy to respond to our thoughts and to fulfil our wishes. The imprints we have in our field set in motion an energetic that searches for a vibratory match and creates coincidences and synchronicities that draw to us what we desire.

The more positive our thoughts and feelings are the better, as what we send out becomes part of and influences the whole. Joy holds a high vibration and when we feel it, it becomes part of the field for us all to enjoy. We become literally 'entrained to joy.' The imprints in the matrix will determine how long it takes us to move through the Covid pandemic and other world crises we are facing. Love is always better than fear and the more love and peace we can project out en masse the better.

I always finish my Level 2 workshops with a group manifestation exercise. The Akashic Records are a dynamic place for manifesting our individual desires but this process is even more powerful in a group. At a workshop when all the participants have their Akashic Records open, are in a state of coherence and holding the space for their own dreams as well as everyone else's, miracles can and do happen.

When Jo, a workshop participant took part in this exercise she focused on her personal relationships. She targeted:

- manifesting a reunion with her son who she had been estranged from for five years

- healing and help for her partner who had addiction issues, and

- a peaceful transition for her elderly mother who had been diagnosed with congestive heart failure.

A week or two after the workshop she emailed me to say that after a trip to the Emergency Department her partner had made a hypnotherapy appointment and was seeking other help for his addictions, her 99 year old mother had passed away peacefully after four days of bed rest with Jo at her side and that she had reconnected with her son who had been a pall-bearer at his grandmother's funeral.

She finished her email by saying, '*This was a powerful weekend starting many healing processes in my life – it was me that needed the healing!*'

Before I begin this group activity, I talk about the process of manifestation. I have learned that it is important to have a clear intention and to have dealt with any beliefs that are blocking what we desire. If we have underlying feelings of unworthiness or of being undeserving, it will be difficult to attract what we want. It is important to come from the heart and to feel the emotions we will feel when our dream becomes reality. It is helpful to visualise it in the mind and to feel gratitude for what we already have as well as for what will come in the future. The most important part of the manifestation process is to let go of all attachment to outcome, to have no idea of how, when and where what we dream of will happen, but to trust that it will and to let it go. It is important to set the energy of our dream or desire free and to know that when the time is right our wishes will come true.

I have been consciously manifesting both big and small things for years with some degree of success. Buying and selling houses has been my forte. In 2003 we had a beautiful home in Thorndon, the oldest suburb in New Zealand. I loved our house but we needed a fourth bedroom and I had a husband who I knew would be happier without a mortgage to pay. The market was tight and property was expensive. I knew we would not find a new house in the usual way. I tuned into my intuition and my daughter Mary and I did a leaflet drop in streets near her school. One house looked too small but the lawns had just been mowed. Its earthy freshness drew us in and Mary popped a flier in the letter box. That night an elderly couple phoned and we were able to buy this house (which had an extra bedroom) at such a reasonable price that we were suddenly mortgage-free. My husband Marty, was able to leave a job he found increasingly toxic and pursue his calling as a Coach and we had enough money to renovate our new home and go on a family holiday to Australia. Several years later we sold it for the exact price I had written down in a pre-sale manifestation exercise which was way above its valuation at the time.

Lynne Mc Taggart says that specific intentions work best. With houses I have often been detailed in terms of price and moving dates. When we left our Thorndon home, I had one date in mind that would suit. I was surprised when the couple who sold us the property asked for a moving date a week later. Soon afterwards they phoned to say they had found a house and asked if they could bring the settlement day forward … to the exact date I had written down. Whenever manifestation has worked for me I have had no doubts about the outcome. Not letting any shadow of doubt enter the mind is all important. As I write this, I am in a peaceful cottage near the sea. From the kitchen table I can see the sand dunes and the ocean waves rolling in. It looks exactly as a visualised it several months ago when I decided that if I was going to get this book written I would need a place in nature with no distractions.

Many of us are noticing that the time between putting out a thought and the universe acting on it is getting shorter. On a good day, when everything is in alignment, I have almost instant wish fulfilment.

The manifestation magic of the Records is teaching me that miracles can and do happen and in the most unexpected ways. They are all around us and if we notice and are grateful for them they will become a regular occurrence. Miracles are our birthright. They are what we deserve and are yet another way that the Akashic Records can help to alleviate our suffering. As we transition more fully into the Fifth Dimension, this powerful vibration will create magic in our lives more quickly and easily. In the meantime, the Akashic Records can connect us directly to this quantum power source. Through accessing this energetic we can magnify our creative abilities and plan and design our lives.

The Akashic Records are the perfect Ascension tool. Their energy can facilitate healing and transformation and help us to create new and exciting realities for humanity. A bridge between the old and the new, they carry the energy of pain, trauma and suffering but they also hold the potentials for a glorious future as a Fifth Dimensional planet. The new energy name for the Records is the Akashic Field. With the power of intention we can tap into its powerful vibration to take us beyond suffering forever.

Chapter 4

Letting Go

The most important part in the manifestation process is letting go of 'attachment to outcome.' If we have zero expectations we can more easily go with the flow of whatever life presents to us. Living in the moment has never been more important especially in this time of uncertainty when we can no longer plan or envision a future based on the past.

In the conscious parenting course I used to teach there were six principles. The first one was 'Accept your children exactly as they are.' It took a while but learning to accept Alice exactly the way she was enabled us both to move forward with our lives. Letting go of any expectations for her future and enjoying and appreciating whatever the moment presented made all the difference.

The Akashic Records have helped me see that there is always more than meets the eye. I have learned to be patient and know that we often have to deal with 'the grit in the oyster' before we find the pearl. Equally, I have learned that what can seem like a disaster, on the surface, is always perfect at a higher level. Last year, I made a second visit to my friend's beach house to devote myself to a week of writing. I plugged in my computer but when I tried to connect the cord to my laptop it would not go in. No charge meant no computer and that I couldn't work on this book. I had no choice but to relax and those days walking on the beach and reconnecting with myself were just what I needed. Everything unfolded perfectly once I let go of my plans. By the end of the week my computer was fixed and we had both been recharged.

Letting go is the theme of the moment. We are letting go of the little things but are also being forced to let go of something big... the past. Covid-19 is a critical moment in our history and nothing will ever be the same. The ripples and repercussions are already spiralling out into the future taking the human race off on a new and, for many people, unexpected trajectory.

At this time of rapid evolution all that has limited us is coming up to be released. This is happening whether we are conscious of it or not. In recent years, wave after wave of high frequency energy has flowed onto the Earth. The consciousness that flourished in the old energy but is too dense and heavy for the new, has been revealing itself. This energy alteration has been challenging for everyone but particularly hard on Old Souls who have thousands of years of distorted thinking behind them. Lifetime after lifetime of living in a dense vibration of fear and suffering, of being persecuted, victimised and attacked have taken a toll. For Old Souls deep feelings of self-hatred underpin sabotaging beliefs like 'I deserve to suffer,' 'I am not good enough, 'I am a failure' and 'It is all my fault.' It has been difficult to carry the light amidst the darkness but Old Souls like myself have persevered. We have kept coming back so we can be here for this moment when finally the energy and life as we know it is changing. Our feelings of shame, guilt and unworthiness run deep.

In our current lifetimes, many Old Souls have chosen difficult experiences early in life, as catalysts to clear and release these imprints once and for all. Birth in this lifetime was traumatic for me. I chose to be born both prematurely and as a twin. I was separated from my mother and sister and placed alone in an incubator for six weeks. From Day One in this lifetime the patterns of behaviour and thoughts I have needed to transcend were triggered. As well as this early trauma, I had a father I adored but whose criticisms I took to heart. This judgement fed into my feelings of unworthiness.

Building on these feelings of inadequacy, from the age of five to seventeen I had an unhealthy friendship with a girl I allowed to dominate and manipulate me. When my child-hood ended I was battle weary and spent but the stage had been set for what was to come. These experiences made me stronger and put me on the path of personal development that has brought me to where I am today. My Akashic Record has given me information about my past life relationships with my father and my childhood friend which makes sense to me. When we meet up with souls we have known before it is easy to slip back into the 'same old, same old' groove of the past. At this time of completion here on Earth many of us are coming up against past life adversaries so we can clear and transmute the karmic energies which have been the hallmark of the Third Dimension.

For the last twenty years 'peeling back' and releasing the energetic layers has been a constant for me, with the process gathering in intensity in the last ten. This ongoing reveal has been a key part of my personal transformation. Alchemists were celebrated for their ability to transmute base metal into gold. All of us on Earth at this time are experiencing these alchemical changes whether we like it or not. To get to the gold we have to let go of the old. For lasting change to occur we have to surrender and release all that is no longer serving us.

Within the safe and loving energy of the Records I have let go of programmes that have had me in their grip for lifetimes. I have also facilitated this process for thousands of people. I often conduct a group session at workshops to help participants release the energetic vibration of the rigid and debilitating thought forms that have limited them during their lives on Earth.

When you state an intention it sets the energy in motion to make it happen. The powerful words I have spoken within the sacred space of the Akash have set the scene for my own transfiguration. These energy imprints almost take on a life of their own as they attract and create the perfect circumstances for us to 'let go.'

Through my almost daily work in the Akashic Records there has been a gradual energetic change. This soul vibration forces us to 'walk our talk' and to live and speak our truth. I now have to alter the dynamics of unhealthy relationships or let them go. Treatment from others that I allowed in the past is no longer acceptable and some of my relationships have come up for review. While I have not stopped caring about people, as a 'rescuer in recovery', I am now putting up stronger boundaries. The energy of the Records has strengthened me. My clarity and sense of self-worth have increased and things I would have kept inside ten years ago are now coming out of my mouth. I know my own mind and am no longer afraid to give my thoughts and feelings a voice.

As the Fifth Dimension beckons us with its pure and enticing energy, the Third Dimensional vibration we have become accustomed to keeps pulling us back. Past life soul expressions are reaching out, dragging us into entrenched behaviours and keeping many of us stuck. Recently, I became aware of a deep-seated fear I had of disappointing people. In 2020, with so many wanting help, I felt like I was no longer in control of my life. I was waking up every day stressed and anxious at the size of my 'to do' list. It was hard to say no to people but every time I said 'yes' a part of me withered and died and I could feel the potential success of my soul mission slipping further away. Out of this turmoil a belief surfaced. 'If I don't do what others want I will die.' I opened my Record and could see where this came from... many lifetimes of being persecuted and even killed for not doing what others asked of me. I discussed this with my friend Caroline over lunch and she said, 'You must break the pattern before it breaks you.'

With these wise words resounding in both head and heart, I called in all of my past life selves who had suffered in this way. There was an army of them! Servants, victims, soldiers, they came in many shapes, sizes and guises. I gave them a 'talking to' telling them that it was time for all of us to let go of this belief and the pattern of self-sacrifice forever.

As I let go of sabotaging programmes, I have also been learning to let go as a parent. Being a mother to my three, now adult children, Alice (32), Hugh (29) and Mary (25) has been my greatest joy and at times, my deepest sorrow. Because of her particular challenges, it has been hardest for me to let go of Alice. To do this I had to first let go of my fears around her suicidality.

The Akashic Records helped me to see that the soul has a choice – that no decision is a wrong one and suicide is a valid option for some when the pain becomes so unbearable that death seems the only way to end it. Several years ago, after yet another midnight dash to hospital, I spoke to Alice and told her that she had to stay alive for herself and not for us... that I had seen how hard life was for her and would understand if one day she decided she had had enough. I told her that on a soul level the soul never dies and if she was no longer here physically, she would still be close.

'I want to live,' said Alice. I felt a huge wave of relief but also a big shift in energy. I was letting go of the responsibility I was carrying for my daughter's life and the belief that I had any control over whether she would live or die. In that moment I held onto the love for my daughter but surrendered all other feelings of obligation towards her. I had given her life but that life was no longer my responsibility. I was handing that over to her.

In 2009 when Alice was in Intensive Care for ten days following an overdose, a nurse removed the small, bone necklace from around her neck and gave it to me. I put it on immediately. It often came undone and I had to re-tie it. Towards the end of that year I secured it with a double knot and it remained around my neck after that. I had become superstitious about the necklace, thinking that if I took it off she might die. A few years ago I realised that the necklace was a symbol of an unhealthy connection to my daughter and that it represented the energy of fear and of the past. On the spur of the moment when Alice was with us I told her that I felt it was time to remove it. She agreed with this. She found some scissors and 'snip' it was gone! This symbolic act instantly energised me. I felt so much lighter that I did something unusual (for me). I went to the kitchen and cleaned and tidied my pantry.

It has been difficult to let go of my feelings of responsibility for others. The whirlpool of rapid change we are currently experiencing on Earth is creating a new paradigm where we have to take responsibility for ourselves. In this new energy, the fall-out and consequences of irresponsibility can 'boomerang' back on us very quickly. In recent years the light has been coming in at such a rate that any way we are acting that is out of alignment is 'in our face' and impossible to ignore. We are being called to step up and take full responsibility for our actions. How we live is our choice. We can no longer expect anyone to save us or to pick up the pieces when we make poor decisions.

Those of us who are people pleasers and rescuers magnetically attract those who are needy. We have much to learn from each other. Being compassionate and kind is one thing but helping those who have no intention of changing or of taking responsibility for themselves is another. Having said that there is always a reason for the way people behave. If people aren't parented properly they can spend their whole lives looking for substitute parents. With clients like that I have come to the conclusion that the kindest thing I can do for them and for myself, is give them tools to heal themselves and send them on their way. The energy of the New Earth and of the Akashic Records is the energy of empowerment. Within their Akashic Record they can find the answers to all of their questions and identify and release limiting programmes. With the help of the Records they can leave victimhood behind forever and take control of their lives.

When I talked with my past life 'victim/servant' selves, I employed a healing method I often use with clients to help them let go of past life beliefs and deep-seated fears that are having a negative impact. In their Record I can see there are past life aspects that are not at peace. They are drawing on their energy and affecting them emotionally and sometimes physically. The information does not come in a straight-forward, linear way but in snippets which I piece together. Once I have the full story I am able to take my client back to the life or lives I have connected with. I guide them to talk to their past life self so they can resolve and release the experience they are still carrying. Most clients get a mental image of how they looked in their former life which they are able to describe to me. I get them to visualise themselves standing in front of their past life aspect. I ask them to hold the hands of their former self and to look into their eyes. I channel through the words that come into my head.

Note: I always tell my clients that:

- they don't need to repeat my words if they don't resonate

- if their own words come through to start talking and I will stop. (It is always more powerful when the words come from them).

I support them as they tell their past life selves that what happened was not their fault and try to get their former soul expression to see their actions in a wider context and a more positive light. My clients then tell their past life selves that they are carrying trauma, beliefs, feelings and fears for them and that it is time to let them go. With my guidance they encourage their past life aspect to release the memory and emotions of the event. They then ask them for help with their work and future path. Finally I get my client to reassure their former soul expression that they will do their best to finish what they were unable to complete. We don't leave the past life persona until they are peaceful and relaxed and the burden of suffering that my client has been carrying for them has been lifted.

Expressions of past life energy have amped up in recent years. We are being repeatedly challenged to let go of self-defeating ideas and behaviours. A simple belief taken on in a lifetime years ago can still have an adverse effect on our present day lives.

When I opened Matt's Akashic Record it was obvious that he was carrying past life trauma. I saw him during World War II as a German rabbi, a warm-hearted spiritual leader who cared for his flock and did his best to protect them. In his current life he is a well-qualified professional running a business that provides a valuable service. Despite this, he admitted he is struggling financially and has had to sell his house because he feels unable to charge his clients what he is worth. Matt told me that when he sends out bills he becomes fearful and anxious and obsessed by the thought, 'If I ask for too much something terrible will happen.'

His life as a rabbi came into view. He was studying a list of those to be deported to concentration camps and on it were the names of family and people he cared about. He decided to take matters into his own hands and begged the German authorities to spare them. His valiant plan backfired. Affronted by his audacity, they not only sent those on the list to the gas chambers, but many others.

It was obvious that Matt had brought this fear and belief into his present life and that it was still affecting him. I guided him to talk to the German rabbi and to let go of this belief so he could overcome this stumbling block and earn what he deserves.

Checking in with Matt some months later he told me that our akashic work had helped him. At the end of our session I recommended that he continue to speak to the rabbi if old fears came up and he had done this.

He ended his email by saying *'I can't remember the last time I felt a sick feeling in my stomach when I sent out my bills.'*

The pattern of self-sacrifice and of being responsible for others runs through many of my lifetimes, and also the female line of my family.

I know it is time to let this go and I have been working hard to do so.

It was also a theme for a client, an open-hearted and compassionate woman named Jayne. She was spreading herself very thinly, struggling to cope with her family's mental health needs, her own wellbeing and the demands of a fulltime job in the health sector. In her Akashic Record I could see that she had lived many lives of devotion to others. She had even honed these caregiving skills, in between lives, by working with those who died suddenly as a result of trauma. Her specialty, it seems, was in helping those that others had given up on. Like many of the Old Souls of Earth she had taken on the difficult assignments. I saw her helping outcasts who had been shunned by society, rescuing and giving drunks shelter in the 1500s and helping prostitutes in the nineteenth century. I looked at her soul contract with her two children and saw they were both souls suffering from extreme past life trauma who no one else had been brave enough to take on.

In this life Jayne was determined to let go of this pattern for good and she had chosen her complex and challenging family situation as a trigger for this. On a soul level Jayne had planned the perfect circumstances to force her to change.

I set my intention and worked with Jayne to remove this energetic. I asked St Germain and the dragons to clear all imprints of the pattern of self-sacrifice and some specific beliefs and fears associated with it. I completed the session by talking Jayne through a physical release process where her body let go of this template as well as the memories of the lifetimes where it had played out.

Just over a year later I had another session with Jayne. There had been many changes since we last spoke. I was thrilled to hear that her family were now content and that she had left her demanding job and found her passion in the healing arts. This had helped raise her energy which had flowed down and had a beneficial effect on those around her. After a short interlude, working as a caregiver, she became disillusioned. The service delivery was not in keeping with her values and she found the courage to leave. She applied for and got a job working twenty hours a week, in an office that was close to home. It sounded perfect. She set up a website for her business, planned to launch some courses and then everything ground to a halt. Her new position was not the part-time job she had wanted and soon she was working longer hours to keep up. It was tedious and draining. She had less time for her own work and before long she found herself feeling stuck and back in a place she thought she had left behind forever.

Many lightworkers, myself included, can relate to Jayne's situation. Honouring our soul work is just the beginning. Once we have stepped onto the path our commitment is tested, particularly if we have a pattern of many lifetimes to shift. These old templates exist energetically in our field and if underlying beliefs of being undeserving and unworthy are not changed, old fears can be triggered which can sabotage our progress.

Opening Jayne's Record again, her pattern of self-sacrifice jumped out in two separate lives. In one, she was the eldest daughter in a large family in England in the nineteenth century. She fell in love with a man in a county 30 miles away. He wanted to marry her and the opportunity for a new life of love, marriage and children beckoned. Her three siblings in that lifetime thought it was her job to look after their widowed father. Succumbing to the pressure, she did what she felt was her duty, broke off her engagement and lived with and cared for her father until he died. By then she was old, resentful and bitter because she had sacrificed her own happiness to meet the needs of others.

In another life I saw her, once again, as a single woman. She was on an ocean liner that was sinking. Passengers were being herded into life boats, women and children first. With the help of my inner sight, I saw her refusing to take her seat on the boat. Once the women and children were loaded, she insisted that young male crew members take her place, and then she watched from the sinking ship while everyone else rowed to safety. Once again she had sacrificed herself for others, literally, this time as she lost her life. To help her release this pattern I took Jayne back to these lives. With my guidance she told these past life aspects that she had a strong sense of duty towards others and a desire to please that was stopping her from following her heart and pursuing her dreams. She told them she had been carrying their feelings and that it was time to let them go. She acknowledged them for their finer qualities and asked for their help and support to live her soul purpose and bring her work to the world. 'I will do it for you and I will do it for me,' she said.

She finished by telling them that putting our own needs first is not selfish but is for the highest good of those around us.

Afterwards Jayne told me she felt like shaking both of the women, in particular the 'eldest daughter.' I told her it was important she didn't allow herself to sink beneath the waves of obligation and duty in yet another lifetime.

Like Jayne, I too have been affected by past life sacrifice. In my first book, *The Magic of the Akashic Records*, I wrote how I carried the shame and guilt from my most recent past life into this one and how these deep feelings of unworthiness affected me. In that lifetime I was a German priest who ended up in a Concentration camp in World War II. Since I wrote my last book I have received the new information that I was a prisoner who, in order to survive, chose to help the SS with some of the grimmer tasks. I was an inmate who was so terrified of death that I worked for the Nazis running the camp. One of my jobs was burning bodies and I tried to do it with dignity and prayer but that does not excuse the fact that I was aiding and abetting the Nazi machine. I sold my soul to survive. When the war was over I could not forgive myself. A depressed and tormented man, I died soon afterwards. When I was in my thirties and forties in my current life, this man obsessed me. I read every book about the Holocaust I could find and battled for a long time with negative feelings which I realised came not so much from me but from the German priest.

The Akashic Records can help us to let go of and lay the ghosts of the past. At this time on Earth, circumstances are also conspiring to assist us to gain closure from past lives that still haunt us. A well-known spiritual medium in New Zealand is a friend of mine. In her last life she was a concentration camp inmate who I cared about, respected and failed to help. Together we pieced together the circumstances of our last life together. Seeing her happy, successful and using her gifts as a force for good has helped me to forgive myself. I have realised that her last life, that was cut short, has set her up for this one. Seeing and understanding the bigger plan has helped me let go of the trauma I have been carrying.

I was able to let go on a higher level and in a more deeply healing way at a workshop I ran in Sydney in 2017. On the first day, it became apparent that many of the participants were Jewish or had connections with the Jewish population in Australia. One young man, called Leon, came to the workshop with the sole intention of solving a family puzzle. His grandfather, who died in the 1980s when Leon was a child, never spoke of the past. After his death, Leon discovered that his grandfather had had another family, a wife and two children he had lost in the Holocaust. Post war, he had migrated to Australia, remarried and started a new life. Leon wanted to know the names of his grandfather's first wife and children so he could find out more about their lives and the circumstances of their deaths. Participants at the workshop helped him with these details and others with Jewish backgrounds were able to tell him where to go for further information. There is a larger Jewish community in Australia than in New Zealand

and I felt the burden of my past life strongly, as they told their stories. I told mine and was enveloped by such a beautiful wave of non-judgement and acceptance that I was able to let go of another huge piece of guilt and sadness. I started this lifetime on the back foot carrying World War II trauma and now with the help of the Akashic Records I have been able to release it.

Those of us who are Old Souls on this planet are surrounded by layers of thoughtforms from many lifetimes. Repeated experiences of suffering and victimhood have left their imprints on our psyche and kept many of us in a holding pattern for lifetime after lifetime. These beliefs and patterns exist energetically in our energy fields and within our cellular structure.

To clear this stuck energy I work with St Germain's Violet Flame and the dragons. This approach is effective, giving instant relief. Often it pops up in yet another layer and shifts us back to a default position of fear and limitation. If we have struggled and suffered for centuries, have built up a foundation of beliefs that support this dynamic, and chosen childhoods that have reinforced this belief system, it is difficult to dismantle the structure. We have to keep working at it. The Akashic Records offer invaluable assistance with this by keeping our vibration high, helping us to identify the blocks and in providing a soul space to heal and release them.

Light Language, a high vibration, multidimensional language of sound and light from other star systems is also effective in breaking down and transmuting this energy. As with any healing, holding the clear and pure intention for what we want is the most important part. My sister, Judy Satori (www.judysatori.com) has been speaking and using Light Language for years and has become well-known for it. I remember my feelings of disbelief the first time I heard her speaking it in 2003. I was in a café with Judy and my twin sister and I didn't know where to look. It sounded weird and I wanted to laugh. It took me a while to appreciate it and to realise its powerful healing potentials. When my son Hugh had a brain tumour in 2013 he let Judy work with him. He had radiotherapy daily for five weeks but I am sure it was the Light Language along with his positive attitude that helped the cancer disappear.

I know that the memory of how to speak these galactic dialects lies deep within my non-coding DNA but as yet have not had the urge to tap into this. I have students in my Soul History Workshops who speak it and an increasing number of them are incorporating it into the soul healing they do with clients. The Akashic Records and Light Language are a potent mix. The Records combined with this high vibrational language, spoken with pure intent, is a powerful string to the bow of any healer. In this new energy on Planet Earth any sort of sound healing is helpful and is coming into its own.

While quantum energy reacts powerfully to words it also reacts to sound. In 2019 I was letting go of some old, emotional stuff and felt out-of-sorts and challenged. I had been working hard and felt intuitively that my field was blocked and that I needed a tune up. I woke up one morning with the words 'sound healing' in my head. I went online and the name of a woman, a friend had recommended, immediately popped up. In four very relaxing sessions she worked her magic with her Tibetan bowls. As I lay there I had my Akashic Record open and held a strong intention for healing.

At a workshop a few months later, I demonstrated my technique for physical healing in the Records with a woman named Kerry. Her issue was constriction and discomfort in her throat which had worsened over the weekend. When I looked into her eyes I saw an Old Soul staring back. I could see and feel the accumulated wisdom of many lifetimes but noticed that when she spoke in front of the group, her throat became hoarse.

I asked about this in the Records. I could see her in a recent past life as a toddler who was being hidden from enemy soldiers. She was a little boy being held by his father in a dark, confined space with a group of family members and acquaintances during a raid. As small children do, he picked up on the emotions of the adults and their fear in particular. This upset him and he started to cry. The next minute he was being smothered to death by his father, who was pressured by the other adults to kill his son, so that they could survive.

I saw several other lives where Kerry had been hung and persecuted for expressing herself in a way that was seen as dangerous. The life mentioned above, however, was the most vivid and the one which appeared to be most strongly affecting her. I worked to remove the energetic imprints and to heal the trauma from these lives. At the end I guided Kerry to say some affirmations e.g 'I speak my truth with love.'

Lastly, I felt it was important that we finish the healing with Kerry opening her throat and releasing the blocked energy with sound. I asked the rest of the class to express their individual soul sound, in unison, to support her. As we did this three times we focused our intention on the healing of Kerry's throat so she could speak openly and without fear. Our combined soul voices 'raised the roof' and lifted us all up, including Kerry. At the end of the workshop she told me the constriction was gone and that her throat felt much lighter.

As an Old Soul like Kerry, I have had much to work on and release. In many of my lifetimes over thousands of years there has not been enough to go round. I have not been able to meet my material needs and it has been difficult for me to get rid of a scarcity mentality. On a soul level I have been haunted by FOMO (the fear of missing out). I have had many lifetimes where I have been shut down and stopped in my tracks. I have lived lives where sharing my secrets has cost me dearly. I have a deep-seated fear that it could happen again.

When I taught parenting I was quite competitive. I was never a well-known parenting expert and I used to compare myself with others and envy their success. The Akashic Records have helped me understand that this competitive streak is something my soul has chosen to work on. I was born into a family of five girls and had a twin sister who was good at most things. We shared a birthday and a bedroom and even had to sit next to each other at school. Full marks to my soul for choosing the perfect life situation for someone with issues of self-worth, competitiveness and jealousy. When I started giving Akashic Readings ten years ago I was, to my knowledge, the only person doing this in my country. I knew I was meant to teach others what I had learned but my conditioning and fears came up at times and I became anxious. There was a part of me that wanted to keep them all to myself, to clutch them to my chest and never let them go. I got over this, as the more time I spent in the Records, the stronger my intuitive messages became and I learned to trust and follow them. I was prompted to share my knowledge and I have now taught many people to access the Akashic Records for themselves and others. In my residential practitioner workshop I give away all my secrets. From being the only Akashic Reader online in my country it has exploded. This proliferation means many people now know about the Akashic Records and can turn to them for help.

Sharing what I have learned in the Records may have gone against some of my baser human instincts but my daughter, Alice, has also taught me that it doesn't help to hold tightly to anything in life and that when you let go something bigger and better comes in to take its place. The demand for my sessions has not diminished. I now have the joy of witnessing many others working with the Records and love the teaching role I am stepping into. None of my akashic pupils work exactly the way I do or with the same people. People are attracted to the person that is right for them. There is enough room for us all.

Competition is old energy. This vibration won't last in the Fifth Dimension. How can we compete when we are all different and do things in our own unique way? If we follow the promptings of our heart and act in integrity, we will be rewarded. Letting go of the Records and sharing their love has given me huge joy and satisfaction and has helped me to learn an important lesson.

As a species, the thing human beings most need to let go of is fear. Writing this amidst the Covid crisis, I am surrounded by it. All of us who are living on this planet, at this time, are being forced, whether we like it or not, to let go. Many of us have a deep-seated fear of change. In past lives it has often spelled disaster. Not surprisingly we are wary of change and resist rather than embrace it. Those who are attracted to this work are almost without exception, skilled lightworkers who have a high vibration. Our intention is all important. If we come from a place of fear nothing will work. The best thing we can do at this momentous time on Earth is keep our vibration high and replace fear with love. The Akashic Records can help us do both of these things.

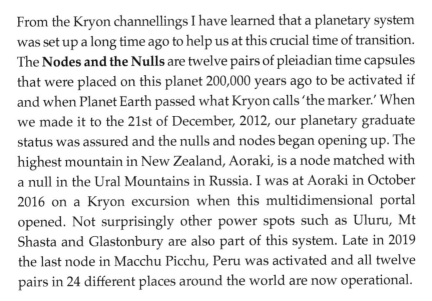

From the Kryon channellings I have learned that a planetary system was set up a long time ago to help us at this crucial time of transition. The **Nodes and the Nulls** are twelve pairs of pleiadian time capsules that were placed on this planet 200,000 years ago to be activated if and when Planet Earth passed what Kryon calls 'the marker.' When we made it to the 21st of December, 2012, our planetary graduate status was assured and the nulls and nodes began opening up. The highest mountain in New Zealand, Aoraki, is a node matched with a null in the Ural Mountains in Russia. I was at Aoraki in October 2016 on a Kryon excursion when this multidimensional portal opened. Not surprisingly other power spots such as Uluru, Mt Shasta and Glastonbury are also part of this system. Late in 2019 the last node in Macchu Picchu, Peru was activated and all twelve pairs in 24 different places around the world are now operational.

The nodes and the nulls of the planet will fast-track our planetary clearing process. They will help sweep up and transmute the energy of suffering. The nulls pull in the negative energies from the planetary grids and push them to their matched node where the energy is then released. This energy is powerful and it works with consciousness. As well as helping us let go of all that is no longer serving us, the nodes and the nulls circulate and magnify any positive energy on the planet. A sudden outburst of compassion, for example, will very quickly be dispersed and leave an indelible mark. In this new energy no one owns anything. It is out there in the collective consciousness for us all to use and increasingly we are being able to do so.

Our rising consciousness and the higher energetic vibration on this planet will also make it easier to shift the imprints of pain and suffering. The more quantum the energy surrounding us becomes, the more readily it will respond to intention and the easier it will be to release this debilitating energy forever. The Akashic Records are a quantum haven. Holding memories of lifetimes of human suffering, they are the perfect container for the planetary process of surrender. With the power of intention we will be able to let go of all that has held us back and rise above our human pain to the place where the truth of our eternal soul resides.

Chapter 5

Trauma

We all suffer from Post Traumatic Stress Disorder (PTSD). It is part of the human condition. In the cells of our bodies and in our merkabah fields we carry the energy of trauma not only from this lifetime, but from many others.

Trauma is caused by a distressing event that overwhelms us and our body's psychological and often physiological ability to cope. The human response to trauma is 'fight, fright or freeze.' When we aren't able to release the energy or integrate and process it, it becomes frozen and stored in our bodies. As Peter Levine, creator of the trauma modality, *Somatic Experiencing*, wrote in his book *Healing Trauma*, when discussing the aftermath of a traumatic event, 'Unless (we) can find a way to discharge the excess energy (our bodies) will keep responding as if (we are) in pain and helpless.' In an attempt to clear and heal trauma our bodies keep responding to triggers (flashbacks) and recreating the original trauma.

Over the last fourteen years I have been no stranger to trauma. Being woken up by a hospital phone call in the middle of the night has happened too often for that. My daughter, Alice, is no stranger to trauma either. Her original diagnosis of *Borderline Personality Disorder* (BPD) has now been changed to *Complex Post Traumatic Stress Disorder* (CPTSD). BPD is characterised by 'emotional dysregulation, an unstable sense of self, difficulty forming relationships and repeated self-harming behaviours.' A diagnosis of BPD carries with it considerable stigma.

A study by Patrick Walker (Adjunct Research Associate) and Jayashri Kulkarni (Professor of Psychiatry) at Monash University argues that BPD should be considered as a complex response to trauma. They say that those diagnosed with BPD all have a history of major trauma and that they exhibit the same behaviours as sufferers of PTSD. They contend that clinicians often discriminate against those with BPD and that if it was recognised as a 'traumatic spectrum condition,' patients would get better treatment. With this changed point of view they would be seen as victims of 'past injustice rather than the perpetrators of their own misfortune.'

This is also the theme of the latest trauma book I have read. Written by Dr Bruce Perry and Oprah Winfrey, they say, the question to ask is *What Happened to You?* (title of the book) rather than 'What is wrong with you?'

During the worst of Alice's illness we made the difficult decision to admit her to our local psychiatric hospital. Family outings to the Psych Ward were the backdrop to my youngest daughter, Mary's teenage years. Alice spent nearly three consecutive years there with little respite and it was horrendous to see her endure so much pain. Our decision saved Alice's life and ultimately brought the daughter and sister we loved back to us. She can't consciously remember much of it now... but we can. The sound of an ambulance siren still makes our hearts race.

Alice's PTSD is certainly complex. I believe it includes all that she has brought into this lifetime from past lives, trauma experienced in early childhood and as a teenager, plus trauma that she endured in hospital and in other institutions when she was fragile. Now at thirty-two years of age she still carries some energetic imprints of these experiences. In the first years of her illness her behaviour ticked all of the boxes for BPD. Looking back, I now believe it was her way of letting go of the cumulative trauma from her human lifetimes.

The scariest thing about PTSD is flashbacks. The body holds the memories of all we can't consciously remember. In the words of author and activist, Marianne Williamson in her book *Tears to Triumph*, 'Traumatic memories... cut through the psyche like razors.'

It is often the sensory experiences of sight, smell, hearing, touch and taste that trigger flashbacks. Like a switch that can be flicked on at any time, they come out of nowhere and put us in a state of fear that can have devastating consequences. Those affected are taken straight to the reactive part of the brain (the brainstem) and communication with the more rational **cortex** is blocked off. These subconscious memories, stored in our bodies, also remember dates. Anniversaries can be a trigger. I have witnessed Alice in this state of unconscious remembrance. Her eyes are different. She is unresponsive and lapses into a dissociative fog and potentially self-harming, default behaviours. We know the signs now. It is happening less often and for shorter lengths of time, but it is still very frightening. The imprints of the trauma are still there and making their presence felt.

Alice's intense suffering gave me the motivation to access the Records. Looking back at my daughter's life I could see that she had come into it with a shadow hanging over her. The storm clouds gathered from a young age as early life experiences triggered memories and fears from the past. Alice was wary of the Akashic Records and of anything spiritual but she did allow me to open her Record and ask about the trauma she was carrying.

In her most recent past life I could see her in a German concentration camp as a sex slave. This sinister aspect of the Third Reich is not well-documented but there is material in some books and online that talks of the existence of brothels in the camps. When I opened Alice's Akashic Record I saw her as a young woman prisoner in a special building where Nazi guards and others came for sexual favours. She was thin and gaunt. She had no control over any aspect of her life and was violated daily by her captors. With my inner sight I saw Alice, as she was then, on a day when the key to the barracks had been entrusted to a fellow female prisoner. With a burst of courage this woman had opened the door and let the other women out into the sunlight. In my mind's eye I saw 'Alice' break free and run straight for the electric fence.

One afternoon in this life, when Alice was four, she played at a young friend's house and came home upset and sore. As I gave her a bath she told me what her friend had done. Although I didn't realise it at the time, this was abuse that was to have far-reaching consequences. I consulted friends who were psychologists and the prevailing view was that Alice's 'friend' was being sexually abused. Her parents were, not surprisingly, very upset when I told them what had happened and inferred this could be the case. I now have a different theory which has been substantiated by my questioning in the Records. The scenario I uncovered was that Alice's playmate was one of her past life rapists and was using objects to act out what she remembered doing then. It is very common for young children to remember, comment on or to re-enact past life memories.

Alice was never the same after this. She became withdrawn and untrusting and a target for bullies. By the time she met the boyfriend who raped her at sixteen, the energy imprints from the trauma of her immediate past life were fully activated. Alice's rape was the trigger for her illness. She has been releasing her accumulated trauma for the last fourteen years. She has done it the hard way. Being locked up in a cell-like room in a psychiatric ward at nineteen, I believe, dredged up subconscious fears and the trauma from the end of her immediate past life. She was vulnerable in the Psych Ward just as she had been in the camp and was raped by a patient.

The ward in those days was run like a military operation. Knowing what I know now it is no wonder my innocent, beautiful daughter was so traumatised. We kept her in there to save her life because every time she had a taste of freedom, she would try to end it. I believe that on some deep level her soul remembered running to the electric fence and held the belief that the only way out of her suffering was death.

Alice has been hugely affected by trauma from both past lives and the present. She has been releasing it in varying ways and in multiple layers over the last fourteen years. She has never been open to things she doesn't understand or that she feels are being imposed on her. Deep down I have always known this is Alice's journey and that it has to be experienced in the way and in the time frame that is right for her. I have respected this and her need for control over her life so have not had many opportunities to practise my own techniques on her. As a mother it has been hard to witness her struggles and pain. In the early years of her illness this process was unrelenting.

To help with her healing, in the last two years, Alice has started *EMDR Therapy*. *EMDR* stands for Eye Movement De-sensitization and Re-processing. First used with Vietnam war veterans, there is growing evidence that it relieves the stress of those suffering from PTSD and anxiety. Using a form of bilateral stimulation, the therapist moves their fingers in front of the client's eyes, while they think about a distressing memory that they talk about briefly beforehand. These lateral eye movements appear to stimulate the area of the brain that has become stuck as a result of trauma and allows the left side of the brain to self-soothe the right side. It re-wires the brain so the traumatic feelings are less acute.

At first, the days following an *EMDR* session, when the feelings were coming up to be released were tough. This intensity has lessened over time and after two years of regular sessions it is obvious they are helping. Flashbacks are happening less frequently and the old painful memories don't carry the same charge. Bessel Van Der Kolk in his book, *The Body Keeps the Score* rates *EMDR* treatment highly and also recommends the following as helpful modalities for the release of trauma: *Neuro-feedback*, the *Emotional Freedom Technique* or EFT, Yoga, Mindfulness, dance, drama and *Dialectical Behaviour* and *Psychomotor Therapy*. Havening, a relatively new trauma therapy is also gaining a following. Using therapeutic touch it alters the chemical balance of the brain and the emotional response of the **amygdala** to threat. This process changes the way memories are stored biologically and seeks to reduce the effects of trauma, anxiety and depression.

At the 'Science and Spirituality Conference' I attended in 2020, Gregg Braden made the important point that body centred healing processes should address the trauma of the heart. He said that there are 40,000 sensory neurites in the heart and that in the healing of trauma, the language of the heart needed to be expressed. I believe that the Akashic Records, holding the memories of trauma from all our earthly experiences and with their soul and heart connection are a perfect place for the release of this pain. After a traumatic experience the energy of the trauma remains in the body. Peter Levine refers to it as 'stuck energy.' Anything that helps to discharge it is helpful. In Levine's book *Healing Trauma* he tells how animals in the wild let go of this energy by shaking their bodies. He describes watching slow motion footage of a polar bear after it had been chased by an aeroplane, shot down with a tranquiliser dart and tagged. The animal started to tremble and convulsively shake. The bear then took deep breaths and moved its limbs rapidly, as if re-enacting its flight from the scene.

For some, the trauma we carry is from our current life, while for others it can be thousands of years old. The energy of trauma does not behave in a linear way. What matters is the degree and intensity of the trauma that our bodies are holding onto rather than when it happened. When I facilitate the release of trauma for my clients I think of it as blocked energy that needs to be cleared and create an intention like this:

It is my intention to completely release the energetic imprints of trauma from all lifetimes, dimensions and time frames·

After I have stated this, I call on St Germain to blaze his violet flame though the cells of my client's body and their energy field removing the imprints and residue of current and past life trauma. With guidance from me, they ask their body to let go of all traumatic memories. I often use my technique of taking them back to a critical incident from a past life so they can talk to their former self and bring them to a place of acceptance. Sometimes, as with the polar bear, I get them to revisit the traumatic experience and create a different ending so it becomes imprinted in a different way in their brain and consciousness.

Adam's face was pale and white on my computer screen. He came to me because he had reached a crisis in his life. His marriage had ended and he was working night shifts which were wreaking havoc with his sleep patterns and affecting his wellbeing. As soon as the session began, I picked up on a past life theme, where he had been given the chance to help others, but his nerve had failed him. I told him that his current life was about finding the courage to get out of his comfort zone. He was still carrying huge feelings of sadness and loss and was very hard on himself. He admitted he was at a low ebb and struggling to reach his potential.

I saw a past life in the trenches in World War I. His battalion was being called to go 'over the top' and he was paralysed with anxiety. Not only did he stay in the trench but he watched as three comrades fell in a hail of bullets. There was a lull and a window of opportunity to drag them to safety, but he remained in the trench, frozen with fear. On some level the trauma was still with him. I could see that he was beating himself up which made it difficult to make positive changes in his life.

In the Records I took him back to the trench. I was prompting him to reassure his soldier self that he didn't lack courage and had done the best he could, in a difficult situation, when Adam started sobbing and yelling at his past life self;

'You can do it. Now's your chance. Get out there and save them.'

As he urged his past life self on, one-by-one he pulled his friends back into the comparative safety of the trench. Adam told his soldier self how proud he was of him and commended him on his bravery. At my suggestion Adam hugged his past life self, pulling the soldier's courage and strength into his body as he did so. After some additional healing Adam told me he was going to take up martial arts training for both himself and the World War I soldier.

As Adam's story shows, within our Akashic Record, we can, with intention, traverse time and create a different ending to our past and current life stories. This gives us a chance to do things differently and provides an opportunity for completion and redemption, as well as the release of trauma. With the rise in planetary vibration, our body wisdom is becoming more closely connected to our Higher Selves, which are pointing us in the direction of soul healing. The potential for these healing methods in the future is, I believe, huge.

Like Adam, many of my clients come to me because they feel stuck and unable to move forward. In most of these cases it is past life trauma that is the culprit. I do my best to identify the origin of the trauma but, as in Adam's case, there is often a theme that has run through many of their lifetimes. Sometimes I see several lives that are still affecting them. Often there is one main life that is pulling my clients back. After they have talked to their past life selves and explained the bigger picture of the traumatic experience, I often utilise other healing methods. I learned a powerful technique for 'alchemising' trauma from a webinar I did with spiritual teacher and writer, Tim Whild. (*Practical Ascension*, www.timwhild.com). I ask my client to close their eyes and to see themselves standing up. I then ask them to see the past life self that experienced trauma, standing some distance away. I get them to visualise a line connecting themselves with their past life self and I call on the unicorns to blaze pure, white light along it, to alchemise the trauma. With their inner vision they see the trauma being broken up and transmuted by the unicorn's high vibration frequencies of love.

Tim's work also inspired another technique I use to help clients suffering from past life trauma. In this method I facilitate the release of the 'pain body.' I tell my clients that their 'pain body' represents and is symbolic of the pain they have accumulated in all of their lifetimes. I ask them to visualise another version of themselves which has the same shape as a human body – head, shoulders, arms, a torso, hips, legs and feet. I then get them to say these or similar words:

> *'Pain body, I have carried you for thousands of years. Thank you for all you have taught me. It is time for us to part. I am grateful for the role you have played in all of my lifetimes. I let you go with love.'*

I then ask them to watch as their pain body leaves and walks into the light.

Working within someone's open Akashic Record makes healing on a deep level possible. It enables us to go beyond the symptoms, to find the cause. The heavy burden of trauma that many of us carry, has no place on the New Earth. The Akashic Records can help us to lighten the load and to leave the bitter legacy of human suffering behind forever.

My friend Rebecca is a soul who experienced huge trauma in a recent past life as a male doctor in both World War I and II. Her current lifetime has been affected by the fall-out from this.

During our session, Rebecca told me that she was a survivor of a large dysfunctional family and that she had been sexually, physically and emotionally abused by her now dead father. In her Akashic Record, I saw her as a medic in World War I. Her young soldier self was so terrified, he ran away from his post. The man who is her father in this life, was her Army superior. He pushed very hard for a court martial but because of her skills as a doctor, 'Rebecca,' was spared that fate.

Twenty-five + years later, in that same lifetime, I saw 'Rebecca' as an older male physician in charge of a large German hospital at the end of World War II. The relentless bombing terrified him, triggering the unresolved PTSD from his World War I experience. Again, he ran away and deserted those he was responsible for, leaving his staff and patients to the mercy of the bombs. When I saw him at the end of his life, he was crippled from the guilt of leaving those he was tasked with keeping alive, to certain death. He was never the same again and did not process the trauma before he died.

Subsequently, Rebecca brought these unresolved feelings into her current life and has been working hard to let the trauma go. On a soul level, I could see that she had also been trying to break a pattern of self-sacrifice and of being overly responsible for others. By running away from her duties in both wars she had managed to do this, but the trauma had sparked a new series of issues: a lack of trust of self and others, a fear of failure and a pervasive feeling of being undeserving. All of these beliefs were preventing her from finding happiness and fulfilment. The deep feelings of guilt, shame and unworthiness she was still carrying from her immediate past life had adversely affected her relationships.

She had a history of partners who were narcissistic and draining, of giving too much for very little in return, and of always feeling like she had to be the responsible one.

It has been a tough road for Rebecca. She has chosen to meet up with many souls in this lifetime with whom she has karmic links. For a father, in this life, she chose her superior and persecutor from World War I. His abuse of her from an early age, added to her trauma energy. This triggered the feelings of unworthiness and the patterns that her soul wanted her to transcend, forcing her to take action to heal herself.

To let go of her childhood trauma she has been working with Peter Levine's *Somatic Experiencing* technique. She is now taking control of the relationships in her life and continuing her medical work with trauma victims which is (not surprisingly) her life's work. Talking of this trauma treatment, Rebecca told me:

'The somatic work is remarkable. You are literally taught to turn your brain off so you can feel safe enough to process fear, trauma, and other emotions. Once I can get myself close enough to where it is stored and I'm given the space and support to access it, I can allow myself to flow with the release of the energy… through my fear and vulnerability to a place of safety.'

Rebecca later told me by email that our sessions had helped her to understand why she had chosen some of her past relationships and had made it easier for her to identify and to let go of self-defeating behaviours. She added, *'It has given me some peace and the space to truly heal and to start building on the parts of my soul that have always been there.'*

She also mentioned that it had helped explain why in this lifetime, with no formal training as a doctor, she has an innate knowledge of medical procedures.

As we leave Third Dimensional energy behind, releasing current and past life trauma is an important task for most of us. Many of us have consciously chosen and planned lives and, more specifically, childhoods, with this in mind. As souls I believe that before each incarnation we think carefully about our circumstances and relationships. If we have a past life pattern of abandonment to clear, for example, we may choose to be adopted out at birth so from Day 1 the issue is 'in our face' and impossible to ignore. At this particular time on Earth, like Rebecca, many of us have deliberately chosen life experiences that will give us the best chance to face our past life demons and release our long-held pain. Other people, like my courageous daughter, have by volunteering to help shift the trauma energy for the planet, chosen on a soul level to play a sacrificial role in moving us beyond suffering.

Young children often show signs of past life suffering and trauma. In my book *The Magic of the Akashic Records*, I described how this has affected all three of my children. My son, Hugh, and youngest daughter, Mary, showed more obvious signs of this when they were growing up. Hugh's took the form of daytime fears and 'night terrors.' In his most recent past life he was murdered by the **Khmer Rouge** at the age of five. When he reached that age in this lifetime he woke up night after night in an agitated state, screaming and unresponsive, and developed a seemingly irrational fear of strange men. Mary was terrified of blood and from the age of eight to ten had a series of fainting episodes whenever she saw blood or it was mentioned. According to the Akashic Records, Mary's most recent past life was during the French Revolution where she witnessed the deaths of many of her friends at the guillotine.

Although I had not fully embraced my current work when my children were young, I had sufficient understanding to talk to Hugh and Mary about this and they were able to let it go. Alice, on the other hand, showed no obvious signs of trauma. As a very young child she had a close connection to Spirit who she saw around her and told me about. As she got older these visions became more frightening and she started sleeping with her bed covers over her head to protect herself. The signs were not as obvious as with her siblings but were more ominous. I dismissed what was happening as a normal stage of child development, expecting her to grow out of it. Unfortunately, she didn't. In retrospect, I have realised that the best course of action is dealing with children's past life trauma as it arises. Hugh's 'night terrors' ended as abruptly as they began. One night, as he re-lived a frightening experience in another time and place, I told him that what he was seeing happened when he was another little boy and that he was Hugh now and he was safe. A simple conversation while the child is in the grip of the trauma, or afterwards, is often all that is needed.

My client, Alison, was also the mother of a five year old son affected by past life trauma. I had difficulty organising a time to teach her how to access the Akashic Records. Alison lives in Malta and the time difference was an issue. Also, she wasn't keen to have the session in her evening as it interfered with her son's bedtime routine, which sounded as if it took time and patience. At first I had my 'parenting' hat on and was a little inflexible. In an email reading I gave Alison she asked about her son. It became obvious that there were good reasons why he needed her presence in the evenings and I rearranged our session times to suit. While I don't give children readings, I am able to access soul information relating to them through the Akashic Record of a parent. I did this in Alison's case.

She asked what was causing her son's irrational fears and behaviours and this was my emailed reply:

In two recent lifetimes you shared with your son he experienced trauma at the age of five. He is of a high vibration and an advanced soul from elsewhere in this galaxy and has had few Earth lifetimes.

You have an ancient connection with him as you both originate from the same star system. There has been advanced planning on a soul level for a series of lives where you will be together.

You agreed to assist him to transition into the Earth plane.

He was very close to you in a life you had as a religious leader in Russia at the turn of the nineteeth and twentieth centuries. He was a great-nephew who became like a son and was someone you tried to shelter and protect.

You were pulled in many directions and had him safe (or so you thought), in the sanctuary of your church building. You went off on a mission to save others, the walls of the church compound were breached and all those inside were killed. Your great-nephew (son), was sleeping peacefully when he was woken up and murdered. He still holds the cellular memory of this event and the trauma.

In a more recent lifetime in World War II you were again, his mother. You went out for supplies and left him in a hiding place with strict instructions not to move. The queues were lengthy that day and you were away longer than usual. He left his safe place, in search of food, just as the Secret Police arrived looking for his father who was in hiding elsewhere. The police harassed your son who was terrified. He couldn't tell them where his father was because he didn't know.

In the end the Germans became frustrated and angry and decided to kill him instead. You came home and found his body and were heartbroken.

How we die is crucially important. The trauma of a dramatic and sudden death can stay in our energy fields and be activated in 'future' lifetimes. It can be triggered by feeling similar emotions to those from the original event and/or when we reach the same chronological age as when the trauma occurred. This is what is happening with your son. On a soul level he is still carrying the trauma which he will release in this lifetime with your help.

I suggested that Alison try these techniques to help her son.

- *In simple words that he will understand, tell him that he has lived with you before, in another time and in another body. Tell him that in both of those lifetimes he was killed by bad men when he was a small boy. Tell him that his body remembers this and is worried that it will happen again. Reassure him that he is safe and protected and that no one can or will hurt him.*

- *Be patient with him as his feelings and behaviours are understandable, given these previous experiences. Meet his needs and let go of the fear that this might go on forever.*

- *Tell him that he can sleep with you when he is scared and that when he feels brave enough to sleep by himself to let you know.*

- *Teach him to visualise his body surrounded by beautiful white light and to say this mantra when he feels scared. 'The light around me loves me and keeps me safe.'*

- *Tell him that there is a beautiful angel looking after him who will be with him always. Talk to him about his angel and ask him to name him/her.*

- *Assure him that he has superpowers and that nothing and no one can hurt him. When he is scared or before he goes to sleep at night get him to send love from his heart (like he is firing a laser), so that anything that is frightening disappears.*

I finished off by saying:

He will outgrow this. The key thing is to accept what is happening, to honour his feelings and fears and not to resist his behaviours or make them wrong. It is important that he is able to take control of the situation. He was unable to do this in the two lifetimes I have discussed. Giving him the tools to do

> *this now will help him to heal from and to release the trauma from the past.*

Just as our bodies remember current life trauma and react to sensory and anniversary triggers, I believe, the same applies to past life memories. Trauma energy is frozen in time. With the help of the Akashic Records we can access, understand and release it. This dynamic will become more common and happen more frequently as the vibration lifts and the veils between dimensions get thinner. In 2017, I had a 'moment' with a workshop participant in Sydney when he released childhood trauma he was carrying from his most recent past life.

On Day Two of the workshop, William came in looking very tired. When I did my morning check-in he confessed that he had hardly slept because his Akashic Record had been open since the day before. He said he had listened as I stressed the importance of slowly building up time in the Records and of closing them before sleep, but he told the group he 'wanted to get his money's worth.' Too much, too soon had meant that William had had a rough night. I try not to tell my students what they should and shouldn't do but there are good reasons behind the recommendations I do make.

He brought a lively energy into the workshop and after a reading from another participant he told us that he felt like he had been questioned by the Gestapo. William was a bit of a rebel and I was nervous when at the end of Day Two we were matched up together for a healing session. I should not have worried. If participant numbers are uneven at workshops I am often on the receiving end and William's healing was sublime. As soon as William opened my Akashic Record he transformed into an **Avatar**. He incorporated Light Language and toning into his healing. Afterwards I felt amazing.

Next it was my turn to work with him. He told me he had physical issues with inflammation in his sinuses. As soon as I opened William's Record I saw that his symptoms were from the cellular memories of a recent past life. In that lifetime, William was the child of a high-ranking Nazi and his wife. His past life brother, sister and mother were his son, daughter and ex-wife in this one. With the help of my **Third Eye** I saw a scene that I described to William.

At the end of the war when all hope of German victory was gone, his mother had tried to get him to swallow cyanide tablets. He watched as his brother and sister took the poison and died. He was traumatised and scared. His mother attempted to force the tablets down his throat. He didn't like being told what to do (still doesn't), and refused to swallow them. His mother hit him repeatedly but he wouldn't do as she wanted. In his panic he escaped and was seen by others who alerted the authorities to his parent's whereabouts. His father was imprisoned and sentenced to death. He was placed in an orphanage and died when he was still quite young.

William told me that in this life when he was seven, he had gone to the dentist and refused to open his mouth. He said that four people held him down as his jaws were prised open and he became hysterical.

He became emotional in this life as well when he talked to this German boy self. As he told this past life aspect who he really was, (an Avatar) he shed many tears and with them the trauma from a lifetime that had left some deep scars.

The human race is going through an intense trauma release. As we move into a higher vibration and our cellular wisdom becomes more acute and our non-coding DNA activates, trauma from our current and past lives is coming up to be cleared. Different layers are being exposed and the body is coming alive with all of the cellular memories that need to be transmuted. It is a necessary process as we transition into a higher frequency.

It is wonderful that new heart-based and body focused trauma healing modalities are appearing and beginning to be used as part of mainstream medicine. Like many of these methods, the Akashic Records, infused with soul energy and holding the memories of all of our earthly experiences provides, and will do so more in the future, an optimal space for the removal of the trauma energy that is testament to our human suffering.

Chapter 6

Intergenerational Family Trauma and Patterns

The dense energies of trauma and all that is not aligned with a higher vibration are coming up to be healed on both a personal and collective level. The families our souls choose to be born into are also giving us the opportunity to discharge these and other heavy energetics. Over the last few years, in many of my client sessions, I have been prompted to facilitate the removal of the imprints of intergenerational family trauma and unhealthy family patterns.

Families are a huge trigger for releasing the toxicity of the past. Some of my clients are unsure why they have come to me. As soon as I open their Records, I can see it is to help their families offload centuries of ancestral suffering and dysfunction. At this time of completion and transition into a higher vibration there is at least one member in every family who has volunteered for this task. These people are often my clients. The vibration of suffering does not sit comfortably in the Fifth Dimension. Whatever has not been healed in the past must now be brought into the light of truth and transmuted. If the trauma in one generation is too great to be resolved, it is passed on to future generations to deal with. The build-up of this lower vibrational energy in most families is huge.

Some of us have a soul contract with our families to resolve karma. Karma is something created by mankind. Simply put, it is an energy imbalance that has governed our experience in countless lifetimes. Hurting someone in one life sets up this dynamic and prompts a soul directive to make amends in the next or a subsequent life. There are many ways that family karma can be balanced.

In the energy of the past, secrecy and denial was rampant in families. Healing family karma sometimes involves re-experiencing a situation our parents or ancestors didn't address so it can be brought to a state of peace and resolution. When we do this we are not only helping ourselves and our ancestors but also future generations. Many lightworkers are being called to this work and it is one of the reasons I have started running my Level 3 residential retreats.

The family arena is where, for many of us, our suffering has been most acute. It provides opportunities for soul growth and evolution. Our biggest learnings come from relationships and from family relationships in particular. As the spiritual teacher Diana Cooper said in a webinar in 2019, 'Our family is our karma.'

Drama spins in families as family relationships are the most intimate and often the most fraught. Many of us have chosen to reincarnate repeatedly within the same family groupings to learn important lessons and to clear and balance karma. As we end one cycle and prepare to move into the next, all that has not been resolved is in our faces and impossible to avoid.

In our energy fields and the cells of our bodies we not only hold the vibrational imprints from past lives and other experiences we have had as souls, but imprints from our **family of origin**. At this time on Earth it is not just soul trauma we are dealing with but ancestral trauma as well. If we choose to be re-born within the same family, as is often the case, these two can overlap.

In the book *What Happened to You?* co-authored by Dr Bruce Perry and Oprah Winfrey, they discuss ways trauma can be passed down the generations. According to Dr Perry, our genes, family, community, society and culture all contribute. He suggests that children pick up on the emotions of their caregivers and 'absorb them.'

Oprah's early years were spent with her grandparents. Her grandfather suffered from dementia and could be violent. When speaking of this and of how her grandmother's fear affected her, Oprah writes: 'I believe it changed me on a cellular level.' They both agree that in Dr Perry's words, 'the language we speak, the beliefs we hold, both good and bad, are passed from generation to generation through experience.'

The growing science of **Epigenetics** looks at how environmental factors influence our gene expression and the way we behave. Perry also believes that epigenetic factors could be responsible for what he calls 'transgenerational trauma.' Epigenetics is a genetic adaptation to an environmental factor. An epigenetic 'tag' is placed on the gene which changes its expression. Dr Perry gives the example of an ancestor who experienced trauma, adapting to it by turning on or off certain genes in an effort to maintain balance. These modified genes, he says, are then passed on to future generations.

Oprah and Dr Perry conclude by saying, 'It is conceivable that the experiences of our grandparents, great grandparents and ancestors, even further back, have had a significant influence on the way we... express our DNA.'

This new science deals with genetic DNA only which makes up 1.2% of the total. It doesn't add in the remaining 98.8% of our non-coding DNA. I believe that ancestral imprints are part of the cellular memory and of our quantum DNA capacity which is being activated in the new energy. I believe that the cellular memory of trauma, patterns of behaviour and anything in the family line that is unresolved is stored in the non-coding DNA and passed on to future generations to deal with. The name Epigenetics supports this. Epi means above, so Epigenetics means 'above the gene,' which implies that something other than our genetic inheritance is responsible for the way we are.

Dr Bruce Lipton is the best known 'New Scientist' in this field. In his ground breaking research at Stanford University between 1987 and 1992, Lipton found, that when placed in varying environments identical cells expressed in different ways. He experimented by placing stem cells into three different culture mediums. The original stem cells were exactly the same but their expression varied producing muscle, bone and fat, respectively. This research, he concluded, proved that our physical and emotional characteristics are not solely determined by our genes and that there are other forces at play. He says that signals from the environment are picked up by the membrane 'mem-brain' of each cell and that we respond to these receptors. In his book *The Biology of Belief*, he argues that it is our consciousness or thought environment that determines our physical expression rather than our genetic inheritance. He contends that it is our environment, particularly in the first seven years of life, that conditions us and programmes our subconscious mind which determines how we live our lives. In this way, our emotions and beliefs become a 'culture medium' that expresses itself differently for each individual.

As Lipton has discovered we are not just our genes. There is so much more to us. These other aspects are being revealed especially now that our DNA is being activated. Non-coding DNA has all the quantum attributes I have discussed in Chapter 3, and most importantly, the ability to respond directly to our consciousness. As Lipton says, we can control our biology. I believe we work not only with the cellular memories from our first seven years of life but from all of our lifetimes. On top of this we are also dealing with the ancestral memories we are carrying for our families.

Scientific experiments are adding weight to the view that trauma and stress are passed from one generation to another. In an online article by Andrew Curry in Sciencemag.org published on July 18th, 2019, he discussed the experiments of Isabelle Mansay, Professor of Neuroepigenetics at the University of Zurich.

Mansay's research showed that female mice placed in stress inducing situations produced offspring who also had a highly developed stress response. To prove that this wasn't the environmental result of parenting by traumatised mothers, the fathers of the baby mice, (who had nothing to do with them and had also been subjected to stress), were tested and also found to be affected by trauma. Their babies showed molecular and behavioural changes that persisted for up to five generations.

Other studies also support the conviction that trauma can be passed down the family line. In an article published on August 17, 2019 on the website of Truthout, A. Abbas Naqu, commented on two of these:

The first study by university professor, Rachel Yehuda, found that the children of male holocaust survivors had lower levels of the hormone cortisol that helps to regulate stress levels and is a risk factor for PTSD. Another study of a group of Australian indigenous Aborigines and Torres Islanders, who carry the bitter legacy of injustice meted out by colonial rulers, revealed high suicide levels, particularly among those under the age of twenty-six.

Mark Wolynn, director of *The Family Constellation Institute* and author of the book, *It Didn't Start With You*, has done landmark work in the field of familial healing. In an online talk on intergenerational trauma in 2019, Wolynn discussed Epigenetics. He said that when we experience trauma it causes a chemical change in our DNA and can change the way our genes express for generations. He says that this alters our DNA which changes the field of energy around us. In this way he says we can become sensitive to situations that are similar to trauma that our ancestors experienced and that this response can be inherited.

My work is proving to me that our soul history is part of the cellular memory within our DNA. I believe that ancestral memories, intergenerational trauma and family patterns are also stored there. This has yet to be conclusively proven by science. However, recent research is revealing a link with non-coding RNA which is a mirror copy of non-coding DNA. In a talk given during the online Ancestral Summit in 2020, Wolynn said that a new line of thought suggests that the non-coding RNA has a part to play in the transference of dysfunctional family patterns and trauma. Separately, in her research (also published in Andrew Curry's online article in Sciencemag.org), Tracy Bale of the University of Maryland has found evidence that suggests that it is the non-coding RNA carried in the sperm of the male mice that is responsible for passing the trauma on to subsequent generations. To me the 'non-coding' attribute of the RNA strengthens the view that trauma and the imprints of family patterns are part of our quantum cellular structure.

In his book, Wolynn gives many examples of unresolved family issues presenting themselves to future generations so the energetic of the repeating pattern can be released and healed. He calls this 'the ringing of the ancestral alarm clock' and says that these symptoms may strike at the same age, when we reach a milestone in our lives, or come up against a fear or trigger that our ancestors experienced. He gives the example of a boy who came to him with a rare neurological disorder. When he was ten, the child began to experience burning sensations on his skin. Mark discovered that at this age the boy's father had played with matches and burned his family's house down. He concluded that the boy was carrying his father's deep feelings of guilt and self-blame which were manifesting as the disorder and skin sensitivity. He cites many other cases where PTSD has been passed down the generations.

The Family Constellation process developed by the late Burt Hellinger and also utilised by Wolynn has helped thousands of people, world-wide, to shift the energy of intergenerational trauma and unhealthy family patterns.

In 2011, I had my own experience of '*Family Constellation Therapy.*' The Family Constellation workshop I attended involved participants choosing a family matter to deal with in a 'constellation.' Others at the workshop were then chosen by the person whose issue was under scrutiny, to represent different family members. Following her intuition and with great skill, our facilitator guided those in the constellation. Through connecting with the energy of past and present she was able to bring a family trauma or dysfunctional pattern to a place of resolution and healing.

It was an amazing process to be part of! As I took on the persona of the family member I was representing, I became that person. I instinctively knew how to act and what to say and so did everyone else. A common theme was of a present-day family member carrying the burden for an older relative or ancestor. The patterns and themes in families were easy to see, from addictive behaviours and poverty consciousness to intergenerational cycles of teenage pregnancy, abandonment and loss.

I was selected for a constellation and I chose to work with Alice's suicidality. The facilitator, Amelia, set up a family grouping. Other workshop participants represented Alice, my mother and members of our extended family.

Amelia asked me questions about my family and I told her that my grandmother had died suddenly when my mother was five years old. As the constellation was acted out it was obvious that my mother had missed her mother terribly and like any child had wanted to be with her. Amelia helped me see that this subconscious 'death wish' was now being carried by my daughter Alice. As this realisation emerged, the energy in the room was electric and I could almost feel my ancestors heave a sigh of relief. Something had shifted. This was not the end of Alice's attempts to end her life, but they certainly slowed down after that.

As my Family Constellation experience shows the process of letting go is happening not just on a soul level but within our families as well. We can work individually to release our negative patterns and beliefs as well as with the energetic overlays passed down through our families. As I said earlier if one family member releases and transmutes this energy, the entire family both past and present, will feel the effects. An energetic shift takes place that helps the complete ancestral line, including those who are yet to be born.

The family story of my American friend, Bonnie, is an example of unresolved trauma being passed on to subsequent generations. Her family narrative includes common themes that have perpetuated suffering in families: abandonment, estrangement, addiction and mental illness. Bonnie told me about her mother Bridget's difficult childhood. An only child, Bridget was effectively abandoned by her parents at an early age, after her father developed crippling rheumatoid arthritis and was institutionalised.

Bridget and her mother, Catherine, moved in with her father's mother who was very hard on her daughter-in-law. Catherine had experienced childhood trauma. Her mother had abandoned Catherine and her brother, leaving them in the care of their alcoholic father and his family. To cope with the stress and her changed situation Catherine started to drink and was kicked out by her mother-in-law.

Bridget wasn't allowed near her mother again. She was never told why she had left or where she had gone. Even though her grandmother loved her dearly and treated her well, Bridget felt deserted and unloved by her mother. She carried this trauma for the rest of her life.

After her grandmother's death, Bridget moved in with an aunt and uncle and met and married a man in the neighbourhood. Their marriage was happy and together they produced eight children. Bridget was very close to her eldest child, a daughter named Maureen. At the age of eighteen, the night before she was to leave for College, Maureen was hit and killed by a drunk driver. This new loss unleashed a wave of trauma and grief and sent my friend's mother into a downward spiral.

Bridget's way of dealing with it was to have another child and ten months later her ninth child, another daughter who they named Molly, was born. My friend told me that her sister Molly has struggled with mental health issues for most of her life and that when she reached the age her mother had been when she lost her child, she became suicidal.

'Your mother was grief-stricken when she carried your sister. Molly picked up on your mother's trauma and sadness,' I told my friend and added, 'If your sister is able to release these feelings she will help not only herself but your mother as well.'

With the help of DNA testing my friend, Bonnie has recently reconnected with her mother's family. Contact with a cousin descended from Bonnie's great uncle (Catherine's brother), has helped to fill in some gaps. According to Bonnie's cousin, Catherine tried to have contact with Bridget for years, but Bridget's grandmother wouldn't permit it. The family feeling was that Catherine had mental health issues that were not addressed. From this rediscovered relative, Bonnie has learned that her grandmother, Catherine, died of alcoholism and was buried in a cemetery for homeless people.

Bonnie's cousin told her that in 1976 her branch of the family had phoned Bridget and asked for permission to re-inter her mother's ashes in the family plot. Apparently Bonnie's mother handed her husband the phone and he said, 'Do what you want, but don't ever call here again!'

Bonnie's cousin has told her that Catherine was a very nice person when she was sober but that she had never got over losing her child.

Bonnie told me she wished her mother had known the truth while she was alive but that she is pleased it is coming out now.

As I wrote this story, I felt the comforting presence of, not only, Bridget and Catherine but of Catherine's mother-in-law (Bonnie's great grandmother as well). One of them was stroking my head.

They are happy that I am telling their story.

As we move into a higher frequency, the truth is rising to the surface and long held secrets are being revealed. This process, happening in every family, is being orchestrated by those beyond the veil and assisted by new technology and family healing modalities such as the Akashic Records.

❀

As I described earlier, I work with clients within their Records to clear them of sabotaging and limiting cellular memories. Like a form of 'Groundhog Day,' these energetic imprints can draw the same experiences to us repeatedly. Sigmund Freud coined the term 'repetition compulsion' to describe, when in an attempt to heal, subconscious feelings compel us to repeat certain behaviours.

There is a similar dynamic within our families. It is possible to clear stuck energies which have kept families in a downward spiral for a long time. Family Constellation therapy is one way to do it and the Akashic Records also provides a safe and loving place for this important process. As I touched on earlier, it is not uncommon for souls to reincarnate repeatedly within the same biological families. This occurrence makes the Akashic Records the perfect place to facilitate this kind of healing.

Within the open Akashic Record of a willing participant, we can hold the intention to clear all energetic imprints of trauma and dysfunctional patterns, not just for them but for their entire family.

Sometimes, as in this case, the family pattern which is held in the body impacts on physical health and wellbeing.

A client came to me because he was finding it difficult to move forward in his life. Nearly sixty-one, Greg told me he felt sad because 'I haven't done what I set out to do.' He said, he felt 'an intense and impulsive feeling inside,' about the need to fulfil his mission, as well as feelings of frustration at the many false starts and dead ends. His passion was 'nutrition farming' or as he told me, 'helping farmers to grow nutrient-dense food.'

He asked me about a physical issue he was experiencing. 'I experience significant tightness through the lumbar region of my lower back and hips as well as very tight abductors, hamstrings and knees. Despite doing regular yoga and stretches, it's proving a challenge to get this area flexible. Is there a cellular memory or thought pattern causing this rigidity and can you suggest what else I can do to let it go?'

I saw that this issue was something he had inherited from his ancestral line in two ways. I sent him these instructions so he could break the pattern not just for himself but for his family in the past, present and future.

'This is familial. There is a genetic predisposition to this. It is also related to a pattern that has been running through your family line for generations; where external circumstances have held family members back and they have not been able to put their plans into action. Many of your ancestors have had dreams they have not been able to fulfil. This same pattern is now affecting you.'

I advised him to say the following every day until he felt a shift in mind, body and spirit:

On behalf of my entire family line, it is my intention to release and transmute a family pattern of 'Dreams being unfulfilled because of factors beyond our control,' which has been carried energetically in our bodies and is contributing to a feeling of significant tightness in the lower region of my body.

I call on St Germain to blaze his violet flame through my body and the energy field surrounding it and also along the timeline of every member of my 'Family of Origin', past, present and future to remove the energetic imprints of this pattern.

115

> *Cells of my body, you carry the memories of many lifetimes where my plans to assist humanity have not come to fruition because of adverse, external factors. You also carry the energetic overlays and imprints of this familial pattern I have inherited. I ask you now to release the stuck energy which has perpetuated this pattern. I ask the cells in the lumbar region of my lower back and hips as well as in my abductors, hamstrings and knees to release the energy they are holding, so present and future generations of my family can fulfil their dreams.*

In a typical family healing session, I identify a past trauma or pattern that is having a detrimental effect on the family. With my client's help I formulate an intention for the healing. I then bring in the Higher Selves of my client's children and their family of origin. I also invite the family's ancestors from their paternal and maternal lines to join us. I ask my client to close their eyes and to visualise the two sides of their family standing in separate chronological lines or sometimes surrounding them in concentric circles.

As was the case with Greg, I prompt my client to state the intention for the healing. I then specify the patterns and/or traumatic memories I am guided to remove. For example: victimhood, premature death, bankruptcy. I then invoke the Violet Flame and call in the dragons to breathe their fire along the ancestral lines to remove the residue of this trauma or of these patterns. I then ask that the DNA of the family, in question, be recalibrated and recoded so that it no longer carries the energetic of what we are trying to release. In the new energy it is possible to instruct our bodies to do whatever is in our best interests. This includes reprogramming our DNA so that we can let go of the imprints of anything that is not serving us or our families. We have always had a genetic pre-set. Now, in our increasingly quantum world, it is possible to do a re-set. To complete the session I do anything else I am guided to. For example, facilitating a conversation with an ancestor (sometimes my client is that ancestor), or releasing family karma. I do whatever is necessary for the family of whoever I am working with to come to a place of forgiveness and harmony. I always end with my client visualising themselves having a group hug with past, present and future generations of their family. I often ask them to name a tree they feel represents their family and to see themselves planting it with their family's youngest members. This work is a fast and effective way of removing the energy of suffering that has been passed down for generations and of setting up a more positive and affirming energetic for the future.

Souls often reincarnate within the same family groupings to clear karma. We are all being given opportunities to redress and rebalance karmic energy at this time of evolutionary change. Animosity and misunderstandings in families can go back thousands of years. Many of us are being confronted by karmic issues in our families of origin and are being forced to deal with their cumulative effects.

There are skeletons in every family closet. As my client Sally described her four daughters' various challenges, I gazed at her in awe. One daughter has a deformed hand as a result of a congenital condition. Another has learning disabilities and depression and has tried to end her life. The father of her children has little contact with his family and refuses to support them. There was conflict between her children and not surprisingly Sally was struggling to cope. I suspected that the younger generation of this family was carrying the burden of their family's unresolved issues.

In the Akashic Records I saw a life where Sally and three of her daughters were again members of a family grouping. They were all women in the harem of the girl's father in this life. In this past life, one by one, 'Sally' and these three daughters had become his wives. 'Sally' the oldest wife was supplanted by one daughter, 'Megan' and then in turn by the other two, 'Paula' and 'Barbara'. There was a great deal of rivalry and conflict as they were played off against each other. 'Megan', was the favourite and 'Paula' and 'Barbara' were jealous. 'Sally' got sick of being 'second best' and took a lover, her present-day boyfriend and first cousin Philip. Her husband (ex-husband in this life), found out and killed her. 'Barbara' and 'Paula' loved 'Sally' who was a mother figure to them and they poisoned their husband. They then committed suicide.

I saw that Sally and her daughters were back together to heal and resolve issues from that dramatic lifetime. There was also a need to clear some longstanding and dysfunctional family patterns in their biological family.

Sally told me that patterns of suicide and sexual abuse have run through several generations of the family. Her children's grandfather on their father's side had recently committed suicide and she had been sexually abused by her father. She added that she was now having an intimate relationship with her first cousin and told me, 'I have fraternised with the dark and am not scared of it.'

Speaking about the intergenerational pattern of incest in her family, Sally revealed that her paternal grandfather had had sex with both of his sons (her father and Philip's father), as well as two other younger family members.

I could see in the Records that in this family the same souls had returned over and over again. I found that Sally and Philip are the reincarnation of their own great-grandparents and that the incestuous behaviour had started with them.

As souls they had begun it in this former lifetime as an experiment and adventure. The intention from a soul and evolutionary standpoint was that once the darkness and dysfunction was released from the family line, they would be opened up to a new octave of creativity and purpose that would not have been possible, otherwise.

Despite their family history, Sally told me that some of her family members were not happy about her relationship with Philip. I told her that there was a higher reason for this, that they loved each other and were here to help change the family pattern from abusive, exploitative relationships to healthy, balanced ones.

Sally was visiting my city for the 85th birthday celebrations of her uncle, Philip's father. She booked a session with me and I knew intuitively that it was time for this family to be released from their past. The arrival of Philip, just as I was preparing for the healing part of our session, confirmed that the timing was right. I facilitated a healing and releasing process with Sally representing the female line and Philip the male. I cleared the imprints of the family pattern of incest and of all dysfunction from the family line, past, present and future.

It has taken time but since this session life has improved for Sally and her children. One by one, her daughters are becoming independent and moving forward with their lives. She recently told me, 'I am happier with everything and am now letting each day unfold with ease.'

Rosie, a young woman of Chinese/Malaysian ancestry has an enduring soul connection and karmic relationship with her present-day father, mother and sister. She told me she had never felt understood by her family, that her parents favoured her sister and that she had been a rebellious teenager who had often run away. She also came to me carrying the energetic of unhealthy patterns that it was time for her family to release.

As soon as I opened Rosie's Akashic Record, I could see she had a highly creative side that needed to be expressed and that the job she was doing in the financial sector was not right for her.

When I told her this she said she had recently started several creative pursuits that helped her feel happier and calmer. She added that ultimately she wanted to find more meaningful work that would make a positive difference to others.

In her Akashic Record I could see the obstacles she faced in making this dream a reality. I told her that there was a pattern in her family of being in survival mode and of having huge fears around security. She confirmed that this was the case. I could see that not only in this lifetime, but in many of the lives she had shared with her parents and sister, that these familial fears had prevailed and they had struggled to survive. Their circumstances in this one, as immigrants intent on creating a life better than the one they left behind, had triggered old fears and reinforced this pattern. In past lives this pressure had often shut 'Rosie' down and stopped her from reaching her potential.

I saw several lives where 'Rosie' had done exactly what the rest of her family had wanted and two other lives where she had stood up to them and been true to herself. Her actions in those two lifetimes had set another family pattern, one of estrangement, in motion.

The first of these lifetimes was one she shared with her current sister. They had lived in China and the two of them (as brothers), had worked in a family business treating people with herbs. Even though this lifetime was several hundred years ago I saw that (she) intuitively had had an understanding that if people were given a small dose of a disease, it could create immunity. 'Rosie' experimented with this and brought it in as part of their practice. Her brother, (sister in this life) was violently opposed and refused to work with Rosie's past life self if he did this. He ordered his brother out of their town and out of his life. 'Rosie' (in that life), left and there was a lifelong rift.

In another more recent life, as a member of the same family, Rosie, then a young Palestinian woman had left her family to elope with the Jewish man she loved. She confided, that even now she was living independently she still at times wanted to escape. Her boyfriend from the UK was offering her the opportunity to do just that. They were preparing to leave New Zealand to settle in Scotland. I could see that these two were meant to be together and that this move would be good for her in many ways, not least in creating the distance she craved from her family. With space she could explore a career path that utilised her creative and healing gifts.

Stuck in a family pattern that had been entrenched for generations, I could see that she had a soul agreement with the same family members to show them a different way of living. That it is possible to do what you love and to still have security and stability. Rosie told me that she found the high expectations of her mother and the guilt she felt in return, oppressive. I helped her see that by honouring her own truth she would be helping all family members, including herself, to let go of behaviours that had been holding them back for a very long time.

Calling in the Higher Selves of her family members, I facilitated a healing to get Rosie's family out of 'survival mode' and to release the associated fears and beliefs, so they could all be liberated. At the end, I asked Rosie to visualise her current family members and herself on the top of a mountain, holding hands. In her mind's eye she saw herself taking a leap of faith into the unknown and trying to take her sister and parents with her. Rosie told me that she took off into the sky while they fell into the ocean below. As she visualised herself helping them out, I told her that every step she takes in the direction of her heart and truth will change the dynamic in her family and help them, especially her mother, as well.

Update: In 2020, two unanticipated events stopped Rosie in her tracks.

Her move to Scotland, with her partner, was postponed because of Covid and she found herself unexpectedly pregnant. Rosie couldn't run away from her family (as she had done so often before) so stayed put and waited for the birth of her daughter, Kaiya. By the time I talked with Rosie in mid-2021, her relationship with her family had become much closer.

'Before I had my baby I had so much resentment I didn't know how to let go of it,' she told me, 'But when I was in labour everything changed. I felt like I understood everything and I forgave everything. I only wanted my mum.' She added that her parents had come and helped her every day for the first six weeks and that her father, after years of being in 'survival mode,' was finally showing his emotions.

'Dad smiles and laughs when he is with Kaiya. She has melted his heart.'

Rosie said that her mother, an ex-midwife, had given her huge support.

'Kaiya has not only helped heal my relationship with my mother but she has healed my mother, who had a troubled relationship with her own mother.'

In Rosie's words, 'My mother wanted to be a mum to me but her own trauma got in the way. Kaiya has been so healing for the whole family.'

This small child is not only healing the trauma from past generations but after lifetimes of misunderstanding and conflict she is helping Rosie and her sister to clear their karma. Rosie told me that her sister also adored Kaiya and that she has helped in any way she can, shopping for the family and bringing them meals. She said that her relationship with her family has been completely transformed.

Although she still has plans to live in Scotland in the future, Rosie said she was grateful she had her baby in New Zealand and told me, 'I don't think I would have coped as well without my family. Kaiya has brought us so much happiness.'

The babies being born at this time are advanced souls who have made a conscious choice to incarnate to help us in the ascension process. Like Kaiya, they hold a high and loving vibration which reminds us of who we really are and heals their families and everyone they come in contact with. These babies are coming in karma-free. Their pure heart energy is pouring healing balm on family wounds and helping their families to transcend them.

As in Rosie's case, Covid-19 has been a catalyst that has brought families together. Many travellers have returned home and the enforced separation of the pandemic has helped many to appreciate and value their family connections. Every family on the planet is being forced to clear the karma and dysfunction that characterised family life in the Third Dimension. We are receiving help with this from the higher realms.

Recently I helped my four sisters clean out our parents' home after our 93 year old mother moved to an Aged Care Facility. As we sorted through drawers and cupboards filled with the minutiae of my parents' lives, I felt the strong presence of my father and of my mother's parents. They were sending their love and support and I felt, orchestrating a process that was healing and perfect for us all. As the items on the trailer and for the charity shop piled up, I sensed an energetic shift and knew that we were lightening the load of our family baggage, not just for ourselves but for our parents, children and ancestors. It was a bittersweet but positive weekend that brought us together as we literally and figuratively let go of the past.

The family is at the heart of human life and has been at the core of human suffering. The pressure is on! What used to take lifetimes to achieve is being forced on us NOW. At this time on Earth many of us have chosen to incarnate with specific souls to clear our karmic debt. Often these souls are members of our immediate families which makes it impossible to avoid them or the work we have to do.

A fresh wind is blowing however, and at long last the ugly legacy of darkness and secrecy which has existed in many families is being exposed and transmuted. Intergenerational trauma and dysfunctional patterns have no place in our human future. They are coming to the surface and many lightworkers are being called to facilitate ancestral healing. Those with soul contracts to help their families are being directed to modalities that can assist.

The Akashic Records with its links through cellular memory to both soul and familial patterns provide a powerful space for this process. As with all healing in our increasingly quantum world, whatever we do for ourselves benefits the whole. By working with one family member we can pull in the many strands from the past, present and future to re-create and reconfigure the family portrait for the highest good of all.

Chapter 7

Completion

As we farewell the old and welcome in the new, we are in a transitional phase. It is an uncertain time as we are called upon to release aspects of our personality selves that we have held onto for a very long time. The end of a cycle of 26,000 years, it is a time of completion on all levels of our being. The Covid-19 outbreak has given a new impetus to this process and is, I believe, one of the higher purposes of this pandemic.

Before we can move forward we must let go of the past. On a soul level this means completing unfinished business and clearing karma.

There is such a thing as positive karma but the karma connected to the Third Dimension has usually involved misery and pain. Each new life has given us the opportunity to make up for things we regret from the past. This spiritual rebirth has gone on for aeons and has strengthened the chains of human suffering that have held us captive. The good news is that in the new energy negative karma can no longer exist. Its vibration is too low. The **New Children** carry no karma, while the rest of us will soon be able to get off the wheel we have been spinning on for lifetimes. It is time to release it and we are all getting opportunities to do this. In the New Earth karma will be no more, and the suffering that has been an integral part of it will be gone forever.

The intense purging process we are undergoing is sweeping away all that flourished in the static and limiting Third Dimensional energy. We are being lifted to a higher frequency and re-born. We are evolving into a new human race of greater love, compassion and power. Completion is the order of the day. We are all getting the opportunity to 'wipe the slate clean.'

The soul is eternal. Through the process of reincarnation our soul comes back to Earth repeatedly. What is not completed in one life can be attended to in the next or a future lifetime. In this intense energy there has been a compulsion to tie up loose ends before we step fully into the Fifth Dimension. This process is being driven by our Higher Self, the soul aspect that has witnessed all of our lifetimes on Earth.

In the energy of the moment, past life behaviours and dynamics that are unresolved are sneaking into the present.

My client, Philippa asked me, 'Why can't I trust my husband?' She told me that he was a wonderful person who she loved dearly, but that she had a nagging feeling about him she couldn't shift. Philippa is an Old Soul who has done things the hard way. She has huge intuitive gifts. Her highest potential is to work as a healer, helping others to release karmic imprints and the cellular memories that are keeping them stuck. She has been undergoing this process herself in recent years and has at times asked me to help her.

In my mind's eye I saw that she had shared many lives with her husband, Dave, and that she was still being affected by a life in Victorian England. In this past life she was a young woman, all alone in the world, who struggling to survive, had become a prostitute. In my mind's eye, I saw her bedraggled, despairing and dirty with lots of missing teeth. Her worst fear was ending up in the workhouse. She had chosen the alternative option of prostitution, in an attempt to retain a semblance of control over her life. I saw that in that lifetime her present-day husband had been a regular customer of hers.

He was also the man in charge of the workhouse. He had a sexual addiction which he tried to hide and which was at odds with his position as the institution governor. I jumped to the future in that lifetime and saw a scene where, destitute and desperate, 'Philippa' arrived at the workhouse, begging to be admitted. Dave, as he was then, recognised her and panicked in case his secret was discovered. He acted as if he had never seen her before and turned her away. She left feeling that she wasn't good enough, even for the workhouse. She lost her will to live and didn't survive for long.

This made sense to Philippa and her current situation. In this life she had discovered that her husband had an addiction to online pornography. She told me that they had dealt with this situation but that it had affected her trust in their relationship. Now, several lifetimes later, they were back together with this unresolved karmic issue still playing out. I told her that, on a subconscious level, she could be reminding him of the past and triggering some old behaviours. In this life, as in the Victorian one, there was a side of himself that Dave kept from others. His reconnection with Philippa had brought up deep and unresolved feelings that needed to be cleared. Their partnership in this life had given Dave the opportunity to face up to his past life guilt and shame and to redress their karma.

Philippa told me that she has trouble believing in herself and that this was stopping her from stepping into her soul work. Like most Old Souls, Philippa has had many lives of feeling unworthy. The build up of energy from these lifetimes has been keeping her stuck. Her husband Dave, has a current life contract to support Philippa with her lightwork and mission in the future.

With my help Philippa talked to her prostitute self and brought her to a state of peace. She then talked to Dave's Higher Self and explained the situation. She promised to talk to her husband, in person, as well.

When I caught up with Philippa sometime later, she said that our session had helped raise her feelings of self-worth and given her the courage to be honest with her husband. She told him that she had been putting his needs first because she was frightened that if she didn't, he would leave. Philippa also said that our session, and the talk with Dave afterwards, had helped her let go of this unhealthy dynamic. She added, 'He has changed because I have changed and our relationship has gone from strength to strength.' Philippa recently told me they have moved to a wonderful plot of land and that, with the full support of her husband, she is now ready to step out with her spiritual gifts.

We all have a back-story. For the Old Souls on Earth this can go back thousands of years. I have had two occasions in recent years where my soul has taken control of a situation. In a short and dramatic moment, centuries of ill feeling and karma and the suffering it has created and recreated have been released.

The first occasion was in the foyer of the Psych Ward during Alice's last stay there. In the early years of her illness, the waves of post-traumatic stress that were triggered were so powerful, her self-harming and suicidal impulses so strong, that Alice was in constant danger. To keep her safe, she spent over a year in the secure ward of our local psychiatric hospital. Carolyn, a nurse about my age, took her under her wing. She became another mother to my daughter at this crucial time and basically saved her life. Despite this, I put up a barrier between us of suspicion and mistrust. In my fragile state I felt that she was judging my parenting. Carolyn was a strong woman who ran a tight ship, in a business-like way. I felt powerless to help my daughter and I appreciated her efforts but the person that I was then felt inadequate and as if I had failed. It was a shocking and emotional time. There was a grudging respect between us but also feelings of rivalry on my part. When Carolyn was helping my daughter I was grateful, but reluctantly so. Over the years I have had a chance to distance myself from the situation and to reflect. I decided that if I ever saw her again I would thank her for her efforts. I heard on the grapevine that she had been through a tough time, with a relationship breakup and the loss of her son. Alice stopped her regular stays in hospital so the chances of us ever meeting again seemed remote.

Alice returned briefly, to the Psych Ward late in 2018. One day, as I was leaving, I walked into the foyer straight into Carolyn. Here was my chance and I made the most of the opportunity. I told her that if she hadn't looked after my daughter so well ten years before she would not be alive. Gratitude came from the bottom of my heart. It is a tough and thankless job being a psych nurse and my words brought her to tears.

During this meeting we squared off at each other but in a different way than in the past. As we looked into each other's eyes there was mutual respect, acknowledgment and empathy for the challenges of our respective journeys.

'I think there is a soul connection between the three of us,' I said. Carolyn nodded and I talked about the spiritual world that Alice's illness had opened up for me. She understood. We were on the same page and it felt good.

'Let's have a hug,' she said. In that instant, centuries of judgement, mistrust and misunderstanding evaporated. It was very powerful. Our hug felt amazing and was healing and liberating for us both, I think. Delving into my Akashic Record later that day, I could see many lifetimes over thousands of years where Carolyn and I had been in conflict, often with Alice in the middle. In one transcendent moment the heavy energy we had carried for centuries was gone. As I drove home I was elated and felt much, much lighter.

Karma and conflict carry the energy of the suffering we have inflicted on ourselves. As was the case with Carolyn we are all being given opportunities to release this. I believe our Higher Self arranges these moments and that there will be more of them. At every point of our human lives we have free choice. It is our decision whether to take the opportunity when it is presented to us or not.

My soul arranged another of these moments in early 2019. About seven years ago a friend and I set up a group for women who are spiritually orientated and would like their work to have a global reach. Our group meets regularly and is the only chance many of us get to talk freely about our dreams, successes and challenges. We take a two month break over summer, so at the beginning of the year I was looking forward to seeing everyone again. The night before the meeting one of our members asked me if she could bring a friend with her. I said that if our host didn't mind it would be fine with me. I was making a cup of tea the next morning when our mystery guest arrived. As soon as I saw her I recognised her as a woman I had had a bad experience with a few years earlier. I was horrified and shocked at her presence in this special group.

It was a Friday afternoon in 2016. As I finished packing my car with everything needed for my stall at a Spiritual Fair, I received a text from a lady I will call Shelley. She wanted a reading immediately. I told her this was not possible but that I would be at the Fair the next day and that if she arrived before 10.30am she should be able to book a reading. At 10.30am the next morning I thought of her, glanced at my booking sheet which still had spaces and sat down with my next client. Fifteen minutes later I was confronted by a very angry woman. Shelley had just arrived to find that I was fully booked. My appointment sheet had never filled up so quickly and I was surprised. I was more shocked by what happened next. I became the subject of the most vitriolic attack I have had in my life. I was told I was inauthentic, a liar, and so it went on. I tried to defend myself from her insults but she was furious and wouldn't listen. She disappeared out the door, leaving me a wreck with a whole day of readings to do. I managed to get through it and to do my best for everyone. I was sitting down at the end of my last session, feeling relieved to have survived, when I looked up to see Shelley walking towards me. She had come back for a reading. She had calmed down but I was still wary. With everyone packing up around me, I gave her one, at no charge.

As she left she said 'You are actually quite good at this.' Followed by, 'You have to believe in yourself more.' This made me furious. I was angry at her sense of entitlement and patronising manner. I was even more angry at myself for allowing this treatment and for not only giving her the reading she demanded but for giving it for free.

I learned a lot from this experience which has helped me since. I had put it to the back of my mind and even forgotten her name and now, here she was, as a guest of the group I had helped to create. Our hostess welcomed her and everyone went around and introduced themselves. Some of the others knew this person and said so.

When I was asked, 'Do you know Shelley?' I had not planned to say anything but my soul had other ideas. From a very deep place the story came out. Starting with, 'I do know Shelley. I will tell you how,' to a hushed audience I told the story as it had happened for me. I am not sure where the words came from but they flowed out of me. As I spoke, I felt as if I had been waiting hundreds, if not thousands of years, to say them. Shelley took it very well.

When she had a chance to speak she said, 'I was going through a very difficult time.'

As I looked at her I felt love and compassion and knew something huge had lifted for us both.

Our soul knows our story and what we as individuals need to do to enable us to fulfil our highest potential. In this situation it was important that I speak and that Shelley listen. As I hugged her at the end she said she would soon be moving across the world.

After many lifetimes of conflict and strife, at the eleventh hour, our souls had arranged an opportunity for us to clear the air. What are the chances of this happening? It was a wonderful letting go of the past which has set us both up to make more of the future.

Speaking my truth is one of my biggest life lessons. In multiple lifetimes I have been a victim and have allowed myself to be manipulated and exploited. In my Akashic Record I found there was a long history between Shelley and me. Through many lifetimes from Atlantis, in the time of Christ, Ancient Rome, thirteenth century France and Nazi Germany we had been antagonists. We had built up a wall of karma that was holding us both back. Suddenly and dramatically, after many lifetimes of suffering, it was gone. I was shocked at the words that came out of my mouth. I have never spoken so honestly to anyone in this lifetime or, I am sure, in any of my recent lifetimes. It felt fantastic.

On a soul level, many of us are getting the chance to complete things we have been unable to in previous lives. In the old energy we all had many lifetimes where we didn't accomplish what we set out to do. Too often events we didn't see coming and didn't expect, stopped us from completing what we planned. 'The rug has been pulled out from under us, 'many times. There is no need to worry, however. The soul is eternal and each new lifetime provides a fresh chance for us to reach our destination.

Some of us have actively chosen to be with souls to finish what we started but have been unable to complete in other lives.

This was the case for Chris and Beth, a young couple I gave separate readings to. The proud parents of a young son they are happy and have big dreams for the future. In the Records I saw they had been together during World War II. In that lifetime, Chris was a young German soldier based in an occupied territory and Beth was a beautiful local girl. They fell madly in love.

'Beth' (in that life), became pregnant and told 'Chris' she was carrying his child. Soon afterwards, suddenly and under a cloak of secrecy, he was transferred to another post. He didn't have the chance to say good bye to 'Beth', who was left, literally, 'holding the baby.' She never heard from 'Chris' again as he died soon afterwards in battle. The baby was adopted out but everyone in her village knew and judged her and 'Beth' carried the shame and sadness for the rest of her life.

When I opened Chris's Akashic Record I could see that he had a belief that he was a failure and a fear of letting people down. Another past life experience had reinforced these convictions. In that life, during another war, I saw him as a teenage boy with his schoolmates in the path of an advancing army. He was given the job of keeping them safe. The soldiers arrived and set fire to the building he had taken his school friends to for shelter. They all died.

In his current life, Chris said he feels huge feelings of obligation and responsibility. These feelings are particularly strong, he admitted, towards his wife Beth. When I shared the details of their recent life together, he said that they resonated. Through circumstances beyond his control, he had been forced to leave his girlfriend and unborn child behind and had not been able to be the husband and father they deserved. Chris shed many tears as I helped him talk to his past life self. He was able to tell him that he had been reunited with his girlfriend and that they were married and bringing up a child together. With my support Chris, was able to let go of the unresolved grief, self-blame and a raft of other feelings he had been carrying from that lifetime.

Another client has continued this theme of a new life providing a fresh opportunity to complete unfinished business. I saw Jenny as a teenage girl in Scotland in the early twentieth century.

She was intelligent and doing well at school. Her dream was to train as a teacher so she could come back to her village to work. She hoped to encourage her young female pupils to follow in her footsteps and get a higher education. She could clearly see the lost potential for village girls who left school early and became mothers and caregivers for their extended families. She wanted a different path for herself and was passionate about inspiring other young women to raise their expectations. Unfortunately, her mother died and her father made her leave school to look after him and her siblings. As if this wasn't bad enough, he also forced her to become his sexual partner. She was broken-hearted, lost her desire to live and died as a young woman from a contagious disease.

All this made sense to Jenny. She shared that in her current life she had been driven by a compulsion to get things done and a fear that she might die early and not be able to reach her goals. She also said she had a fear of intimacy and that she had been married to a controlling partner who she had recently, with great difficulty, managed to divorce. Her ex-husband (I saw), had been her father in the Scottish life. I told her that she had done the right thing, that it had been part of her soul's plan for her to stand up to him in this life and to end the relationship. I was not surprised when she told me that she works in a high school mentoring and encouraging young women to make the most of their abilities and to reach their potential. Over one hundred years later, in another lifetime, she is finally making her dreams come true.

I have given several readings to a young woman called Bella. When I last saw her she had just finished writing a book which she hopes will give inspiration to other young people dealing with the complexity and challenges of modern life. She told me she has recently started writing another book: a detailed account of a woman's life in Mexico several hundred years ago. She said one day she felt compelled to meditate and that this story began to come through. She said she can link in with the woman and her life whenever she likes and that the book is taking shape very quickly. I found this very exciting, especially when she reminded me of a reading I did for her in 2015 which told of a past life she had as a wealthy, young woman in Mexico. In that lifetime she had plans to assist the poor in her community. This never eventuated as she married a man who took control of her life and her money. Here is an extract from that email reading:

A long time ago you had a life in Mexico as a powerful and beautiful woman. You inherited a great deal of money when your father died. You cared deeply for the poor and wanted to use your wealth to help people who lived on the streets.

You had advanced plans to provide them with food and shelter and then met and were swept off your feet by a young man who acted like he desired you but really wanted your money. You married him and lost control of it. Your wealth was never used in the way you intended but squandered by your new husband. You lost your power and deeply regretted your decision to marry.

My young friend told me that the Mexican lady she is writing about (herself in that past life), had many dreams that never came to fruition. As well as projects to relieve poverty, she wrote a book which was never published.

A theme that keeps coming up in Bella's readings is the crucial importance for her, this time round, of having the freedom to express herself, especially in relationships. She is doing this through her writing and is now connecting with this former soul aspect of herself to tell **her** story. This will not only help Bella in this life but her past life self, who will finally be able to get her message out and to help others.

It may take lifetimes but our soul's agenda is for healing. Our souls work beyond existing time lines to master-mind this and bring us back into balance.

Now that we have greater access to the Akashic Records, the opportunity to integrate our unhealed aspects, and to resolve past life issues has become easier.

Karen, another client, had a past life that was troubling her. She phoned me wanting an urgent reading. Her twenty-two year old son, Jack, had recently met and fallen in love with a young woman called Josie. When he introduced her to his parents, it was love at first sight for Karen and her husband Pat. They felt huge love for this young woman who they had only just met. When Josie left, Karen said the feelings she had were indescribable. She was overwhelmed by a deep sadness and the fear that Josie was going to die. She kept having visions of imminent death and these words came into her head. 'Make the most of every moment. Every moment counts.'

Karen felt as if she could lose this lovely young woman at any time and in her panic called me to see if I could help. I accessed Karen's Akashic Record and saw a life in the early 1900s where she had been married to her current husband, Pat. They lived with her father-in-law and were in their early 40s and childless. For years they tried to have a baby and lived a grim and joyless existence. Then a miracle happened. 'Karen' became pregnant and produced a beautiful daughter who became the light of their lives. I saw this gorgeous girl sitting on her grandfather's knee in a household that had been transformed by love. The next scene was of the little girl lying in bed, dying from diphtheria. Next to the bed was her heartbroken mother who was in denial, refusing to believe what was happening. Well-meaning relatives and neighbours were trying to prepare her by saying, 'Make the most of every moment. Every moment counts,' but she didn't listen. The little girl died and the three people who loved her the most never recovered. Their life had been bleak before the birth of their baby but to experience three years of great joy and then have it snatched away, was far worse. Sadness overshadowed the rest of their lives.

Two lifetimes later, Karen has been reunited with her beautiful baby girl in the form of her son's new girlfriend. Her husband, Pat has been reunited with the soul of his lost child and her son, Jack with his dearly loved granddaughter. Jack was 'Karen's' father-in-law in that past life and the child's grandfather.

I facilitated soul healing for Karen. When I asked her to close her eyes she saw her past life self holding tightly onto her dead child.

With my prompting she introduced herself by saying, 'I am Karen, a future aspect of you.' She then told her 'past life self' that she had been an excellent mother and that she had lost her child because it was not the right time for them to be together. She explained that her baby was of a higher vibration, a soul she had known from the stars, who had been eager to reconnect but had come in too early. Karen continued, telling her past life self that they had been separated thousands of years before and that the plan was always, when the vibration on Earth was high enough, that the soul of 'Josie' would return. Karen assured her past life self that 'Josie' would come back into her life and the lives of her husband and father-in-law at a future time. Karen told her that she had carried the grief over the loss of her child into her current life, that it was holding her back and that it was time for them both to let it go. In our minds, Karen and I both saw the mother handing over her child. Karen cried uncontrollably, releasing the grief she didn't know she had. Afterwards she felt much happier and she told me that her past life self was also smiling and at peace.

I looked into the potentials for Karen and Josie in the future. I saw the loving family unit back together and the possibility of them joining forces to bring in a higher consciousness to the world. Reflecting on this experience in a recent email Karen wrote:

'With the assistance of the Akashic Records what was deeply traumatic for each of us has now been returned to love. We are all moving forward with renewed vigour, a deepened passion for life and a heightened multidimensional connectedness.'

Karen is a healer who can easily connect with other dimensions. The words she heard were not relevant to today but a 'bleed-through' from another life. Bleed-through experiences are happening more frequently on Earth as the vibration is lifting and the veils between worlds and dimensions are getting thinner. These inter and multi-dimensional experiences will become more common in the years ahead.

I had an interdimensional experience of my own, in Europe in 2017, where I was given the opportunity to heal and release some fears and sadness from one of my past lives. The main reason my husband and I took the trip was to see our son, Hugh, and to meet and spend time with his new Spanish partner and her family. Since late 2015, Hugh had been living in the UK which is where he met Marta.

As part of this trip we walked the last five days (117kms) of the Camino in northern Spain with Hugh and Marta, her father, mother and brother. As we flew into Santiago de Compostela, before beginning our pilgrimage at Sarria, I received an energetic download of information about why it was important for us to complete this section of the walk. I was told that we were carrying the trauma and pain from a much earlier lifetime we had shared. Together, we had embarked on this same pilgrimage and been attacked and killed near the end of our journey. I was told that it was important we finish it together so we could lay the sadness and fear from this past experience to rest. This is the information that came to me:

> *You have trodden that path before in another life and in another time. You were one of the early pilgrims in the nineth century. You were murdered before you reached Santiago. You came from France across the Pyrenees after the death of your son (Hugh in this life). Your grief was immense and you felt you were losing your mind. You had heard of the remains of St James in the holy city of Santiago de Compostela and decided to embark on this pilgrimage. With you were your spiritual advisor, a priest with gnostic leanings, (Marta), your brother (Marta's father), sister (Marta's mother) and Hugh's grandmother (Marta's brother). 'Hugh', (or whoever he was in that life), was your only child and his father had died of a fever. He was all you had. He had such promise and was deeply loved by all. He died suddenly and your family feared you would die too.*
>
> *Your faith was strong and it was decided to set off on the walk. Five days out from your destination you were ambushed by Moors who killed you by slitting your throats. You knew you were dying and it was a grisly and traumatic end. You experienced this together. It is now important on a soul level that you reach Santiago safely.*

It was a huge feeling of accomplishment when we reached the Cathedral. I am someone who has neglected my body in this life and the physical challenge of it was big but my feelings went way beyond that. The past life significance explains why. Although I am not a church goer, the ceremony we attended the next day in the Cathedral of Santiago de Compostela, was magical. As we watched the **botafumeiro** swing from one end of the church to the other and breathed in the sweet smell of incense, the exhilaration I felt on both a soul and a physical level was massive. The trauma from an incarnation long ago had been released. Not just for me but for all of us.

❀

As we enter a new era of existence, many old cycles are coming to an end. In the Third Dimensional energy lifetimes of obstacles, persecution and unexpected events have sabotaged our progress. In the post 2012 vibration we, at last, have a clear run. We can finish what we set out to do in other lifetimes and existences. This new energy is clearing karma, healing rifts and discharging the lower vibrational legacy that has reigned supreme on this planet. As we move from one cycle to the next, we are getting the opportunity to complete experiences from other lifetimes and soul expressions. Things are coming full circle but we have to complete the old one before we start the new. This situation is challenging. All that we have been running away from is catching up with us. The universe is making sure that all of our unfinished business is attended to. People we have distanced ourselves from are now, sometimes literally, knocking on our doors. Our unhealed family stuff is taunting us and our **Inner Child** is screaming for attention. Often we are compelled by feelings beyond our control to do and say things that have no logical explanation.

It is the pure and vibrant energy of the Akashic Records with their soul overview that drives this compulsion. The Records know what is missing and can help us fill in the gaps, not just in our knowledge, but with experiences that return us to a place of balance.

When we make peace with the past we create space for the new. As upgraded versions of ourselves, we will soon be able to step into and take our rightful place in the centre of a new circle and cycle of evolution.

Chapter 8

Physical Healing

To go from tragic to magic and to move beyond suffering we have to heal and bring into balance the emotional and physical afflictions that cause us pain. Within the Fifth Dimensional frequency of the Records we can release and transmute the stuck energy we are holding in our bodies that perpetuates suffering. As I said earlier, with the help of the Akashic Records it is possible to identify and isolate the past life causes of beliefs and behaviours that are adversely affecting our physical and emotional wellbeing. We can then state a strong intention to clear these and ask our bodies to let the cellular imprints go. As our vibration rises, our non-coding DNA unlocks and our consciousness changes, our bodies will respond more quickly to these commands. The more quantum we become, the easier it will be to let go of the past and to create lives of harmony and joy.

As our DNA capabilities are being upgraded so are our abilities for self-healing. Talking to the cells of our bodies we can instruct them to release all distortion, **dis-ease** and the beliefs that create illness. We can connect to lifetimes where we had perfect health and to the genetics of ancestors who lived long and healthy lives. We can even ask for a genetic predisposition to hereditary ailments to be released. It is time to take control of our biology. According to Gregg Braden (Kryon 'Science and Spirituality Conference,' 2020), we are the only species capable of doing this.

We have these healing abilities but at the same time many of us are disconnected from our bodies. They are making the best of an increasingly difficult situation. Facing an onslaught of inactivity, poor nutrition and a mindset where negative beliefs about aging, illness and disease are strong, our bodies still work tirelessly and to the best of their ability to keep us healthy. They need to know we love and appreciate them. They need us to listen to them and to value what they have to say. They want to work in partnership with us for perfect health and vitality. They are waiting for and listening to our instructions. If the only messages they receive are e.g. 'You are ugly, You are fat, You are failing me' or, worse still, if they receive no messages at all, they will give up, 'go rogue' and illness can be the result. Our wisdom is in our cells and it is time to communicate with and to listen to this intelligence.

In his channellings, Kryon calls our cellular intelligence, the innate. He says our bodies respond to our conscious and sub-conscious thoughts, that they like being told what to do and need clear guidance.

I often say these simple phrases from Kryon when I talk to my body:

- 'I ask that the purest DNA that I have ever possessed be placed upon the attributes of my current health.'
- 'I hereby break any disease inheritance in my body. I no longer have it in my blood.'

Bruce Lipton is bringing Cell Biology and Quantum Physics together. As discussed in Chapter 6, he has proven that our physical bodies are affected by our consciousness and respond to our thoughts, feelings and beliefs.

At the 'Science and Spirituality Conference' in 2020, another New Scientist, Dr Todd Ovokaitys, said that DNA is more than just chemistry. The structure of DNA, he claimed, 'consists of physical coils which are able to pass on electromagnetic frequency information to DNA elsewhere in the body.' In this way, he said, 'We can instruct our DNA to do what we wish.'

In an article (The Living Internet Inside of Us, 2002), Barbel Mohr summarises the work of Russian researchers Grazyna Fosar and Franz Bludorf who found evidence that our bodies understand and respond to language. The Russian scientists led by Pjotr Garjajev, found that our DNA plays a crucial role in data storage and in communication. They also discovered that the genetic code follows the same rules in syntax, semantics and grammar as our spoken human languages.

The Russian researchers asserted that Human Languages did not develop coincidentally but 'are a reflection of our DNA.' They further concluded that as the structure of alkaline pairs and of language are the same, no decoding is necessary and that 'DNA can be influenced and reprogrammed by words and frequencies.' Experiments with living DNA have shown that they respond to 'language modulated laser rays' if the frequency is set the same. Fosar and Bludorf have suggested that this is why high vibrational programming such as positive affirmations, and hypnosis can have a beneficial effect on the physical body.

I believe it is the quantum aspects of our bodies, the cellular intelligence which is a part of our non-coding DNA, which most readily responds to words and instructions. Being in the quantum energy of the Akashic Records accelerates and enhances these processes. Non-coding DNA and cellular wisdom (innate), are also quantum so it is only natural they respond to consciousness – our thoughts, feelings, beliefs and intention.

Human suffering and physical pain are inextricably connected. Sooner or later, any emotional pain we feel will be manifested in our bodies. They carry the burden of our human discomfort and the blockages in energy that result in dis-ease. The feelings that exist as an energetic in our Merkabah Field will eventually manifest as illness. Unresolved emotions build up and overcome our body's resistance and sickness is the result. We create our own reality on every level of our being, in the physical as well as the emotional, mental and spiritual. The health of our bodies is a direct reflection of our wellness in all areas of our lives. Louise Hay recognised the crucial link between emotional and physical wellbeing. In her pioneering book *You Can Heal Your Life*, she identified the feelings and emotions behind specific ailments and conditions.

Our Akashic Record can also help us to identify the underlying causes of ill health. They are a direct link to the memories of past life physical weakness and conditions. In many lives I have had respiratory ailments. Since my late 40s in this lifetime, I have suffered from the conditions of asthma and sinusitis. When I conduct physical healing for myself, I open my Akashic Record and begin with a clear intention for what I want to happen.

'It is my intention to heal completely from my conditions of asthma and sinusitis and to bring my body into a state of balance, physical harmony and perfection.'

I also talk to the cellular memory and the intelligence in my body and ask:

- that all current and past life emotions and memories that are impacting my physical body be released
- that I be connected with all lifetimes where I experienced perfect health
- that my life force be fully returned to me
- that the high vibration template of health and perfection, a blueprint that exists in the etheric, be activated and anchored into my physical body.

I use these same techniques with my clients.

My open Akashic Record not only provides a quantum healing space, it also makes it possible to travel backwards and forwards in time, as part of the healing process. In this lifetime I have taken myself back to when I was younger and the time just before I developed asthma comes to mind. I was writing a conscious parenting course for a parent organisation in New Zealand. At a meeting for those involved, I was upset to hear that my colleague's husband had become seriously ill. He was confined to bed and unable to work. The thought went through my mind that I had never really been unwell in my life. I wondered how that would feel and it brought up some fears. In that precise moment, I believe, I gave my body permission to get sick. Unknown to me, at that very same time, Alice had just been sexually assaulted and her life was starting to unravel. We were so connected that I am sure that Alice's trauma was also a contributory factor.

Shortly after this meeting I became ill with asthma and sinus conditions that have plagued me ever since. It has been helpful being able to pinpoint that moment. When I am in the Records I often take myself back to the time just beforehand and give my body a different message. This practice and connecting with myself earlier in this lifetime when I was young, energetic and healthy is helping me to recover.

❀

In several readings I have shared past life information with clients who have worked in the Temples of Rejuvenation. As far as I know these temples existed in the Fifth Dimensional civilisations of Lemuria and **Golden Atlantis**. Kryon and others say our bodies are designed to last longer and that an increased life span is one of many positive physical changes we can look forward to in the future. Kryon has identified a 'Youth Template,' which exists in our bodies which he says is activated by other multidimensional energies. Being in the Fifth Dimensional vibration of the Akashic

Records not only boosts our healing potentials but makes it easier to access this template.

As well as saying healing affirmations to my body, in the last few years I have been instructing my telomeres to stay the same length. As we age they naturally shorten. They become damaged when our cells replicate and we eventually lose them altogether. When our chromosomes reach a point where they can no longer divide because there is no telomere left, the result is degeneration and eventually death.

Scientific experiments with mice are proving that rejuvenation is possible. In an article in the December 15, 2016 issue of *Science* magazine, Mitch Leslie reported on recent discoveries. Scientists found that by activating genes associated with embryos, the adult cells of mice could be reprogrammed into stem cells that returned epigenetic markers to their youthful settings. Additionally, a study by Juan Carlos Izpisua Belmonte of the *Salk Institute* in San Diego with mice afflicted by the premature aging disease *Hutchinson-Guildford Progeria Syndrome*, discovered that their life spans were boosted by more than a third when the stem cell genes of these mice were switched on.

In the summit *Pleiadian Passport to Earth*, in 2021, Dr Todd Overkaitys talked of the pioneering rejuvenation and regeneration research he and other scientists are conducting with stem cells. They work with small embryonic stem cells that have been circulating in the blood and in a dormant state since birth. Because the telomeres of these cells don't divide, they don't replicate and they don't age. Using advanced sound and light (laser) technology, they are getting excellent results with regenerating the body and reversing biological age. Dr Overkaitys summed up this ground breaking work by saying, 'A very small stem cell has the potential to extend life that we can engineer and manage intentionally.'

Like many things we have not believed possible, rejuvenation is happening and it is happening now. The potentials for this will only increase as our vibrations lift and our DNA capabilities are restored.

❀

Healing is never a certainty. Healing must be a partnership between the healer and those they work with; a conscious connection built on trust, faith and mutual respect. As healers and lightworkers it is important to realise that we can't help everyone. Our ability to assist others is in direct proportion to their willingness to receive that help. Healing is a two-way process and can't occur if the person on the receiving end is not open to it. They must believe it can help them and believe in us. We can set the scene, create the intention and bring in the energies but we have no control over the outcome. We can play our part but whoever we are working with needs to play theirs as well.

It is also important to understand that sometimes it is not for a soul's highest good to heal at a certain time. Their physical or emotional condition may be part of a karmic inheritance or present lessons and challenges that they have chosen to experience. It may even be their time to die. At this crucial time on Earth souls may be needed elsewhere and can often be of more use in the spirit world than as human beings trapped in ailing bodies.

The new energy is making it easier for those on 'the other side' to communicate and help us. Many have chosen to serve their loved ones in this way at this decisive moment in history. Everyone needs an angel in heaven and we all have them assigned to us as we navigate huge change on the planet. I feel my father who died in 2013 around me often. He is helping with editing and urging me on as I write. My close friend Robyn who died in 2018 and was a great support to our family when Alice became ill, is doing her best to help as well.

✤

Healthwise, my chronic sinus problem lasted for years. It still flares up at times and I take it as a message from my body that I need to slow down and look after myself. In my efforts to heal I have tried every remedy and healing modality possible. Many of my clients and the participants at my workshops have offered me advice on what to do. At my first Two Day workshop, as I farewelled everyone at the door, every single participant had advice for me on how I could cure my sinuses. Their suggestions were different but they all resonated with me on some level and I was confused over what to do. I kept being told 'You can heal yourself.'

While humanity certainly has potential for self-healing, my healing is not happening overnight. It is a work in progress. The Akashic Records have helped me raise my vibration and to rid myself of sabotaging beliefs and behaviours. I feel that focused intention and the repetition of words and phrases are creating a structure in the etheric, which, at the right time will be transferred to my body. When I am resonating at a higher frequency it will be easy for me to bring in and to lay down this energetic. I have had to persevere with this work which has been difficult at times. When I am letting go of the imbalance and disharmony within my body, my health conditions sometimes get worse and my body doesn't cope well with stress. The years of being on 'high alert' with Alice have left their mark and I still have to pace myself. I know that this damage is reversible and that the Akashic Records are helping me to turn back the clock. I have friends who are 'battening down the hatches' and registering for retirement homes but now in my early 60s I feel better than I did a decade ago. In my speech on my 60th birthday I told everyone that I was not winding down but winding up. In many ways I feel my real work in this lifetime hasn't even begun. Every time I am in the energy of the Records I hold the intention for healing, my vibration lifts and every cell in my body benefits from their energy. After eleven years of this it is no wonder

I am feeling younger and more energised. Watch this space. It can only get better.

❀

What happens in our bodies is not just determined by what exists energetically around us. What exists within our cellular memory is also very important. The cells of our bodies remember everything from our current lifetimes and others as well. They hold trauma and trapped emotions from the past as well as the more positive memories. Kryon calls this energetic our '**Akashic Template.**' Physical weakness, as well as having an emotional link to our current life, often has a direct connection to past lives or lifetimes where we have suffered injury in that part of the body.

A client asked me why she was experiencing discomfort in the vertebrae of her middle-back and with her heart.

I saw her in a recent lifetime, as a reluctant soldier in an African army. It was a time of political upheaval and prolonged drought. In order to provide for his extended family, my client (in that life), became a mercenary for a ruthless dictator. In her email reading I told her:

You were lured into the army by promises of money and only agreed to it to support your family. You were subject to the whims of an unstable ruler. It was a miserable existence. You knew that if you refused to follow orders you would be killed and that your family would suffer. You were caught between 'a rock and a hard place.' The atrocities you witnessed weigh heavily on your soul. This trauma and the memories of your death, in that lifetime, are still affecting you.

You were betrayed by a fellow soldier who knew your true feelings. When he was hauled in on a breach of discipline, to save himself, he turned the spotlight on you. You were beaten

> *on the back until your heart gave out. Your body holds the memories of this and when you are feeling 'boxed in,' or as if there is no way out of a difficult situation, these pains return.*

A friend who came to see me had two broken arms. His injuries had occurred shortly after he had been bullied at work and made redundant. In the Records I saw him in a past life stretched out and being tortured on a rack. My friend told me that the work situation, he had just left had felt like torture.

A woman I met in Sydney, in 2017, told me about a terrible accident she had had in Russia that year. She was knocked over by a teenager on a bicycle in St Petersburg and broke several ribs and damaged her lungs. While she was recovering in hospital, her 'far memory' kicked in. She saw that in a previous life she had died after being run over by a horse and carriage in the exact same location. The body remembers. Cellular memory can be triggered by being the same age or in the same place as when the trauma happened or by feeling emotions similar to those felt in a past life when we suffered an injury.

As I said earlier, the innate is intelligent and quantum and takes direction from us. Our cellular wisdom, the smart body, is awaiting our instructions and will follow them to the letter. In the words of Adironnda, channelled by Marilyn Harper (www.adironndaspiritualhealer.com), what we think, feel and believe is our 'purchase order to the universe.'

Our non-coding DNA is also quantum. According to Kryon, Layer Nine is a healing layer presided over by St Germain and right next to this is Layer Eight (our Akashic Record). These energy strands are a powerful combination for both emotional and physical healing. In this high vibration space, with the power of intention and faith, anything is possible.

I have been most successful in facilitating physical healing when my client's ailment has been linked to past life experience.

Often physical symptoms become more acute as a cellular memory is being released. With longer term ailments, time, patience and repetition is often needed. Our intentions and words have to bypass our subconscious thoughts and beliefs. Our bodies must know that we mean what we say. There are huge potentials for physical healing in the future, especially as our DNA capacity increases. According to Kryon we are currently vibrating at a level of 35%. He says that when we are firing at 44%, disease will no longer exist in our bodies as our frequency will be too high. The resonance of this energy will cancel out anything lower and dis-ease will be eradicated.

As we become more closely connected to 'the field' that both surrounds us and lies within us, healing ourselves will get easier. Using our own tools to heal ourselves is the way of the future. We can utilise the quantum energy of the Records for this and there has been a proliferation of other healing methods that also draw on this energy. The days of being reliant on others to 'fix us' will soon be at an end.

Some of my students are combining the Akashic Records with existing physical healing modalities, with excellent results. The Records allow healing to occur on a deep soul level and provide a quantum portal to other Fifth Dimensional healing techniques. Healing in this energy is just as effective from a distance as in person. Some of us Old Souls have vague recollections of lifetimes of working in this way in Atlantis and Lemuria. The wisdom and knowledge of how to do this is in our DNA from these lifetimes and from those off planet.

Many healers are now calling themselves quantum. Dr John Ryan of Ottawa practises and teaches *Unity Field Healing*. This modality works with our non-coding DNA and uses a quantum field light template to connect and align clients to their deeper healing potential. Ryan says that in the quantum DNA field 'there is information about all elements of your life, your healing and wellbeing and your soul journey through time.' This healing method was first channelled by Dr Ryan in meditation. He was shown the Unity Field Healing template which he uses to recalibrate the human energy system to its original blueprint.

Along with Quantum DNA work, for some healers all that is necessary is for them to have a high vibration that cancels out lower frequencies and to hold a powerful intention for their client. Richard Bartlett with his healing modality, *Matrix Energetics* and Richard Gordon, both demonstrate and teach this. Richard Gordon with his healing method, *Quantum Touch*, uses the heart to raise the vibration of healer and healee. Coming from his heart, he surrounds those he works with in a powerful energetic of love, before he directs his intention and healing energy to the area of physical pain and weakness. The body of the other person then starts to resonate at the same frequency which makes it easier for healing to take place.

I have a friend in the US who works within the quantum field as a healer. She told me that when she conducts sessions she holds the intention for complete healing for the other person. She says to her clients, 'I am taking you into the quantum field and I am asking your body's intelligence to organise itself around my touch.'

She told me that all quantum energy has a Zero Point field and that it is when you get to Zero Point that the healing and miracles happen. She said that this healing method has been around for 30 years and confirmed that it is getting easier to access this field. Quantum techniques such as this and *Unity Field Healing*, are empowering, eliciting the help of the client's body wisdom to heal. In Dr Ryan's words, healing in the new energy is about connecting to the intuitive intelligence within us and bringing everything into balance, coherence and alignment.' These and similar techniques will make it easier for us to heal ourselves in years to come.

Information and guidance I have received while working in the Records suggests that as we move into a new cycle of life, exciting changes are afoot. Heightened abilities which go way beyond the parameters of modern medicine are being activated, including the ability to heal ourselves. Words from Kryon such as these spoken as part of a 2021 online class on 'The Twelve Layers of DNA,' support this. He said that in the future we will have no need for chemical drugs and remedies as 'within your own biology there is healing for almost every disease that ever existed and what isn't there is available in nature.' Miraculous healings are becoming more common. A key question to ask is, what is stopping these miracles happening for everyone?

1. Our belief system:

Any resistance or doubt will affect the outcome. If we don't believe we can or deserve to have good health and be healed, we won't be. Telling patients how long they have to live doesn't help either. My friend Robyn, died almost five years to the day, after being told she had a rare lung condition and at worst only five years to live. In spite of my best efforts she believed everything her doctors told her and her deterioration and death proved them right. Medical prognoses are based firmly on what has gone before. The new energy is all about moving beyond the limitations of the past and the belief system that sustained us in 3D.

Lynne Mc Taggart and Joe Dispenza, both teachers working with 'the field,' are pushing the boundaries of established healing practice. They have individually demonstrated that healing is possible through the power of the mind. Some participants in Mc Taggart's 'Power of Eight' groups and intention experiments and attendees at Dispenza's retreats and workshops are living proof of this. With focussed group intention and a mindset that is free of doubt they have witnessed many miraculous healings.

Doubt about alternative healing methods has been implanted in many of us and often it is this scepticism that prevents a positive outcome. In the new energy with the right conditions, healing or the creation of a zero point field can be a simple process that is instantaneous. This may seem too good to be true but instances of 'spontaneous remission' are increasing and I believe they will continue to do so.

Despite my belief in the power of alternative healing methods, I hugely admire the skill and wisdom of the medical profession. They have saved my life as well as the lives of my children, Alice and Hugh. Heroes of the Covid-19 crisis, it takes a special soul to choose such a path. I am not suggesting that the expertise of doctors be replaced. Many of them are divinely inspired as have been many of the world's life-saving scientific discoveries. Like everything else, as we transition from the Third to the Fifth Dimension, new structures are growing up alongside the old. There is a place for conventional practices as well as alternative methods of healing that have been forgotten as a more scientific approach has taken hold. There is plenty of space for modalities which work with the new energy. The labels given to non-traditional medicine reflect the changing nature of healing dynamics. Alternative Medicine has become Complementary Medicine which is now evolving into Integrative Medicine. This suggests that all modalities can work together to find the healing solution best suited to the individual.

2. Our DNA is not firing at a high enough level

As I mentioned earlier our DNA is currently working at a level of about 35%. As more of our DNA is enabled and our capacity increases it will be easier for us to heal from emotional and physical afflictions.

3. Timing:

Timing is everything, especially in this new energy. Even though we may be doing all the right things, talking to our bodies, saying positive affirmations and releasing emotional imprints from past lives, if the time is not right nothing will happen. We all come into our lives with things to work on. For me, as with many of my clients, patience is at the top of the list and faith and trust are close behind. Our life experiences feed into the lessons we are here to learn. The Akashic Records don't exist in linear time so it is impossible to give a time frame for when things will happen. The potentials of future life events are there but when and if they happen depends on other factors like soul growth, learning and divine timing.

4. Soul Choice

Sometimes it is part of our soul plan to face a health challenge or a life-threatening disease or illness. There is a higher agreement for us to die young or to be physically dependent on those close to us and nothing can change this. For many healers their own experiences of ill-health set them on a quest for healing. They learn techniques along the way which they then use to help others. These soul choices are often made to help ourselves and / or those around us to learn specific lessons, evolve faster, or to redress karma. In these cases our condition is part of our path.

❈

Our bodies want to work with us. They know when something is not right and do their best to tell us. If we don't honour them they will give up and illness can result. As we move into a new energy and a new era of individual empowerment, however, there is cause for optimism.

Healing ourselves in mind, body and spirit will take us beyond suffering. Finding the root causes of ill health and disease will help us to alleviate it. Illness and health are a 'Catch 22'. When we move beyond suffering we will no longer create physical illness and once we have reclaimed perfect health we will no longer suffer.

Within the quantum container that is the Akashic Records everything is amplified and the potentials for healing are huge. The Records are a high vibrational space where we can more easily connect and work with the quantum elements of our bodies. We can work, beyond linear time, to create and bring in the highest vibratory templates of perfect health in existence. Given its quantum nature there is a natural affinity between the Akashic

Records and many new healing modalities. With the help of the Akashic Records we can take responsibility for our own health and work in partnership to heal and rejuvenate our bodies and to lengthen our lives.

As we connect to the field and our non-coding DNA these abilities will be accelerated. We will no longer be victims of random disease or of our genes. We will have an open and honest relationship with our bodies, a working partnership of mutual appreciation, optimum health and perfection where physical suffering can no longer exist.

Chapter 9

The life purpose of the Old Souls and the Millennials

I always look at life purpose when I give a reading. It is the question that excites me the most. I like to see my client's highest potential and mission and to share it with them. Sometimes there are many details and sometimes just a few. As with everything in the Records there is fluidity and flexibility. Too much information can be limiting and confining and it is often best just to tell them the broad sweep of their purpose. There are always many different ways that it can play out. Life, as we know it, is changing so quickly, that with my current understanding I often can't conceptualise or describe the work a client may do in the future. All I can do is repeat the words that come into my head. At the beginning of a session the details are often sketchy. By the end, I have usually managed to fill in some of the gaps. As with everything else at this unprecedented time of change, our life purpose is not set in stone. It can be renegotiated throughout our lives and it is our choice whether we fulfil it.

This life purpose of a client I gave an email reading to lacked specific detail. There are many ways it could manifest in her life.

Your divine mission is to assist humanity to find the light within and to beam that light out to the dark places on Earth, so that humanity can bask in it, be healed by it and start to

> *love themselves so the need to hurt others is gone from our psyche and from the planet. You have all the soul attributes to be a leader to others and to show them a more evolved and humanitarian way of being, where we live in harmony with nature and with each other.*

To another client I also gave a generalised description of her life purpose:

> *Broadly, your mission is to overcome fear and to free the planet from its debilitating effects and all fear-based beliefs, behaviours and actions. Fear is a Third Dimensional construct for which there is no place in the New Earth. How you work with this will become clear as time goes on. Firstly, you will be guided to let go of all your personal fears. When you have mastered this you will assist others in this process and be guided to places on Planet Earth where the fear vibration is locked and stuck within the grids. You will be able to work with St Germain to liberate people and the planet from an energetic that has kept us imprisoned for a very long time.*
>
> *You have speaking, writing and teaching skills from other lifetimes which you will draw on for your mission. There are a number of possibilities for how this work could manifest but your brief is to assist in replacing the fear vibration with love in peoples' hearts and on the Earth.*

We are all here at this time, 'on purpose,' to assist with an elevation in consciousness and the transformation of the planet to a place of greater love, compassion and unity. We all have different jobs to do. On a soul level none is more or less important than any other. Our chosen task is usually a perfect reflection of who we are and who we have been as souls on Earth.

There are a group of Old Souls who have been preparing for this moment for aeons. They have lived many lives here and had every human experience possible. They have felt extreme emotions and have done their best to hold the light amidst the darkness. Most have been persecuted and have suffered for their beliefs in every conceivable way. They still carry these memories on a cellular and energetic level and have been releasing them over the last 30 years since higher vibrational energy first arrived on this planet. These are the healers, the Old Souls who have agreed to be the pioneers and to lead the way. They are all too familiar with the aspects of human nature we are determined to transcend. In many times and places they have been on the receiving end. The Old Souls have experienced the extreme consequences of greed, competition and the lust for power and are here to assist humanity to move beyond it. I know, because I am a member of this group. We are battle-scarred but not defeated. Deep down we know the time is now. Buoyed by feelings of anticipation and disbelief, we are ready and willing to do what we have been preparing for for lifetimes.

This time things are different. We have support. The younger generation, the so-called Millennials and The Children are here to help us. The Old Souls have been here forever and understand the way things work. Born in the shadow of World War II we know only too well what we are dealing with. Our job has been to lay the foundations for planetary transformation and to set things in motion.

The Millennials are not weighed down in the same way. Sometimes called 'Indigo' or 'Crystal' children, they are not only here to bring down the old but to create new structures. Many have not had as many lives on Earth as the Old Souls and are closer on a soul level to other star systems. Their potential is huge and their feelings of unworthiness not so deeply ingrained. Despite this, they still struggle with the low vibration of this planet, with the misery we inflict on each other and the suffering that surrounds us. They are acutely sensitive and feel the pain of man's inhumanity, deeply. Some of them find this unbearable and are desperate to escape. While some choose suicide, many avoid their feelings and dull their senses through addictive behaviours. We are in a time of transition and I believe there are forces present that are trying to stop our advance to the light. Some of our young people are easy targets and are being disempowered through technology and substances, unhealthy food, and mind control through social and other media.

This younger generation is bringing our awareness to some of the worst aspects of our human existence e.g. addictions, mental health issues and environmental catastrophe. Many have volunteered to serve in this way. They have strong convictions and are here to take the human race into a new epoch. Young leaders are emerging all over the world who are not intimidated by the **'Old Boys' Club'** that has held power for centuries. Unmotivated by greed, ego or self-interest, these young people are not afraid to speak their truth or to take action. The Millennials are an unstoppable force.

The Old Souls and the Millennials share a common purpose and both have a connection to the stars. The Old Souls are the original **starseeds** who volunteered to come to Earth thousands of years ago in the era of Lemuria and in some cases, even before that. For most of that time they have had no conscious links to, or memories of, their galactic past and have chosen to reincarnate repeatedly in human bodies. As for the Millennials most, but not all, have had past lives on Earth. Born in the 1980s and early 1990s, they connected with a higher planetary vibration at birth and have maintained close links with their souls and to experiences they have had elsewhere in the galaxy and beyond. Because of this they have a store of wisdom available about the technology and the higher vibration consciousness of these star systems. They are beginning to draw on this knowledge.

Coming closely behind the Millennials are 'The Children.' Sometimes called **Rainbow Children**, they are souls from other star systems who have never been on Earth before. They are here to bring in the light and to support and assist the older generations. Much of what I have said about the Millennials applies to them, especially their energetic sensitivity to harsh environments and to addictive influences.

On a soul level we all have similar memories as our souls are eternal and the ascension process is nothing new. We have been through this before in other times, places and universes. The difference is the Old Souls of Earth carry the energy of this planet and its past more heavily. This weight makes it harder for them to rise above their Earth pain and to connect with their soul truth.

The Old Souls are here to clean up the mess from the past. The Millennials and The Children, with their closer connection to stellar wisdom, are here to 'roll up their sleeves' and to finish the job. They astound and delight me with their lightness of being, their self-belief, innate wisdom and ability to create effortlessly and easily. We go about things differently, however. Where they come from they are used to instant gratification. There is no time lapse between a thought and its manifestation. If Millennials want something they want it now and can find it difficult to wait. This can be frustrating for Old Souls who have spent lifetimes cultivating patience. Millennials can seem unreliable and undisciplined as they go from one thing to another as the mood takes them. The reality is they know how to live in the present and to flow with the passion and enthusiasm of the moment. Their confidence can be scary as is their ability to utilise and to project themselves on Social Media. Old Souls want to hide. Many Millennials have no such problem. Those that can tune into their soul wisdom speak it with an authority and maturity that is both impressive and terrifying to the Old Soul.

We are all teachers. As an Old Soul I prefer the written word or teaching to a live group of people in a workshop setting. My millennial friends are more relaxed online, using platforms such as *Instagram*, *Facebook Live* or *YouTube* and nailing it with a minimum of preparation. It is important to remember that we are in this together and have much to learn from each other. The Old Souls have done things the hard way. Suffering has been our calling card. Millennials have also suffered. Many have felt homesick and as if they don't belong. Their existence in a world not ready for and that doesn't understand them, has caused great anguish. The Old Souls have had these same experiences but they go further back. They represent the past and the Millennials the future. It is time for us to work together to build a new world order.

A favourite Millennial of mine is Australian, Will Connolly (aka Egg Boy). His spontaneous act after Senator Fraser Anning inferred Muslim immigration was to blame for the murder of 51 worshippers at two mosques in Christchurch, New Zealand, in 2019, highlighted high level xenophobia. To register his disapproval, Will threw an egg at Senator Anning. This action captured the public imagination. A trust was set up to pay his legal fees and a lawyer offered to act for him for free. Every cent of the $100,000 he was gifted was given by Will to the Mosque survivors. As he said at the time, 'I am pro-humanity, not political.'

There is a different brand of young leaders stepping forward in many countries, my own, included. New Zealand's current leader, Jacinda Ardern is demonstrating leadership that is inclusive, far-sighted and comes from the heart. She has become known and respected globally for her response to the massacres at the Christchurch Mosques as well as her leadership during the Covid pandemic. She stresses the importance of kindness but is not afraid to make tough calls. For example, far-reaching **gun legislation** was introduced after the massacre. Her lack of ego has meant that she has been able to work with experts and others to develop and coordinate a response to Covid-19. At this stage of writing in August, 2021, New Zealand has had 26 deaths.

❀

One of my favourite teachers of the older generation is Patricia Cota-Robles (www.eraofpeace.org). She works on an energetic level to bring forth higher consciousness to the planet. In her 'Activities of Light,' she assists others to bring into manifestation the higher vibrational potentials and Fifth Dimensional templates of Earth, which exist in the etheric, or as she puts it, 'the realms of cause.' In 2018 she talked of the activation of the **Consciousness Codes** of the Millennials and The Children which took place in August of that year. The activation of these codes has given the younger generation a surge of energy and purpose that is impossible to ignore. They are doing things differently and tackling the ills of society head on. This group still has high levels of depression and anxiety but the tide is turning. Within my family circle, many of the younger members are vegetarian or vegan and practise yoga and mindfulness. My daughter, Mary, has taught me about the dangers of soft plastics and one of my nephews has lectured me about racism and adopting a vegan diet. One Easter I hosted a vegan dinner for the younger members of my family that, as I said at the time, 'Would make my father turn in his grave.' Environmental issues are coming to the fore. This generation will not be silenced and are protesting on the streets. Rallies organised by school children the world over, highlighting the issue of Climate Change, are evidence of this.

Whether for the Old Souls or the younger souls of Earth, I love looking at my client's highest soul potential. In every single case I am blinded by the light. We are not on Earth at this time by accident. We all have a higher purpose and plan in place and as human beings the freedom to follow it... or not. I have noticed that those with the more ambitious missions often have the most challenging paths. For many this pathway is like the initiations of old. It is laid out before us but we have to take the first step. When we do we are rewarded but our resolve and commitment is tested at every stage of the journey. Spirit comes in to assist us when we agree to follow the highest plan for our lives, but we still have to put the effort in ourselves. We all have huge potential but it will only become reality if we follow our inner promptings, take the leaps of faith and work with our unseen helpers to create it. If we ask for help we will get it but it is us, as individuals, that have to make the first move.

There is no compulsion to fulfil our life purpose or to follow our soul path. Most of us, myself included, have had lifetime after lifetime of turning our backs on our destiny. Fear, self-doubt and circumstance have held us back. It will not be the end of the world if we don't realise our potential this time around. There will be more opportunities in the future. Stepping off the safety of the riverbank, into the flowing water, takes courage and we have to be ready. Having said that, at this time on Earth, it is easier than ever to hear the whispers of our soul. Many people are braving the icy waters of uncertainty and following their hearts. My husband and I have both done this and as a parent it is the example I am most proud of. The more people who do this, the easier it will become for others, until making our passion our life's work is mainstream. For me there is no greater satisfaction than seeing those I have worked with living and breathing their purpose. It's why I keep doing what I do. For many clients what I share about their life purpose resonates. This confirmation gives them the 'green light' to start moving forward.

For Old Souls there is often a redemptive quality to their life purpose. There is an aspect to it that allows them to do some karmic balancing and to atone for the past. As I said in Chapter 7, we are in a time of completion and for Old Souls there is a lot to resolve. In my own case, the way I am living this life is being strongly influenced by the last one, where I was a German priest who ended up in a concentration camp. In order to survive, I assisted my captors in running the camp. I did this to save my own skin but the irony was that after the war I was so tormented by this involvement that I gave up on life. At the end of that lifetime I was depressed and defeated. I carried feelings of shame, guilt and unworthiness with me into this one. On a deep level I felt I had a lot of making up to do.

My Akashic Record has revealed a soul pattern of watching on from the sidelines and not having the courage to speak my truth. I have done what I needed to survive, often turning a blind eye to the suffering of others. I have been afraid to stick my neck out and to stick to my principles. This time round I know I have to do things differently and this is one of the reasons I am writing this book. After lifetimes of playing it safe and staying silent I am finding my voice. Hopefully, I can redeem myself.

I have been driven by a desire to help humanity move beyond pain and hatred, to help others understand the truth about human life and to give people tools to rise above their 'shadow' aspects and human misery. From a very young age I felt I had an important mission this time round. Many of my clients can relate to this feeling. There has been an urgency about this lifetime that has kept us going through our toughest times.

I have had many lives on this planet over a long time period. Some I am proud of. Some I am not. With the help of the Akashic Records I can see not one life in isolation but the series of lives that have led me to this point. I know that without the agony and trauma of my immediate past life I probably wouldn't be doing what I am today. It was a springboard for this lifetime. This is what drives me as well as the knowledge that I have been preparing for this moment for a very long time… since I first stepped into a body on Earth in fact.

The Holocaust has come back to haunt me many times during sessions with clients and in Alice's struggles. In many ways my life purpose is providing the perfect opportunity for me to slay my personal dragons and to atone for the past. As well as helping others, my work in this lifetime is assisting my own healing on a deep, soul level. Against the backdrop of many lifetimes, how I am living my current life and what I am doing makes perfect sense.

This is also the case for many of my clients. One of them, Cassie, as a teacher of children with special needs, is being given the opportunity for redemption and for the healing of soul trauma from her most recent past life.

When I opened Cassie's Akashic Record, I saw her in twentieth century China, as Shanghai was being attacked by the Japanese. She was an Amah who looked after preschool children from ex-pat families. She was totally devoted and dedicated to her charges who she loved dearly.

'Your children were your life. You created a safe and loving space for them,' I told her.

When the bombs dropped she didn't get out in time and was unable to save the children in her care. As she died, she realised what had happened and she took acute feelings of failure and regret and a heavy burden of trauma with her.

Deep-seated feelings of responsibility have affected Cassie in her current life. She told me she has been overly responsible in her relationships and in the work place and that when she was younger she found it difficult to leave unhealthy situations. Cassie is a special person and is already intuitively doing what she needs to do, on a soul level, to heal and to move forward. She confided to me that in the last few years she has left her marriage and also two jobs that she didn't enjoy. In this lifetime she has chosen to work with children with disabilities and special needs. I told her that these children are almost without exception from the stars and are wired differently.

'Their DNA expression is different. They have been coming into being in larger numbers since the turn of the century and have had labels slapped on them. Your life's purpose is to work with these children to help them adjust to Earth and to feel safe and protected.'

I told Cassie that being able to give these children, what she was unable to give her charges in Shanghai, would help her to release the pain and to heal her heart. Under my direction she talked with her past life self and brought her to a state of calm and resolution.

Some time later Cassie, told me that our session had touched her deeply and given her a greater understanding of her life purpose this time round. She added that she had recently begun to 'privately tutor a young dyslexic girl.' She saw this as the beginning of lightwork, where, in her words, she would be able 'to assist beautiful souls on their earthly journey and help them not just academically, but spiritually as well.'

We all have regrets. Whether it is within the context of one life or many, making mistakes is a part of being human. Each life is a fresh start, giving us the chance to do things differently and the opportunity to redeem ourselves. Cassie was not able to save the children in her care in Shanghai, but she is making up for it now with a new generation of children who will benefit from her love and devotion.

Our chosen life purpose can give us the chance to:

- make up for behaviours and actions in past lives that were harmful to others
- finish off a job that we started but were unable to complete
- utilise past life learning and strengths to contribute in a hands-on way to 'the shift.

They can also help us to break out of a long-standing pattern and to heal and overcome personal past life trauma. This was the case with Ellen, an attractive woman with a big smile and lots of love in her heart. Born in Canada, Ellen had lived in New Zealand for 30 years.

Opening her Akashic Record I saw a soul history of being displaced and uprooted many times, as a result of both natural and man-made disasters. In her most recent past life she had also been married to her current husband, Dan. Members of the nobility at the time of the Russian Revolution, they were forced to flee for their lives. In my mind's eye I saw her in a small, dingy Paris flat heating up soup on the stove. This was just one of the many lives where Ellen had lost everything: possessions, family and security. In this Russian life she and her husband had owned a large country estate. They regarded those who worked for them as 'family' and treated them with kindness and concern. They were happy and settled in their lives until the Revolution. In 1917 they lost everything. It was the loss of their 'family' that hit them the hardest.

Digging deeper into Ellen's Record, I could see that this pattern of loss had begun in Atlantis. In her last Atlantean life, she had again lost everything of importance to her and the energy of that trauma had remained as well as the core beliefs, 'I always lose those I love' and 'The good times never last.'

In this lifetime Ellen is doing her best to heal from the past and to utilise the wisdom from her past life experiences. She has a business helping migrants to settle and adjust to life in New Zealand.

'I help them feel at home, they become family,' she told me.

As well as helping displaced people to feel secure, Ellen and her husband Dan have managed to create a happy and stable life for themselves and their two daughters.

Despite a comfortable life and fulfilling work, Ellen told me that she has never really felt at home on this planet. I saw her as one of the early wave of starseeds who have been searching for a place to call home on Earth and never quite found it. I could see the potential for Ellen to take her work to a new level and to pursue a more consciously spiritual life. The soul work she has come to do, if this is her choice, involves helping young people who have had few or no human lives to feel safe and settled here. I told her that this is of vital importance, if they are to fulfil their soul missions. She has been busy helping newcomers to our city, to adjust. Now it is time to take her work up a notch to help new souls to the planet to feel safe and comfortable. She was open to this and very excited.

Ellen's work in this lifetime is enabling her to continue a theme from the past, of creating stability for others and supporting them as family. This is helping her put the learning and skills gained from difficult past life circumstances to good use. She is living a secure and happy life with her husband, children and grandchildren far away from her Canadian birthplace. As in her Russian life she is family orientated and her definition of family goes way beyond the traditional.

❀

The life purpose of the Old Soul involves dealing with the debris of the past while the Millennials are here to lay down a new template for the future. With its buoyant, future-focus the millennial life purpose has a more positive vibe.

This is definitely the case with 23 year old Ella who asked me about her life purpose. I could see that she has a big job to do in this lifetime if she chooses.

'You hold a lot of light and a lot of power... you are a bit like a high voltage energy socket,' I told her.
I saw that she could be a leader and role model to young people struggling with mental health and/or addiction issues.
'Your mission is to help lost souls to find their way,' I said.
She agreed that she wanted to help her own generation and the children coming along behind. She shared her vision, which was to put the idea of manifestation into a context

that they would understand and to teach them how to be responsible for their thoughts.

'I want to help them to align their heart with their mind, body and soul so they can understand who they are and put out their thoughts and manifest in a positive way. This is my journey at the moment and I want to document it,' Ella told me.

'Many of the younger generation are wavering,' I replied. 'Some have never been here before. They have come in to help but it is much harder than they thought. They are getting into things that are taking away their potential.'

'I am seeing that everywhere,' Ella said.

I continued, 'They are worrying whether they have the energy and motivation to accomplish what they signed up for. Your mission is to help the younger generation remember who they are, why they are here and what they are here to do. This will give them the incentive to keep going.'

I could see the potential for her to access this audience on Social Media. She told me she worked in Social Media and Marketing and had a YouTube channel but hadn't started posting yet because she needed to get clearer on her message. She added that she and her boyfriend had bought a camera the previous weekend.

'You have contacted me because it is time to start,' I told her.

The best teachers are those who teach from their own experience and I saw that as well as having a strong online presence as a positive 'influencer,' Ella had the potential in the future to write books and to teach.

I finished the session with the following, 'The younger generation will love what you have to say. They are here to change consciousness which seems a gargantuan task when all around them people are living in unethical ways. You will give them a lifeline. As you get older your life purpose will morph into something bigger. There will so much change in your lifetime. By the end of it you will be living on a completely different planet.'

Ella has very important work to do in the years ahead and she is definitely up for the challenge.

❀

The fact we are embodied on the planet at this time is not a random event. A call was put out to the far reaches of the universe to assist with this planetary upgrade. Many souls from other **Star Nations** and universes volunteered to help. There were numerous applications. As with any job opportunities, only the best were accepted. The Old Souls answered the call thousands of years ago and have immersed themselves in Earth experience by way of preparation. The reinforcements, The Children and Millennials, are in most cases more recent recruits. For Old Souls, having support is making all the difference. We no longer feel alone and misunderstood. Fresh off the boat from other star systems, The Children and some Millennials are not weighed down by lifetimes of trauma and low self-esteem. They are not afraid to speak up and out against injustice and hypocrisy. Conscious or not we all have a vested interest in a successful outcome. Now more than ever we need meaning in our lives and can sense the excitement of what we are creating.

Whether we are an Old Soul or a Millennial, understanding the larger purpose of what is happening on the planet and our part in it, will make it easier to put our suffering in context. Viewing our mission and purpose against a succession of lifetimes on Earth, and what is happening in the galaxy and beyond, will give us the motivation to carry on and to take our planet into light.

Chapter 10

The Magnificence of the Soul

Our Higher Self is the aspect of the soul that has been in charge on Earth. It is the soul piece that has been present in all of our human lifetimes and can see and understand the 'bigger picture.' Our Akashic Record is the expression of our Higher Self that reflects and contains an overview of our soul wisdom and experiences on this planet. Being in the Records helps us to connect with our soul and to live a soul-driven life. The incoming Fifth Dimensional energy is making it easier for our soul to communicate. After thousands of years of the lower vibrational limbo and limitation of the Third Dimension, our soul is tapping us on the shoulder and saying, 'Remember me.' It is becoming increasingly difficult and will be impossible when we are fully in the Fifth Dimension, to live a life out of alignment with it. The Akashic Records are a safe and easy place to link in with our soul and its plans for us.

The soul is magnificent and multidimensional. As we live our lives on Earth, aspects of it are in other places at the same time. They can be on the 'other side of the veil,' in another part of this galaxy or other galaxies. They can be living past, future or parallel lives or existences in other places and elsewhere on the planet. For souls wanting to evolve more rapidly it is not uncommon to choose to live more than one Earth lifetime at once.

The Akashic Records are not linear and neither is our soul. Our soul does not inhabit one human body and then when we die go to 'heaven' and return in another human body, over and over again.

A piece of our soul does this but there are always other aspects elsewhere doing other things. This is a difficult concept for us to grasp, but as the vibration on Earth rises and the 'curtain between worlds' begins to open, our multidimensional aspects are becoming a greater part of our reality.

Many people feel sure they were a well-known person in a past life, that they were Joan of Arc or Mary Magdalene or even Jesus. There is a car in my street with the number plate 'Nefertiti.' The first time I saw it on my daily walk I thought to myself, 'Not another one!' I have met several self-proclaimed reincarnations of Nefertiti over the years. So how does this work? Apart from being a direct reincarnation of a famous person, (very rare, I believe), the work I have done in the Records has taught me that there are two other ways we can feel connected to a famous person from the past.

1. Well known and illustrious historical figures represent archetypes that carry a special energy that we can connect with. These archetypal beings pass on some of their soul essence to twelve others who can then pass this on to up to twelve more, a total of 144 in all. (Information from the Akashic Records has provided confirmation of this as did Diana Cooper in a Zoom class on September 22, 2019).

2. Before beginning a new incarnation, we can choose to take on some of the soul attributes of a person we revere from history. If we admire Joan of Arc, as many of us do, we may ask for some of her finer qualities to help us in the lifetime to come.

In an email reading for a woman who asked about her past lives, I received the following information:

You are connected to the soul essence of the biblical prophet Elijah. As such, the memories of his lifetime are part of your DNA. The soul that was Elijah has split and there are others that carry this energy and these memories. Human lifetimes are linear but the soul is multidimensional and that is how this can happen.

And for another:

You carry the energy of St Francis of Assisi. You are an aspect of the same soul. Our souls are multidimensional so one soul does not have one life and then another life in a linear fashion. As many as 144 beings can carry the essence of the originating soul. You have held back a part of yourself on Earth as a form of protection. Your greatest achievements have been as a soul in your true home, off-planet.

I asked her to say the following words, to bring in a larger piece of her soul to help her moving forward:

I ask that I be fully reconnected with my soul and with the energy and gifts of St Francis of Assisi. I ask that this magnificent soul aspect guide me on my journey and assist me onto my path of purpose so I can become the highest expression of myself in this lifetime. I ask that a larger piece of my soul come into my body to give me the confidence and the energy and determination I need to fulfil my mission.

I then told her to close her eyes and to think of St Francis. I asked her to connect in with the energy of his heart and to pull it into her body until she was fully vibrating with the compassion, wisdom and peace that he emanated during his lifetime.

This was my email answer to a client, George, who said he had been told he was a reincarnation of Alexei Nikolaevich, Tsar Nicholas II's son who was murdered by the Bolsheviks in July, 1918. In this life George, works with and sells crystals.

You carry the archetypal energy of Alexei. You are an aspect of him. His life epitomised some of the worst facets of the human condition: powerlessness, suffering and atonement for karmic misdeeds. He was a very pure soul with a loving and open heart. In his short life he did much to balance out some of the worst excesses of his ancestors. He anchored a high vibration and a more compassionate frequency within his extended family and within Russia as a whole. His energetic is still there and will eventually help Russia to become more loving and to re-chart its course on the world stage.

You carry some of his energy as do other souls on both sides of the veil. Like Alexei you are here to purify the planet and to show others simple ways of raising their vibration. Alexei embodied the pure crystalline energy which you resonate with and hold. You chose to take on some of his essence before being incarnated, to assist you in your mission to help others to connect with the light-filled crystalline vibration.

My client asked for further clarification and this was my reply:

You were not Alexei in a linear sense but you carry his energy. He is a historical figure of archetypal importance. He symbolised suffering, innocence and grace in the face of evil and this is the essence you also carry and which will help you in your mission to restore a purer vibration to Earth.

Before your current incarnation you knew what you were up against. You connected with Alexei's energy to prepare you. You carry his wisdom and the memories of his pain and the lessons he learned. There are many famous people in history whose Akashic Records can be accessed and remembered by others. Before each lifetime, we have the choice to connect in with the energies of those who have lived before, who symbolise an aspect of the human experience that may serve our path. You took on some of Alexei's energy before this incarnation as it was thought it would assist you in your mission.

Most of us find it difficult in the current vibration to carry too much of our soul. In recent years, I have had a series of clients (usually advanced souls), who have fallen suddenly, inexplicably and madly in love. They describe feelings of unbelievable chemistry and an almost indescribable passion. They feel a powerful bond and a strong urge to do whatever it takes to be with the other person. It is difficult for me to tell them this, but the potentials for a long-term connection aren't good. Usually my client tells me that the relationship has already hit some road bumps and while the highs are sublime, the lows have been challenging.

In these cases I often find that the being they have connected with is another aspect of their own soul. The feelings are immense and the relationship consuming and difficult to sustain on Earth, at this time. I don't enjoy sharing this, but on a deep level they usually know it. The purpose of these relationships seems to be so an exchange of soul energy can take place, that will give them a lift and allow them to move forward in their lives, with renewed vigour. I believe that in the future these relationships will be lasting and that integrating the pieces of our soul from all dimensions is a process we will all go through.

In an email reading a client asked me about a relationship she had with Alan, a man she had recently met. She told me that the connection with him and the feelings it triggered, had been intense. On opening her Record I could see that she had begun this soul integration process.

This was my message for her:

He is from the same soul and has come into your life to show you a part of yourself you have yet to embrace. The connection feels strong and at times overwhelming because he is another aspect of you. He began human life at the same moment, but then split off from the soul source. At this time on Earth, we are beginning the process of soul integration and this is what is happening for you.

She asked me about the purpose of this relationship:

You have come together to help each other on your journey. You are two parts of the same soul which for a very long time have been on separate trajectories, having different human experiences.

To each other you represent a facet that has been lost during your Earth lifetimes. There are qualities and aspects to Alan's personality that you can emulate and integrate to help you move forward and vice versa. He has a gentler and more creative approach to life which your soul is wanting you to reconnect with. He could benefit from more focus, self-belief and inner strength and that is what you have to offer. Try to see him as a mirror aspect of you that is reflecting back some attributes and a way of approaching life, that can help you now. The personal characteristics you find most attractive in him are ones that would be useful in your life.

I talked about her relationship in the context of the soul integration process that is occurring:

As human beings, many of us have been working to heal our Inner Child and to reintegrate pieces of our human psyche, in order to become whole. This theme is now expanding to the integration of the soul, where different aspects on Earth and elsewhere are coming back together, so we can achieve soul expansion and completion. This is the purpose of this relationship and your reconnection at this time will help you both to move forward rapidly in your respective lives.

She asked me for guidance in navigating the relationship:

This relationship is meant to be an intense union for a short period of time. There is a magnetic pull between you and understanding why that is should help you to navigate it.

It is important at this time, in both your lives, that you meet and that there is an exchange of energies. Your energy will give Alan something he has been missing and his energy will do the same for you. Such a relationship is extreme and difficult to sustain in the current vibration on Earth. Try to see it as a special gift, know that it is divinely guided and enjoy it in the moment without worrying about the future.

The highest purpose of this relationship is that it will be a catalyst to strengthen your connection with your soul which will then take your life and work to a whole new level.

The new energy is facilitating a process of soul integration. Some of us are meeting up with aspects of our soul that have spun off in other directions and had different Earth experiences. At this time of completion, I believe we will all (in this or most likely in future lifetimes), have the opportunity to reconnect with all of the pieces of our soul. The integration will happen as we become more evolved spiritually. The human aspects that have been experiencing life on Earth will be reunited first.

❀

Many of my clients ask me, 'When will I meet my soul mate?' With due respect to them, this is not my favourite question. I am far more interested in looking at what they came to Earth to do. I can only see the potentials for the future and these are based on the energy of the client at the time of their session. If we don't have a deep love for ourselves and feel that we deserve to be loved our chances of finding a soul mate are not good.

My work in the Records supports my belief that there is not just one soul mate. My definition of 'soul mate' is loose and broad and includes every soul we have ever been close to in any of our incarnations. Because we have 'free will,' I feel there has to be more than one soul mate option. If Plan A doesn't work out there must be a Plan B and sometimes a Plan C, D and E as well. A soul mate could be someone we have loved and lost or a past life enemy. The common denominator is 'shared experiences' in other lives.

Clients also ask about Twin Flames. The information I have received from the Records is that sometimes when a soul aspect of our greater or over soul first comes to Earth, they split into two. There is a part of the same aspect out there and the reunion can be divine. These pairings have a greater chance of success than those described above.

Here is information about Twin Flames that I received from the Records:

In certain circumstances when a soul first comes to Earth some split into two. This was a conscious soul choice by those who wanted support during their earthly lives. In many different lifetimes, these souls have come together for mutual assistance and to mitigate the loneliness and suffering which has characterised human life. This has made the soul journey and the precession of lifetimes easier but it has also acted, at times, to slow down individual progress and learning. Not all of us chose this option. Those who didn't have had a tougher time, but have experienced more rapid soul growth and are often stronger and better prepared to offer their gifts to the world.

Those who have a Twin Flame know it deep inside and are driven by this inner yearning to find their 'other half.' In the new energy these twin flame pairings are often choosing to work together for a common purpose. Sometimes one will pass over before the other and continue helping with their joint mission and endeavour from the other side.

A man came to me for a past life regression. A modern day Māori avatar, he was humble and authentic with mana (a Māori word used to describe someone who has authority and commands respect). The dictionary definition is (in Polynesian, Melanesian, and Māori belief), 'an impersonal supernatural power which can be transmitted or inherited.'

I have conducted many regressions and this was the only time I haven't been able to regress someone to a past life. I persevered for a while and then decided to open his Akashic Record to find out what was going on. I connected with his soul which was immense and, in particular, a piece of it that resided in another galaxy. I realised that my job was to act as a conduit to bring in this larger part of his soul. It was able to exist in the higher (post 2012) frequencies and was ready to join him. I could see that it was an important part of my client's future path to have more of his soul in his body and that his Higher Self had directed him to me so that I could facilitate this process.

As I understand it, before we are born we decide how much of our soul we will bring into our physical world. It is important to get the balance right. Too little and we might be ungrounded and find human life a challenge. Too much and the intensity could be so great that we will also find human life a challenge. The higher vibration energy that is now flooding the planet is making it possible for us to bring in more of our soul strength to help us in our lives.

The so-called Rainbow children, who since the year 2000, have come to Earth for the first time, carry more of their soul energy in their bodies. For many of them, the early years of their lives are difficult as they have been born into a lower vibration, are sensitive and find the human pain that surrounds them difficult to handle. As we move into the Fifth Dimension their lives will get easier. They will resonate more with the frequency of the Earth and feel more comfortable.

These children don't fit any pre-existing mould. Many of them are considered to have learning and other disabilities and to be on the **'spectrum.'** They all have special gifts which will help with the evolution of this planet. Their presence is prompting change in all areas of society and helping us to become more inclusive, compassionate and tolerant of diversity.

Many of us have done Inner Child work and the Akashic Records is a safe place to conduct it. I find it easier to connect with 'past' and 'future' lives in the Records but the information from our current lives is there as well. I am not a trained psychologist and if it is obvious that a client has significant mental health issues and/or childhood trauma I send them to qualified, mainstream practitioners. Past life trauma is more my specialty, but it is often linked to early experiences in a client's present life. Because of this I sometimes incorporate inner child healing into a session.

With their Akashic Record open I ask my client to close their eyes and to imagine their child self, sitting on their knee. The age when their childhood wounding began comes into my head and I pass this on. I guide them to talk with their child self. They tell them they love them, that they are special and that what happened wasn't their fault. I end by getting my client's adult self to tell their younger self that they are no longer alone, that they are safe and that they now have someone to love, understand and protect them. I encourage them to find their own words to talk to their child self.

Inner child healing is part of the journey back to wholeness where we make peace with our **subpersonalities** (the Inner Child being one) and integrate the lost pieces into our human psyche. As I mentioned in Chapter 5, all of us, especially the Old Souls, carry trauma not just from our current life but from past incarnations. Trauma can drain our vitality and affect us on a soul level, with pieces of our soul splitting off to protect us from pain. This process is called **dissociation** by psychologists and is often a result of post-traumatic stress. Lifetimes of unresolved trauma can impact the soul and can result in aspects of our soul going into hiding. In a process similar to Inner Child work, Soul Retrieval can also help us bring the damaged and lost pieces of our soul back into our bodies.

Shamans in indigenous cultures have long worked in this area.

They utilise ancient rituals and complex processes to restore the life force. In the new energy, with purity of intent, it is a simpler procedure to bring back the integrity of the soul and to reintegrate the missing fragments. We are more powerful when these lost aspects have been returned and their trauma has been released.

To help clients clear this trauma, I facilitate a process to re-integrate the splintered aspects of their psyche. I set an intention similar to this:

> *It is my intention to assist xxx to completely release all energetic imprints of trauma from all incarnations and to reintegrate all soul fragments that have split from the whole so that xxx's life force and the full integrity of their soul can be restored in all directions of time.*

I then ask my client to open their heart and to attune to the frequency of love. Once they are holding a high level of this vibration, I guide them through a process of releasing the trauma and welcoming their fragmented soul aspects home.

❈

Our souls are making their presence felt. If we are not listening or following our highest plan sometimes they will stage an intervention. This happened to a client of mine called Sue.

> In Sue's case the motivation she needed was (literally), a sore shoulder. She had come to me several years earlier but had not managed to make many of the changes I suggested. She was currently working as a restaurant manager in a spa town. She had considerable gifts as a healer which she had the potential to use. I could see that her services would be in demand in this spot, where tourists go to relax and to enjoy the mountains and thermal pools. She wanted to leave her

restaurant job and loved the idea of healing work. Two years later the restaurant was still taking up most of her time and energy. Nothing much had changed, so her soul intervened in the form of an accident, where she broke her arm and shoulder.

Sue was now unable to work and had weeks of enforced isolation and inaction in front of her. The restaurant owner employed several people to replace her and she hunkered down at home.

Here at last was a chance to use her healing gifts. I could see that she had the potential to heal her own injury and to assist others to heal themselves. She told me that before her accident old feelings of failure and unworthiness had been surfacing.

'I felt that life was a constant struggle, that I was not getting where I wanted to go and that time was running out,' she said.

I opened her Akashic Record and saw her as a teenage boy after the 1949 communist takeover, desperately trying to escape mainland China. He was clinging to the side of a **junk**.

I described what I was seeing in my mind and told her:

'In that life you were the hope of your large extended family. They had all been through a difficult time of struggle and deprivation. As the young male of the family, you felt huge feelings of responsibility and obligation towards them. You were desperate for freedom and paid for an illegal passage on a boat leaving China. As you left you carried the hopes, dreams and expectations of your family on your shoulders. You knew it may be impossible for them to join you, but hoped that if you managed to escape you could send them money.'

'The boat was a human circus, crowded with refugees and there was no room for you. You clung desperately to the side. Even though you had paid for a seat, the people on the junk were brutal. They hit you repeatedly on your shoulders and arms. You held on for 'dear life' but eventually, after your arm was broken, you let go... and with it the hope you had for yourself and your family, as well. You died feeling traumatised and carrying huge feelings of failure and unworthiness.'

If we have a sudden and traumatic death the feelings can stay with us. I could see that part of Sue was still clinging to the side of the boat. These old feelings and a fear of being in situations she couldn't control had been triggered by her job at the café and were keeping her stuck. Her body remembered the same emotions from that recent past life. It was no coincidence that the weakness in that area of her body had resulted in injury to her arm and shoulder. In this life these old feelings as well as strong feelings of responsibility and obligation had kept her in her restaurant job. In her Chinese life she had not been able to keep hold of the freedom she deserved. I hoped that once Sue's injuries healed she would be able to reach out and grab this with both hands.

Two years after she hurt her shoulder, I talked with Sue. It has taken a while for her body to heal but she has put her down time to good use. She has completed several healing courses and is now working with clients to help them to move from the head to their heart. She connects them with their bodies and asks them to breathe into what needs to be healed. Sue is thrilled with the results and says she is trusting more in Spirit and in her mission.

'I didn't believe I could do this, but I am finally stepping out and it feels wonderful,' she told me.

As I write this, we are in the midst of a global intervention. Higher forces with the agreement of every soul on this planet, are staging an intervention, in the form of a pandemic, to bring us back into alignment with our true soul nature. Many of the things that I believe now would have seemed crazy to me ten years ago. There is still so much we don't know about the soul. We are being drip-fed information at the time and pace that is right for us. It is difficult to see and understand multidimensionality through 3D, linear glasses. As we put our 5D specs on, a whole new world is opening up and with it the potential for a brilliance we have not believed possible. Kryon, channelled by Lee Carroll talks of the 'New Human' in this context and hints at many of the capabilities that are there for us to reclaim.

In the book, *The Twelve Layers of DNA*, Kryon gives more specific information. From this book and an online class, I learned that the Twelve layers of DNA are grouped into four groups of three and that they are all in their own way infused with soul energy.

- Layers 1, 2 and 3 relate to the innate intelligence of the body.
- Layers 4, 5 and 6 connect us to the angelic realms and our Higher Selves.
- Layers 7, 8 and 9 link us to our Pleiadian and Lemurian pasts and to the Akashic Records.
- Layers 10, 11 and 12 connect us to the divinity within.

As more of our non-coding DNA is enabled, we are becoming purer expressions of our soul. Lee Carroll also talks of the residual that has built up over the years he has been channelling, Kryon. He speaks of how it has made possible a soul merge between his human self and his higher soul aspects.

The Akashic Records, like everything else at this time, is reflecting the new energy we are part of. It is opening us up, not just to our soul, but to our true multidimensional nature.

As we become more quantum it is getting easier to cross time, space and dimensions to connect with other aspects of our soul. In the years to come this theme of soul integration will become more common and we will take wholeness and healing from the human to the soul level. We will be able to reunite with aspects of our soul and bring them in to help us. Soul integration will help us to bring our soul and human selves back into balance. It will set the stage for a new era where our soul gifts come to the fore and our true magnificence can shine through.

The Akashic Records are a gateway to our glorious soul potential. They have helped me to lead a more soul-directed life. In the future, the activation of our non-coding strands of DNA will accelerate the soul integration process. They will allow us to recognise and use our soul gifts so we can become co-creators with our spiritual core. Suffering is a human construct. On a soul level all is perfect. The more aligned we become with our soul the less we will suffer and the easier it will be to create magic in our lives.

Chapter 11

Multidimensionality

A long with many long forgotten gifts and talents, our soul is beginning to reveal itself in all of its multidimensional splendour. Quantum energy is opening us up to new realms and parts of ourselves we didn't know existed. From the beginning the Records introduced me to multidimensionality, but more recently there has been an upsurge in this trend, for both myself and my clients. My work in the Records, has me travelling interdimensionally on a regular basis, as I describe existences in other time frames and places. I see clients in past lives, sometimes parallel ones or I catch a glimpse of their potential in a future life. While I work mainly with their human Akash, I can get information about their star origins, especially if it is relevant to their current incarnation.

Working in the Akashic Records isn't boring. As my mother liked to say, 'There is never a dull moment.' I find it is best if my human self steps aside. It is a bit like driving a car with our body while our mind is off somewhere else. That I only remember what happened in a session for a short time afterwards, tells me I have been in an altered state. I don't find this scary. Usually the words come out of my mouth in a steady stream. I have spent this lifetime talking without thinking (got me into trouble as a child), so it comes easily and naturally to me.

The Akashic Records are a doorway to a quantum world of alternate realities. Moving through time and space, we can connect with other soul aspects. It is also easier to communicate with those who have passed on and with beings that are off planet. Multidimensionality is difficult to grasp as we are still bound by linear time constraints, but in the higher dimensions, time is fluid. There is only the present or the 'now' moment. This means that every life experience our soul has had on this planet and elsewhere is happening at the same time. This is hard for us to understand from our current reality, but it does make it easy, especially when we are in a soul space like the Akashic Records, to link in with other soul expressions we have had or will have. We can connect in with their energy, talk to them and bring them in to assist us.

As I mentioned in Chapters 4 and 9, much of my current lifetime has been overshadowed by my last one, as a priest in Germany. In my audio programme *Soul Magic* there is a visualisation where I guide listeners to meet three past life aspects that can help them in the present. I have listened to this many times and each time three different versions of myself have come forward. They have all had messages for me that have been relevant and helpful to me at the time. In the visualisation I ask those listening to see themselves sitting in a railway carriage. One by one (as they stop at three stations), different soul expressions join them.

One day I was doing this meditation and was surprised, but also delighted, when the German priest came in and sat opposite me. When I have connected with him in the past he has been unhappy. My efforts sending him love, compassion and forgiveness across time must have helped, because he sat in front of me and looked me straight in the eye. He wasn't smiling, but he was at peace. I got the sense of a gentle man with high ideals and principles that were not fully integrated. He had removed himself from the harsh realities of life and the cruelty of human behaviour and when he was faced with them, he couldn't cope. He became unstuck because he couldn't reconcile his light with the darkness into which he had suddenly descended. He implored me not to make the same mistake. He told me that while it was important to hold a higher vision, I should also be realistic and open to accepting and integrating both my own and humanity's shadow aspects. I could see he had wonderful ideas and a talent for expressing them in words. I asked for his guidance with this in my current life time. He promised to help me to simplify my thoughts and beliefs so they could be easily understood. He told me he was proud of me and I felt his joy and love.

The first time I met him he was a man in bed with his face to the wall, full of self-loathing and desperate to die. Now he has been transformed and is no longer suffering. All the efforts I have made to heal and to understand myself, have helped him as well. I believe this is also the case for all of my other soul aspects. The German priest, is ready to assist me to finish what he was unable to do, with his wise words, open heart and huge compassion. He is a special being, now at peace. He is cheering me on as I write this book and I know he will be with me in the future every time I think of him and ask for his help.

As Old Souls some of us have lived on a Fifth Dimensional Earth before. In Lemuria and Golden Atlantis, we taught and lived by core human truths and used the healing gifts that are now being returned to us. We are reconnecting with souls we know from these Fifth Dimensional civilisations and the restoration of this energetic bond is, for many of us, unlocking our sacred gifts and knowledge.

Before my first Level 3 *Soul History Workshop* in January, 2020, I knew it was important that we have twenty-two people. I had a waiting list and there was some fluctuation in numbers, but on the first day of the weekend there were twenty-two of us, all women. The energy of these beautiful souls was amazing. It felt like a very special reunion. On a deep level we knew each other and it was wonderful to be together in the same place. I felt like I had been waiting a very long time for this.

These feelings didn't surprise me. Before the weekend, I had received the information that we had been together before, as High Priestesses in Golden Atlantis. The workshop, was one I had been prompted to run, for those who had completed my Level 1 and 2 training and who were working or wanted to work as healers in the Akashic Records. Most fitted the latter category but not all. Deep down, I knew they all had to be there, and that it was important we come back together. The highlight for me was the ceremony that I was guided to hold on the Saturday evening. In a beautiful setting, surrounded by tall trees, we were reunited. It felt so natural and just like old times as Marie and Jasmine, both proficient in Light Language, led us into the clearing, invoking sounds and proclamations that were ancient but which sounded familiar, and sent chills down my spine. There was no prior planning for this but it was superb, most in the circle playing their part, instinctively knowing their role and what to say and do. The soul singing of Tracy from Australia was surreal and the words of all participants were perfect. In those magic moments, it was as if we had stepped collectively beyond existing timelines, through an interdimensional portal and into a shared past. As the sun went down and the wind blew softly around our heads, we were once again Priestesses of Golden Atlantis. Together we had travelled to another dimension to reconnect with an experience from long ago.

I thought the main reason I was prompted to organise the weekend was to share my healing techniques with others, so they could take them out into the world. That was certainly part of it, but as with everything in the new energy construct we are stepping into, there are many layers. It allowed the twenty-two of us to forge an energetic link with each other and to bring back long forgotten soul gifts and abilities which will be utilised in the future. Some of my fellow Priestesses have stepped straight into a higher octave of their work. Others will do so when the time is right. Personally, it gave me a much needed boost. As I said to them, 'This can be a long, lonely road and I don't feel so alone anymore.'

We keep in touch and this friendship is certainly helping me and I hope helping them as well.

As we co-create a Fifth Dimensional planet we are linking in with aspects of ourselves that we have been unable to express for a very long time. Many of my clients are having multidimensional experiences. Most often in vivid dreams, but a few are able to tune into the crystalline grid to see into realities that have existed in the 'so called' past.

During a session with a young friend called Eliza, she told me of several unusual experiences she has had. One was when she visited the Palace of Versailles and saw a young woman sitting on a window ledge, reading. Eliza knew she was from another time because of her hair style and the clothes she was wearing. She tuned into the girl's emotions, which were peaceful and happy. As Eliza was looking at a present-day men's toilet, it morphed into an old-fashioned kitchen. Out of the kitchen walked two men, one who Eliza knew was the girl's father and one who she knew the girl loved very much. She was shown a glimpse of them enjoying the palace gardens.

Eliza also asked me about a vivid dream she had several years ago of a past life in the New Zealand city of Rotorua, at the time of the 1886 Tarawera eruption. In this dream she was standing on a balcony watching the acclaimed geological wonder, the *Pink and White Terraces*, being engulfed by mud and lava. In Eliza's Akashic Record I saw the potential for this talent for interdimensional travel to increase in the years to come and for it to be an important part of her path.

Eliza is able to connect with events that have happened in different times and places. As we become more multidimensional, our ability to link in with other soul experiences, is making its presence felt in what is called 'bleed-through.' It is easier to connect with energetic residue from the past if there is strong (positive or negative emotion), attached to it. In Chapter 7, I told how my friend Karen re-experienced traumatic memories from another lifetime where she lost her beloved three year old daughter. The feelings returned with a frightening urgency and she could even hear the words that were spoken to her then. When we behave in a way that is out of character and which seems inexplicable and even irrational, bleed-through may well be the culprit.

I had a case of this recently. In the Records I could see that my client, Alex had had three lifetimes in a row where she had left home at a young age and been forced to grow up very fast. In a lifetime in Nineteenth Century England, she had been sent away to boarding school at the age of eight. In the next, she became a scullery maid in a stately home at the same age. In the third she had entered a Tibetan monastery, again, as an eight year old. I laughed as she told me that when she was near this age in this lifetime, she had packed her bags and wanted to leave home. She shared with me that as a child she often felt alone and misunderstood and that after a recent break up these feelings had become stronger. I told her that when we feel intense emotions, it is often our Inner Child needing attention and that in her case, she had a chorus of eight year old voices from past lives to deal with as well.

I called in all four eight year olds and took her through a healing process which took inner child healing and multidimensionality to a whole new level.

❀

Emily is a massage therapist but when I opened her Akashic Record I could see she was so much more than that. The potentials for her mission in this life were dazzling. One of the questions she asked me was 'Why do I sometimes forget what I am saying when I am talking to my partner?'

I saw that she had a close connection with the incoming quantum energy (it is her soul mission to work with it), and that it was pulling her out of her body, into other soul experiences and timelines. She was relieved when I told her she didn't have early onset Alzheimers, but was a healer, who in this new energy is finding it easier to access multidimensional aspects of herself. At this time on Earth the two operating timelines are separating out. For many of us there is a 3D pathway which is often presided over by fearful past life aspects and a 5D one which holds the magic of who we really are and the richness of who we can become. Every time Emily had a glimpse of her highest potential, 3D soul aspects from the past, came in to sabotage her progress.

In her Akashic Record I saw that one past life self, in particular, was holding her back. A teacher in England at the turn of the nineteenth and twentieth centuries, I called him 'the schoolmaster.' He was passionate about his work and devoted to his pupils. Living and working at the school, he poured his best years and love and knowledge into his 'boys.' World War I began and he watched on in horror as the war machine devoured his students, one by one, and with it their potential and hope for the future. Already insular, he became depressed and more introverted. At the end of his life, devastated by the loss of a generation of young men, he was not in a good space. He felt he had failed and that all his efforts had been in vain.

Emily told me that her partner wanted her to move to a larger overseas city and that she felt conflicted and was resisting it. She told me she felt there were two parts of her:

One part knew her potential and wanted her to spread her wings and step into a more expansive vision. The other was keeping her stuck in a confined space and was urging her to live a 'normal,' safe life. I immediately recognised the influence of the schoolmaster and took Emily back in time to talk with him. She helped him to see his life in its wider context and to understand that he hadn't failed and that he lived on in her. She asked for his help in fulfilling her mission. With the support of her schoolmaster self, by the end of the session, Emily was ready to step out of her comfort zone and to embrace her soul purpose. Helping her teacher self had enabled Emily to help herself as well. In the Records I received this information about her life purpose:

'Your highest potential in this lifetime is to introduce new ways of teaching which will help people to see their true magnificence and to go beyond it.'

Emily has since moved overseas and all is going well. In accepting her mission, she will not only be able to carry on the schoolmaster's legacy, but help him to find the peace he deserves.

It is important that our soul aspects work with us, not against us. I have had clients that have multidimensional expressions that are so draining on their energy that they find it difficult to move forward.

I had an interesting session with a woman called Rachel. On opening her Akashic Record, I immediately saw the potential for her to work facilitating healing and integration on a soul level. She told me she was well-known as the 'angel lady' in Australia, but had stopped this spiritual work since returning to her home country, New Zealand, because of physical challenges. She had developed Arthritis after a Near Death Experience (NDE), nine years earlier, when her oldest child was born. Shortly after this, her father had died and she had developed coeliac disease and become gluten intolerant. I saw this was related to a past life where her father had been her grandmother. In that life 'Rachel' was a young man who craved adventure. His elderly relative had dementia and was his sole responsibility. He poisoned his grandmother, in a way that couldn't be detected, so he could join Napoleon's army.

Rachel told me that her father (now dead), had also suffered from dementia. I could feel the guilt, self-blame and feelings of unworthiness of Rachel's soldier self. I knew that Rachel was still carrying these feelings for him and that her father's death had triggered those emotions and cellular memories, from the past. When her father died in this life, her body had reacted by becoming allergic and resisting a foreign substance, gluten. The gluten was now poisoning her in the same way she had poisoned her 'grandmother.'

These ailments, as well as severe allergies and chronic fatigue, were stopping Rachel from moving forward with her mission. She also shared with me that the loss of a twin brother at birth and sexual abuse, as a child, had clouded this lifetime.

I was told that aspects of her that were existing elsewhere were sapping her strength and contributing to her extreme tiredness. I could see that I needed to bring these lost fragments home so they could work in partnership with her. I identified five main soul aspects from different dimensions and time frames that were causing her issues and which needed to be brought into balance and harmony.

I shared this with Rachel and also the higher reason for these challenges which I felt was connected to her life purpose. I saw she had the potential to work with others to facilitate the integration of soul aspects that had split off through trauma and which exist in other dimensions or in the words of the Records:

To work in a multidimensional way, moving across time and space, to reconnect others with soul pieces of themselves from 'the other side of the veil' and from other lifetimes and galaxies.'

Together Rachel and I set this intention for her healing:

It is my intention to fully integrate all of the soul aspects that are drawing on my energy and impacting my wellbeing, so I am balanced, healed and able to move forward rapidly with my soul mission in this lifetime.

Rachel read out this intention and I called in the five multidimensional aspects. With my help Rachel brought them all to
a place of peace and understanding.

She talked to them individually, telling them what she needed,
and asking them for help with her mission. She then talked to
them as a group.

'I am pulling in your energy and I ask that all the
multidimensional soul aspects that we have gathered here
today, work through me in unison. This will help me develop
the work I am here to do and teach others how to harness the
gifts, the strengths and the love of all the multidimensional
aspects of themselves, for their highest good and for the
highest good of humanity.'

I finished by asking her to put out a heart-felt intention to all
of her soul aspects to blend in so they could exist in resonance
and harmony.

I talked with Rachel recently and was thrilled when she said,
'You gave me the key to the door of my multidimensional story.'

She told me that after our session she had become a grand mag-
net that was able to draw in all of the aspects she had been grappling
with. According to Rachel, we sparked off a process where she was
able to retrieve and integrate past life aspects that had experienced
soul loss in many lifetimes. Rachel realised what she was dealing
with was huge and enlisted the help of an osteopath and a homeo-
path. With this assistance she did 'deep work' to ground this energy
into her body. She told me:

'Once the energy was back in my body, I was able to take others
through a process to access and integrate their multidimensional
selves.'

Rachel works in this way with clients but has also begun to
express her multidimensionality through stunning artworks; 'living
paintings,' which carry light and healing codes and are able to

transport the observer to other dimensions. Rachel has been on a difficult journey but the rewards have been great – improved health and vitality and the vibrancy and joy of multidimensionality in all its glory.

There are always those who agree to incarnate a generation or two early so they can prepare the way for an influx of people, with a similar gift, who will come later.

I had a session with one of these souls, called Shayne. What I discovered when I opened Shayne's Akashic Record was extraordinary and rare. There were so many powerful multidimensional aspects that I could see that growing up in the Third Dimension must have been immensely difficult for her. Even now with the new energy coming in, it was obvious that she had chosen an arduous path. She laughed as I told her there were other people like her on Earth but that most of them were in psychiatric hospitals. I identified four main soul aspects affecting Shayne:

1. An indigenous woman: Shayne said she already knew her as a Māori woman with a **Ta moko** on her chin and a **tui** bird on her shoulder and that she had a painting of her. She told me that two weeks before, she had felt compelled to take the portrait out of storage, frame it and bring it home. This picture was in her room as I conducted the session.

2. Hollow Earth Elf: From **Agartha** (Hollow Earth). Shayne saw him as a short, masculine, elfin entity.

3. The Venusian Master: From Venus. Shayne saw him as a blue, light energy.

4. **Ashtar Command**: A member of the intergalactic group, the 'Ashtar Command,' which travels the Earth protecting the planet and its inhabitants. Shayne described him as very large and tall and wearing a white space suit.

I told Shayne that they were benevolent aspects of her

soul that existed in different realities, who were all here to help, but were not working as a team. This was causing her inner conflict. I could see that the purpose of our session was to make her aware of them and to introduce them to each other, so she could feel more in control and harness their gifts. I shared that the 'indigenous woman' aspect of Shayne connected her to her Lemurian and Pacifica soul and biological roots. I told her that she had a soul contract in the first part of her life, to carry and release the pain of these indigenous peoples. The idea of this specific soul agreement made sense to Shayne, who said that this, coupled with her gift of accessing other dimensions, had made her life hard.

She was relieved when I saw that this old contract was coming to an end and that it was time for her to begin a new one. This new work would involve helping others, particularly from the younger generation, to understand and embrace their similar gifts. Firstly, however, Shayne had to show these dominant soul aspects who was in charge.

With this in mind I helped her to:

- Bring them all into her conscious awareness.

- Make them all aware of each other.

- Integrate them all into her current physical reality (as Shayne).

- Talk to them and ask them to use their combined strengths to assist her to help others to accept and integrate their own multi and interdimensional aspects.

I guided Shayne as she talked to them one by one.

She asked them individually how they could help her and then introduced them to each other. They each had a message for her which she relayed to me.

The indigenous woman promised to help her to:

'*Understand the distinctive vibration of each indigenous group on a core essence level.*'

'*Understand and to discern and speak the various energetic languages of the different groups so you can communicate with them and so they can be heard.*'

The Elf from 'Hollow Earth' asked Shayne to:

'*Go outside more often to connect with nature and to give your energy back to the trees and the Earth.*'

The soul aspect from The Ashtar Command promised Shayne that he would:

'*Provide a clear and pure vibrational link to the galactic side of who you are, to allow you to access that energy, so you can utilise it moving forward with strength, grace and integrity.*'

The Master from Venus said:

'*We will allow you to come from your highest place and to always act with love in your dealings with people.*'

He reminded her that:

'*It is this energy that can bring true, lasting changes and shifts in individuals here on the planet.*'

I ended the session by asking her to stand in a circle with these four soul aspects and to say the following:

'*We are all part of the same soul. We have an important job to do. We carry the same light and the same intention. It is time for my work to really begin. I will do it with your support and help. I love you all. I honour you all and I thank you all. It is now time for us to work as a team, for the highest good of all who live on this planet and in this galaxy and beyond.*'

I asked Shayne to visualise herself pulling the four separate energies into her body so they were united and able to work together and to say:

'*I am part of you and you are part of me. We will work together in harmony to transform this planet. We have*

> *merged together as one united force for good.'*
> The session ended with a group hug.

This email I received later that day made me smile:

'My heart is filled with sooo much joy tonight, and all four aspects seem to be sitting quite comfortably inside me (human Shayne) with minimal fuss and a lot of camaraderie. I feel laughter and many simultaneous conversations going on between them. They have so many stories to share and are melding together. Sleep tonight won't be easy.'

When I heard from Shayne some time later she was still on a high. She messaged me:

'Our session seems several lifetimes ago. Re-reading this again made me cry tears of joy. All that has unfolded for me since has been magically transformative. Having all aspects in complete alignment within a human vessel is a truly miraculous outcome.'

'Mining the Akash' is connecting with past life gifts, abilities and talents that can help us now. I borrowed this phrase from Lee Carroll who channels Kryon. Our lifetimes have not all been full of suffering and disaster, even for the Old Souls of the planet. They are rich with human experience and along the way there has been joy and love and lives where we have fulfilled our potential and easily created abundance. We have been leaders and teachers and everything in between. The Records are a safe space to connect with past life and multidimensional aspects of ourselves that are supportive and can give us assistance in the present. I had a very interesting session with a client, who specifically asked to be connected to positive past life experiences and attributes. I opened her Akashic Record and eight lives came up:

1. A galactic gate keeper before her soul came to Earth.
2. A healer in Lemuria.
3. A Greek philosopher.

4. An Egyptian building a pyramid.

5. A Druid carving intricate symbols on stone.

6. A nun caring for children in a convent orphanage.

7. A young woman, an acclaimed ballet dancer in Russia, who got pregnant out of wedlock.

8. A university professor who was intellectual, studious and analytical.

My client is a beautiful soul and her humility, innate wisdom and pure and open heart shone through in all of these lives. Not surprisingly, the life where she experienced the greatest soul growth, was the hardest. A gifted dancer who was the pride of her Russian village, she went from 'hero to zero' after she was seduced by a married man and became pregnant. Her baby was handicapped and she could have given him away and returned to the stage, but she loved him deeply and chose to bring him up herself. Her family and community shunned her completely and gave her no support. (During the reading I got a mental image of a young woman, very much alone, pushing a boy in a primitive wooden wheel chair).

Her strength of character, courage and compassion came through and with it the understanding that she had chosen these difficult circumstances to learn the true meaning of unconditional love. I got my client to close her eyes and brought in all of these past life selves. She connected with their energies and pulled in the vibration of their different attributes and talents which were:

- the gift of manifesting in the physical realms through the power of intention from the galactic gate keeper

- balance between the head and the heart from the Lemurian healer

- intellect and communication skills from the Greek philosopher

- patience and the importance of building strong foundations to leave a lasting legacy from the Egyptian pyramid builder

- the ability to communicate through symbols and using multidimensional energies from the Druid

- an optimistic outlook and complete faith from the nun

- an open heart and unconditional love and compassion for all from the ballet dancer

- self-discipline and focus from the professor.

Afterwards she shared that as I connected her to these past life selves she had different physical and emotional sensations. This is what she told me:

- Galactic gate keeper: 'I felt energy pouring into my head.'

- Lemurian healer: 'I felt an incredible sensation of lightness and agility of the physical body.'

- Greek philosopher: 'I felt like there was a finger touching each of my temples.'

- Nun: 'My hands got warm.'

- Ballet dancer: 'I felt very emotional.'

It was an honour to help my client connect with these past life attributes and abilities. They resonated with her. After two quite solitary lifetimes, (ballet dancer and professor), she now has a team of past life helpers that she can draw on for support with her mission and purpose, in this one.

When I asked for her permission to publish these details, she told me that she is still connected to these heroic past life selves. She calls on her Egyptian self when she needs patience and often thanks her nun and ballerina selves for her deep love and compassion.

After thanking me she added, 'Knowing about these gifts and talents within myself has been very empowering.'

❁

The difference between 'reality' in the Third Dimension and in the higher dimensions we are moving into is, as Kryon has said, like moving from black and white into colour. As we move through the Fourth Dimension into the Fifth it is opening us up to different realities and as a friend of mine said, 'to different aspects of the hologram.' It is easier for us to link in with alternative realities: past lives, parallel realities and different universes within the multiverse. Our multidimensionality is making its presence felt and it is becoming easier for us to have inter and multidimensional experiences.

In Chapter 8, I mentioned a healing technique where I take clients back in time to just before they became unwell, to try to alter the outcome. In Chapter 5, I wrote about Adam who was still carrying the trauma from a past life in World War I. I took him back to the pivotal incident and with very little prompting from me, he created a different end to the story. Instead of cowering in the trenches, he found the courage to take advantage of a short lull in the fighting to pull his wounded friends to safety. This technique where I 'project a new reality into the hologram' is called **retrocausality**. The Akashic Records lends itself to this type of healing.

I used this in a session with Maddie, another client of mine.

Maddie told me she had worked as a lightworker for nearly 30 years but that in 2010, after a trip to New York, everything in her life had unravelled. She stopped her spiritual work, her marriage ended, she lost her savings and now after moving south to a new job, was being bullied by her workmates. After a run of unbelievable bad luck she was stuck in a deep groove she felt she couldn't get out of.

In her Record I saw that there were two past lives that were still affecting her. I saw her as a male immigrant to America who arrived at Ellis Island, full of hopes and dreams. Before he had a chance to set foot on mainland soil, he was killed by a man who stabbed him from behind. I told her that her trip to New York in 2010, had triggered memories of this other lifetime when things had come unstuck. Maddie told me that on this visit she had gone on a harbour cruise and hadn't wanted to get off the boat when it stopped at Ellis Island.

The other life I saw, was one as a single woman who looked after her grandmother. In that lifetime Maddie had healing gifts. She was happy not to marry and have children and was quite content living in a cottage with her elderly relative, who she cared for with loving devotion.

When the grandmother died, family members found that many of her valuable items were missing. Suspicion fell on her granddaughter. Her extended family and the rest of the village loved the old lady and word got out. Because of these rumours and the fact that Maddie was different to everyone else, she became a target for persecution. She was accused of stealing and of selling her grandmother's things.

'The whole village turned against you,' I told her, as with my inner vision I saw her being chased and flogged to death by her family and the villagers.

I added that their treatment of her had been unjust. Her grandmother in that life had had dementia and had (unknown to her granddaughter), given the lost items to peddlers and passing travellers who knocked on her door.

Fast forward to this life and Maddie has moved to a smaller town and a new job where she is mistrusted and mistreated.

'The same situation is happening in my life right now,' she told me.

As we move into a Fifth Dimensional reality and into a different time zone there are many aspects to the hologram and with my help Maddie went in and changed it. I took her back to both of these lives and she created a different and much happier ending to these stories.

We went back to the life in New York, just before her migrant self was stabbed. I listened, enraptured, as Maddie regaled me with details of a life of incredible, good fortune. Her past life self, disembarked at New York. He met and married a beautiful woman, had two children and created a successful and profitable business before dying of old age (with a smile on his face), surrounded by his loving family.

In the other life, the caregiving granddaughter inherited her grandmother's house and became a pillar of the community. She was loved and supported by the villagers. People came from miles around for her healing and compassion and she was respected and revered. She lived a long, happy and peaceful life and helped many people with her gifts.

I told Maddie to hug her past life selves and to pull in their qualities and the new memories and then I said, 'We have got their lives back on track and now it is time for you. It is time for you to create a new ending to your own story.'

Maddie vividly described an abundant future where she has reconnected to her gifts, dreams and plans. She created a template for the rest of her life that involves establishing her own business; a retreat where people can come for rest and healing. The successful migrant businessman and the sought after healer will both be with her, I am sure, as she creates this new reality.

Speaking with Maddie several months later she told me that she had moved towns and changed jobs. She said that our session had been a 'tipping point' which had helped her transition to more positive energy and that she loved her new life.

'I have finally found the place where I can let go and breathe.'

She shared her passion for her new job where she gives valued service to the community.

'It has everything on my wish list. Life is finally coming together for me.'

❁

The Akashic Records have given me and my students a gentle introduction to multidimensionality and a taste of things to come. They are a safe place to explore this new arena. The quantum attribute of entanglement means that energy can be in two places at once and still be connected. As we become more quantum this will start happening for us too. As a bridge to this energy and the soul, the Akashic Records are the perfect place for multidimensional exploration. The many and varied aspects of our soul are here to help us. We can utilise their gifts and attributes and harness their strength, as a support team, to help us in all areas of our lives.

We are on the brink of a breakthrough in human evolution. The increasing multidimensionality of human life will take us beyond suffering forever. With the help of the Akashic Records, we can heal, elevate and integrate our multidimensional aspects, so there are no longer any parts of us (from lower vibrational soul experiences), dragging us down. Any progress we make on a personal level will help all of the other aspects of ourselves in existence. Our own healing and transformation will benefit not just us as individuals but by imprinting new energy into the matrix, the entire human race.

When I am on an akashic adventure, I am still very much aware of the core part of me that is sitting in a chair speaking the words. I have become used to this and it doesn't frighten me. Eventually, we will all be able to embrace the different realities that are part of our soul nature. It won't happen overnight and will happen, first, to those who are open to the possibility. It will greatly enhance our lives.

At last we have a 'get out of jail card.' Reconnecting with the truth and grandeur of our multidimensional selves is like being released from prison after a lengthy incarceration. We have done our time. Freedom is ours!

Chapter 12

Out of the Darkness

As I begin this chapter, I am observing the suffering as the Covid-19 pandemic sweeps the world. Let's hope this is our final wake-up call. I am devastated at the loss of life this virus is causing and the sadness for those losing loved ones. I am hoping that this is the last swish of the tail, and that the wave of fear that is engulfing the planet will help to take us beyond it and suffering, forever. Already, this situation is bringing out the best in many of us, and opening up our hearts and minds to what is important and what it is possible to create together.

It's crunch time. The world is changing before our eyes and will never be the same. There is disbelief, fear and panic. Together we are sharing a collective dark night of the soul, a mass awakening that has the potential to take us to a much better place. The busyness and structure of our normal reality, friends, family, routine, work, childcare and even fast food have gone. The world has shut up shop. It has pulled down the shutters and it is not business as usual. The diversions we have used to numb our pain have been taken away. We are in the eye of the storm and being forced to go within. We are waking up, not only to our own truth, but to some bigger truths about life on this planet.

As souls on Earth we have been through a lot over thousands of years. There are many facets to who we are. These layers are being removed and as we open up to our inner wisdom, this can be painful. It is possible to access the Akashic Records of places and when the pandemic hit, I naturally, turned to the Records for answers. In a reading I gave for Planet Earth I received this information:

> *It is a catalyst for change and a necessary part of the ascension process. Personally and collectively, it is triggering rapid growth and transformation. It is removing the old to make way for the new. On a higher level it was planned to empower and to bring humanity back into balance. There is huge learning in this situation. It is necessary to change the consciousness on the planet and to bring us into closer alignment with Fifth Dimensional energies.*

As Franklin Delano Roosevelt once so wisely said, 'The only thing we to have to fear, is fear itself.' The low vibration of fear has enslaved us for centuries. It has been used by the dark to control and manipulate. It has kept us small and mired in victimhood and has perpetuated suffering. It has no place on the new Earth. Fear is running rampant. Conspiracy theories, panic about the future and the crumbling of old social and financial structures have reached fever pitch. As I said in an online post at the beginning of the crisis, thought viruses can be more scary than real ones and the worst and most contagious (and deadly), of these, is fear.

Ironically the one person that does not seem unduly affected is my daughter, Alice. Fear is an old adversary of hers. Over the last fourteen years in many places and guises she has stared it in the face and won. The level of fear in the air is normal for her. After years of living in its grip, just as everyone else is firmly in its clutches, she is (at long last), letting it go. To my husband and I, this is no surprise. When she was a child and we asked her to do something, she usually did the opposite. We learned to ask for what we *didn't* want and practised reverse psychology on her with great success.

Fear has held humanity captive for thousands of years. As one of my favourite teachers, Tim Whild, said in a Zoom webinar, 'We must separate ourselves out from the 3D matrix of drama and chaos.' Fear is not our friend and it comes in many forms. I believe that our greatest fear is the fear of ourselves and what we are capable of. We have lived many lifetimes in **duality**. We have played in the light and played in the dark. As souls on Earth we have all done things we are ashamed of. I described in earlier chapters how the pain of this is now coming up to be released and how the Akashic Records can help with this.

The turbulent energies swirling around are helping us to release our shadow aspects. 'The shadow' is at the heart of human life. Carl Jung coined this phrase to describe the aspects of our personality that we disown or don't accept. The shadow takes shape in childhood. On a primal level children feel their survival depends on the approval of the adults around them. They change their behaviour to feel loved and accepted. By the time they have grown up, the difference between who they really are and who they have become to please others, is huge. As the author John Bradshaw wrote in his book, *Homecoming: Reclaiming and Healing Your Inner Child*, 'the wonder child becomes the wounded child.' Children disconnect from their soul truth, becoming who they feel they need to be to survive. This separation causes pain and plants seeds of self-doubt and unworthiness.

The child's authentic self that is shut down and repressed, becomes the 'shadow.' We all have one. How we react to those around us gives clues about what lurks in our shadows. What triggers us in others is almost always something we have to work on ourselves. It is not surprising given that Planet Earth is a place of duality and of light and dark, that the shadow is and has been an integral part of our human experience.

At this time of transition and clearing, our shadow aspects are glaringly obvious. Only once we recognise, accept and integrate them, will we be able to move beyond the suffering we have created and have been recreating for lifetimes. This process of integrating our different aspects (subpersonalities) including our Inner Child, is a crucial part of the process of healing and restoring ourselves to wholeness. As I have discussed previously, the Akashic Records with the memories of all our human experiences, is the perfect place for identifying and integrating the disparate aspects of our soul and self throughout different time frames and dimensions.

The shadow side of humanity has always existed. In past generations it has (often), been expressed as a masculine tendency to control and dominate and as a feminine tendency towards victimhood and helplessness. The two world wars of the twentieth century bought these impulses to a head. The 'cannon fodder' and shell-shock of World War I was swiftly followed by the mass murder and social dislocation of World War II. Since then we have been dealing with the fall-out. The worst excesses of human nature came into focus and in the ensuing decades no one wanted to talk about it. Many of my generation carry the pain and scars of our parents and grandparents, who lived through this period.

The way to deal with it in the 1950s, 1960s and early 70s was to act as if it had never happened. But it did, and many of us were affected by our parent's trauma which was rarely expressed in healthy ways. Every family had secrets, including my own. The public face was often very different from the private one. We were not ready to accept the ugliness within our family systems and within ourselves.

The hypocrisy and darkness did not go away and was expressed in the Western world at least, as male supremacy, alcoholism, racism, homophobia, sexual abuse, materialism, secrecy and general dysfunction. These masked and threw a cloak over the pain of our parents and grandparents' generations and left a legacy of shame that was so acute, that my generation and our children, have been compelled to take action. In the western world it started with widespread therapy and psychoanalysis in the 1960s and

1970s. Since the 1980s and 1990s there has been an increasing trend towards personal development and self-awareness.

As many of us know, suppressing the truth only makes things worse. As a child I was often puzzled by the mixed messages from the adults around me. Some of them had 'two faces' and could be vicious. I was sent to the local convent for piano lessons with a nun whose mood and behaviour were mercurial to say the least. One week she would be on a charm offensive, while the next she would be sadistically rapping my knuckles for playing wrong notes. It ruined the piano for me. The lessons left me so upset that during the week I tried to forget about them. Practising was a stark reminder. It triggered my anxiety and pain so I stopped. Week after week, as the benevolent statues of Jesus and Mary watched on in silence, I was screamed at and punished. Afterwards I would jump on my bike and ride shakily to school, crying all the way.

In my first teaching job I didn't have a voice. The Headmistress of my school was also a confusing mixture of light and dark. At first glance she seemed a sweet, old lady. A 1980s version of Queen Victoria, stocky and big chested, she had grey hair in a bun and rosy, pink cheeks. She too was driven by fear, however, and had a strong shadow side. At staff meetings she addressed us formally as Mr, Mrs and Miss and while she could be warm and friendly, she could also lash out in brutal and bullying ways. One day after witnessing a physical attack by one girl on another, I went straight to the top. Shocked by what had happened, I walked into the Headmistress's office without knocking, interrupting a meeting with the Hostel matron. These two didn't get on and the full ire of my boss's wrath was unleashed on me. I became a quivering wreck, (in front of the violent pupil who went unpunished). This was how it worked back then. Bullying and narcissism were everywhere and the 'Old Boys' Club' (to which many women also belonged), was firmly in control. The Old Boys' Club has existed for aeons. Representing humanity's shadow side, fear has been their weapon and centuries of human suffering has been the result.

For a very long time the human race has been dominated by fear-based thought forms and entities that have enslaved and crippled us. Manipulated and indoctrinated, we have passively acquiesced to actions that have had disastrous consequences.

In the final days of Atlantis there were dark forces at play. Advanced mind control technology was developed and used to 'mess with the minds' of the masses. Those from the darkness, masqueraded as beings of light and successfully exploited and duped many to follow their lead. The corruption and ego-centred greed and hunger for power, set forces in motion that resulted in the cataclysm that destroyed Atlantis forever.

I have worked with clients who still carry the residue from this time in the form of energy implants in their brains and I have removed these etheric 'tumours', on their behalf. In 2014, my son Hugh, had a real brain tumour. In his Akashic Record, I found that one of the reasons for this was so he could release an energetic he had carried through many lifetimes, which was the result of brainwashing he received in Atlantis:

In Atlantis you worked tirelessly for the light but towards the end there was a group who brainwashed people by tampering energetically with their minds. You had a loving and trusting nature and got fooled by these people who reprogrammed you. They removed energy templates and replaced them with new ones. In subsequent lives you were affected by this 'energetic lobotomy' and you lost touch with your inner truth and to some extent your ideals. Your brain tumour was a physical manifestation of this Atlantean energy and it has now completely disappeared. With it a veil has lifted and your spiritual gifts and wisdom have been fully returned to you.

I am sure it was no coincidence that my son's tumour was attached to his pineal gland, which some call 'the seat of the soul' and is the quantum antenna that connects us with our Higher Self or that his surgery was the day before his 22nd birthday. Twenty-two is a master builder number that empowers us to turn our dreams into reality. The removal of that old energy has opened him up to his full power and potential.

Many of us, who are living now, were there in those final days. Spiritual teacher, Tim Whild, has talked of a group of nine souls who took on the dark roles at the end of Atlantis. I believe, that some were prominent figures during World War II and that others are current leaders. They have wielded power for thousands of years and won't give up without a fight. These souls don't play by the rules. They have survived through corruption in many forms and a 'divide and rule' mentality. They are not going to change now. Surrounded by higher vibration energy and in a world where there is now an obvious difference between leaders that care about people and those who don't, however, their game is up.

It is not difficult to see the similarities between the last days of Atlantis and the present. Mind control through hypnotic speaking techniques, the secrecy of a power elite with a hidden agenda. Tim Whild calls this group the 1%. He says that this 1% have held the wealth and power on our planet for thousands of years. Since Atlantis, their weapon has been fear, which they have exploited to create societies of people living in survival mode, with little energy and inclination to question the status quo. In the digital age where information is available via the World Wide Web and we have an easily accessible platform to express ourselves, this is changing fast. Just like 'Sleeping Beauty' in the fairy tale, humanity has been asleep for a long time (much longer than one hundred years). After a harrowing journey through a thick and dark forest our prince has finally found us and is kissing us on the lips. Individually and collectively we are finally waking up. As always the timing is perfect.

❀

In the last few years there have been many unsavoury revelations about the actions of those in power and there will be more to come. The 'Me Too' movement is a prime example of the exposure of bad behaviour and also the efficacy of collective energies for positive change. In the Covid time, the difference between leaders who are self-seeking and corrupted by power and money and those who have reverence for life and work for the highest good, has been easy to see. The blinkers are coming off and the truth of what is happening, and has been happening for thousands of years, is being revealed. With the rapid influx of light on this planet, the darkness has nowhere to hide. In the ensuing panic its true nature and agenda is being uncovered.

Only last night on the TV news, two male icons of power were confronted. Now in their eighties and extremely wealthy, both men were respected and honoured by my parent's generation. One was being taken to task by a woman about his racist comments and the other was on trial for possessing large quantities of child pornography. With the assistance of online technology, the Millennials are calling out these behaviours in a very public way. This trend will continue. It takes only one person with the courage to stand up, to create a revolution. The world of the 'Old Boys' Club' is disappearing fast. A beautiful metamorphosis is taking place. Humility is the new currency, the new gold.

In the Covid era 'essential workers' have become the champions. Those on the supermarket checkout and medical workers, who know all about selfless giving, have put themselves at risk for our survival. Our shared circumstances and the ease of social media has allowed many unsung heroes to shine. Many people, who have not previously had a voice, are rising up and receiving recognition and accolades that are long overdue. There is empathy, compassion and kindness. We are embracing and celebrating diversity and difference. Finally and not before time, as Jesus prophesied, the meek are inheriting the Earth.

The Old Souls have paved the way for the Millennials and The Children who do not have the same level of fear, and are tackling the shadow aspects of this planet head on. This generation are fully aware of what is needed for change and are here to do the work. It is their job to expose the shadow and to bring it into the light of day, so we can go beyond it.

This process is also happening for the younger generation on a personal level. They are taking self awareness to new heights, sharing their deepest and darkest secrets on social media. They have no time for hypocritical, dishonest or abusive behaviour. They are 'whistleblowers.' It is part of their collective soul mission to uncover the dark practices that have reigned supreme for too long. They are helping humanity's shadow aspects to emerge into the light so they can be transmuted and released.

Can we leave our shadow behind forever? To do so we must acknowledge and accept it. We must look it squarely in the eye and stare it down. The Akashic Records, as a tool for self-examination, can help us do this. Many of our shadow aspects have been created by past and current life selves that have experienced trauma. We have carried them from lifetime to lifetime in what Kryon calls the 'Akashic Template' and Patricia Cota-Robles calls the '**Karmic Birth Template**.' Within the safety of the Records we can explore the deepest and darkest recesses of our soul and psyche. We can find the missing pieces of the puzzle and join the dots so we can become whole. We can bring the dark and the light together in healthy ways so we no longer have to be scared of ourselves or anyone else.

There is hope. So much is happening on different levels. Like a recurring wish that eventually comes true, things have to happen in the etheric first. In 2020, Patricia Cota-Robles, spoke at the '34th Annual World Congress on Illumination' about the lifting of the 'enslavement codes.' After what she calls humanity's 'fall from grace,' and our descent into the Third Dimension, she says, we created a patriarchal consciousness that was no longer anchored in love. We lost our connection to our Higher Selves, our balanced male and female aspects and to our fully enabled twelve strands of DNA and acquired a 'Karmic Birth Template,' which has perpetuated lifetimes of pain and suffering. Cota-Robles says that in late 2019, early 2020, the links connecting us to this template and to the 'enslavement codes' were cut. This, she says, has enabled every person on Earth to release the energy of suffering and the energetic links to our ego selves that have perpetuated it. She says, that our lower human egos no longer have command of our bodies, but that their dramas are still playing out because 'old habits die hard' and it will take time to let them go. Patricia says that this process has healed the wounds and paved the way for humanity to move into a new frequency. As part of the 'Congress on Illumination' in October, 2020, lightworkers from all over the globe joined together to anchor our highest soul aspect, which some call our 'I Am presence', into the hearts of every person on Earth. This act of service will help us to navigate the rocky roads ahead.

At this momentous time on the planet, consciously and un-consciously, we are all, in our own way, helping humanity to leave the darkness behind. Some like my daughter, Alice, and a client, Dawn, who lives in the US have had a more hands-on role.

When I opened Dawn's Akashic Record, I saw that she had reached a turning point in her life. She had gifts as a writer and a story to tell. Dawn told me that she had journaled regularly before taking leave from her job the year before. She mentioned she had been living on disability payments after an incident in her work place forced her to take time out and said,

'I had a difficult childhood and I crawled my way up. The thing I loved most about my work was helping people. For twenty years I poured my heart and soul into my job, until the company was sold.'

Her new bosses got rid of some long-term employees and insisted their workers meet almost impossible targets. Dawn's American dream fast became an American nightmare.

She continued, 'They told me what I had to say and pressured me to work in a way that was against my principles. It was all about money and greed. I was being forced to sell people things they didn't really want and need. It was immoral.'

This and the fifteen hour days got to her. At a work meeting she was honest about her feelings. Her words were not well received. She told me that no one supported her and that she felt, not only that it was her problem, but that she *was* the problem. She burst into tears and told them she couldn't do it anymore. Dawn was offered the choice of resigning or of taking two years leave.

'You made a stand. Even though they treated you as a pariah, you were the only sane one,' I assured Dawn.

In her Akashic Record, I saw that her highest potential was to write a book exposing unethical business practices.

I continued, 'You have the ability to put into words what others are thinking but haven't the courage to own or express. It is time for the behaviours of the Old Boys' Club to be revealed. You can do it. Others will come in to support you. The energy on the planet is very different than it used to be. It is no longer the energy of deception, deceit or inauthenticity. It carries the light of truth, justice and compassion. In the new energy darkness can't thrive. It will be flushed out.'

Dawn replied, 'I spoke my truth and they didn't like it. I am usually never afraid but this has made me very fearful.'

In the Records I could see why her experience had been traumatic. What happened had been a replay of other lifetimes where she had stood up to those in power and been killed for it.

'You have been hung. You have been burned. You have been

shot. They haven't wanted to hear what you have to say,' I told her.

Her most recent past life was still affecting her. In this life, as a Japanese soldier working in a Prisoner of War camp, she had witnessed the barbaric and degrading treatment of Korean women who were kept as sex slaves. Her soldier self had documented everything and when the war was over, planned to tell the world what he had witnessed. He didn't get the chance. In my mind's eye, I saw him drinking rice alcohol. This relaxed him and he shared his feelings, confiding in someone he thought he could trust. Soon afterwards, he was shot.

It was easy to see the parallels between what happened then and what was happening now.

'In both lifetimes you had the courage to speak out about how sickened you felt. You were then scapegoated and betrayed by those you worked with,' I told Dawn.

She shared with me that she had shaken uncontrollably when she had confronted her bosses.

I replied, 'You are still carrying the energy of the trauma from that last life. You have had many lives where you have been ostracised and persecuted because you have spoken your truth. Your body went into shock as deep soul pain from those lives was triggered. In that lifetime you were killed so you couldn't tell the story. In this life you have lived a different version of the same story, but you are still here and have years to tell it. Your story is one that is being played out all over your country and across the Western world. You have been mourning your old identity, but now it is about creating a new one. Your life is not over, it is just beginning. You have the potential to be a powerful voice.'

I saw that as well as writing and speaking, Dawn's work in the future could also involve advocating for others who were refusing to 'play the game' and being squeezed out of organisations.

I finished with, 'It's your time to stand up and speak out. You will feel empowered as you heal from not just one lifetime, but many. Taking on the power elite will give you momentum and strength. You are here to help change the consciousness of the work culture in the Western world. It won't be a few people you will be helping. It will be many. It is finally safe to tell your story.'

Like Dawn, my friend Debbie also has a soul agreement to help us overcome the darkness:

In recent years Debbie has travelled to different parts of the world on various spiritually inspired expeditions. The anticipation before these trips and their reality have not matched, as every single one has been debilitating, both physically and emotionally. Opening her Akashic Record I could see that she is an acutely sensitive being who can link in with the energies of the crystalline grid, magnetise their imprints of pain and suffering directly to her and transmute them for the collective. Her 'holidays' were far from relaxing, as she was not only confronted by the energy of suffering in the places she visited but by her own past life misery. I saw that she had experienced difficult past lives in many of the places she travelled to. Connecting with a deep vein of human suffering in these places, as well as her own, had been very hard on her.

Even a trip to Nepal and a monastery in Tibet had dire consequences for Debbie. In the Himalayas she re-experienced a life time where she froze to death while on an errand to get medicinal herbs for someone who was seriously ill. In a lifetime in Tibet, as a reluctant young monk, she became a target for the frustrations of many in the monastic community, who, like the boy she was in that lifetime, had their life path chosen for them.

I told Debbie that she has a contract to help humanity to move beyond suffering and that, as is usually the case, this agreement fitted in perfectly with her soul work.

Debbie asked me about various quantum healing courses she could attend. I told her that she didn't need to participate because she already knew what to do. Just as she has the ability to magnetise and transmute the suffering in the crystalline grid of the places she visited, I saw that she had innate knowledge of effective ways to assist individuals to release their imprints of pain and suffering. I told her:

'Just hold the intention and bring it through your mind, heart and body and you can work miracles. You have been preparing for this work for years. You will be able to take people, very quickly, to a place where they can release their pain. You can communicate with the cells of people's bodies and ask them what they need and will be able to work inter and multidimensionally.'

The residents of certain places on Earth have a soul agreement to help, in a special way, while we are in the transitional phase of the ascension process. The city of Christchurch, in New Zealand's South Island, is one such place. Still recovering from two destructive earthquakes in 2010 and 2011, on March 15, 2019, the city took another blow when fifty-one Muslim worshippers in two separate mosques were murdered by a young, white supremacist gunman. Jacinda Ardern, New Zealand's Prime Minister flew straight to the city, and wearing a scarf on her head to express love and solidarity, visited the survivors and their families.

'They are us,' she declared. Her compassionate leadership in the wake of the disaster, united our country, undermining the gunman's agenda of division and hatred. In the 2011 earthquake the central city was destroyed and the cathedral at its heart, irreparably damaged. Shortly after the massacre, I opened the Akashic Record of Christchurch and got this information:

The city has already been through so much. The earthquakes in 2010 and 2011 transmuted negative energy and set the stage for greater love and cooperation between people. There are many special souls in Christchurch. Some have always lived there, but in the last eight years many more have been drawn to this place. Some of these people will have a positive global reach and influence in years to come.

The city has chosen to be of service to the world and to show us what is possible when people come together from the heart. Christchurch has always been imbued with the sacred and high vibration of golden, christed energy. Over time overlays and undercurrents acted to block this energy. The earthquakes released it. The clearing and transmutation of the crystalline grid means that the higher consciousness energies of Christchurch can now flow freely from this place to the rest of the world.

*Christchurch will demonstrate a new model for living in harmony and without fear. The people of Christchurch are laying down a new template of **Unity Consciousness** which will ripple out to the rest of New Zealand and the world. How this city deals with adversity, will be an inspiration to us all, and will demonstrate a higher way of living and being.*

I was proud of our country's response to this tragedy. With spectacular leadership from our young Prime Minister, we were forced to acknowledge the darkness in our midst and a huge wave of grief, love and compassion engulfed us all. A sea of flowers extended from one end of the country to the other and a tide of love washed out from our country to distant shores. As I mentioned in Chapter 9, our government swiftly brought in new legislation banning military style, semi-automatic rifles and establishing a gun registry to track every gun in the country and to ensure that only 'fit and proper' people can hold firearms licences.

❃

As this planet and its inhabitants begin to move out of the darkness, Alice and I are also leaving suffering behind. The trauma of the past is receding and (thankfully), also the drama. The experiences of the last fourteen years return to trouble me less and less. Seeing Alice locked in a urine-soaked police cell, being treated with disdain by a cocky policeman, in 2008, was one of the worst. She had just tried to kill herself and this young man was berating her for being attention seeking and wasting his time. Days (and weeks) spent at hospital bedsides, have been no fun either.

In the early years of Alice's illness, Marty and I went into overdrive trying to fix her, pulling out our best parenting and coaching techniques. No stone was left unturned but it seemed the harder we tried the worse she got. Sometimes she would appear to be listening to the advice we gave, but it was seldom taken. Books remained unopened and an army of well-meaning family and friends (often healers), who were eager to help, were pushed away. Eventually we realised that this was Alice's journey and although we could walk alongside her, it was not our job to take the lead. It was up to Alice to find her own path… and she has.

Gradually she has connected with her own tribe, mostly online. In their inimitable, millennial way, they have introduced her to many of the things we have been talking about for years: positive thinking and affirmations, mindfulness, meditation, yoga, self-help books and more. She is finding her own teachers at the right time for her. It has been a gradual process but now we are the ones getting recommendations for YouTube, Ted talks and books. Although she still has moments of mind-numbing anxiety and sadness, Alice is slowly but surely finding her way out of the darkness. Every step is a victory and it is so exciting after years of being lost in the wilderness to see her coming home to the truth of her soul.

The positive change in Alice is thrilling and information I received about the 2020 pandemic is also helping me to remain positive about our wider, global future:

Covid-19 will help expose any flaws in the system, leaders for whom human life and wellbeing is not a priority and the questionable practises which helped create the virus in the first place. It will break down old structures and will usher in a new generation of leaders who aren't motivated by self-interest and a desire for power and control.

The war is not over but the gloves are off and victory is at hand. In my (current), lifetime there has been a massive attempt to understand the past and to explore our darkness. All that has been hidden is being revealed, from secrecy and corruption to addictions, sexual impropriety and religious and racial intolerance. We are creating a different world. A world where light will be able to replace the dark because we have acknowledged the darkness within humanity as a whole and within ourselves. It is only through understanding who we are and, more importantly, who we have been that we can move beyond suffering.

A repeated message from Kryon in the last few years has been 'Don't judge the present by what has happened in the past.' The 5D energy is ushering in a new age. We can harness this energy to create a world of peace, love and joy. We have been waiting a long time for this. It is the reason the Old Souls have gritted their teeth and kept returning again and again. It is the reason some of the younger souls of this planet have come from all over the galaxy and beyond, to be here as we let go of the old and co-create the new. It is important we do this without a backward glance. There is so much to look forward to. With the help of the Akashic Records we can understand and integrate our past and walk boldly into the future.

Seeing my work spiral out into the world gives me great satisfaction. The Akashic Records are exploding. A reservoir of the old energy, they also hold the potentials for the new. They can help us move from the suffering of the past into an exciting, multidimensional future. It is my wish that they become a tool for teachers, healers and people everywhere. It is time that doctors, psychiatrists and psychologists recognised the role of the soul in influencing our mental and physical wellbeing. The burgeoning rates of stress and anxiety on this planet, particularly among young people, is symptomatic of another global pandemic, that of 'soul sickness.' The life force has been sucked out of many of us by bad food, screen addiction, prescription medication, drugs and alcohol. As we step up in vibration it is no longer possible to leave the soul out of the equation. It is time to restore it to its rightful place.

The Akashic Records can help with this. They carry the new energy that will make everything possible and provide a direct link to our soul and its wisdom. With intention, they can be used for all forms of healing and to create all that we dream of. They are a safe place for us to farewell the past and to step into our true soul nature. The Akashic Records or Akashic Field is a gift that has the power to alter the trajectory of humanity in miraculous ways.

Chapter 13

Into the Light

Change is at hand. 2020 was a watershed year. As I said to my husband at one point, 'The world is like a powder-keg waiting for a match.'

Fear was raging and society became increasingly polarized. Whereas in the past we kept quiet and were happy to sit on the fence, now our true feelings bubbled to the surface. Social and other media became a battle ground and did much to incite these divisions. The gap between generations, races and belief systems, in many places, became unbridgeable. We looked at the world with new eyes and with this 20/20 vision, the gaping wounds in society were easy to see. Nowhere was this more obvious than in the United States where the intensifying Covid crisis and the growing political divide, culminated in a close election which revealed even deeper rifts. We all know the pain that separation can cause. Our souls yearn for unity and evolution not separation and revolution. Our planet has been in crisis-mode.

As a recovering victim I know how easy it is to get pulled back into the mire of negativity, judgement, complaining and blame. In the game of life we all get dealt bad cards. Yes, we have suffered and some more than others, but I know from the Akashic Records that on a soul level we have chosen this. Instead of allowing our suffering to define us, we can use it to create a new identity. Some who experience a dark night of the soul stay stuck in the blackness. Others find meaning in their suffering. In the words of the poet and visionary, **Kahlil Gibran**, 'Out of suffering have emerged the strongest souls. The most massive characters are seared with scars.'

Last year I attended the unveiling of the grave headstone of the beautiful daughter of one of my oldest friends. The heartbreak of my friend and her husband was plain to see. At the age of nineteen, Sophia, was crushed by other students rushing to leave a party, after a rumour spread that campus wardens were on their way. My friends could have 'pointed the finger' in many directions, but from the outset they were determined to turn their tragedy into something positive. Woken at 3am, the first thing they did after flying south and viewing their daughter's body, was meet with the University Vice Chancellor. They discussed the support being provided for the other students and ways that they could help and then met up with Sophia's close friends. Together, they organised a gathering in the local gardens, where the young people affected could share their memories of Sophia and give each other support. After this they met with the young men who threw the party and comforted them and assured them they were not to blame. They also encouraged an immediate initiative to clean up the streets in the student quarter of the city.

More significantly, they have spearheaded 'The Sophia Charter.' This is a multi-agency agreement between various stakeholders including the University, Students' Association, Emergency Services, the local council and property owners and managers. Designed as a 'circle of support,' it aims to promote community responsibility and to enhance student wellbeing. My friends have also set up two scholarships, in perpetuity. One for a second-year female student in financial need, who excels in Maths and is community minded (like Sophia). The other for a second-year female student of any subject.

I have huge admiration and respect for my friends, who, while shouldering immense grief, have honoured their daughter's life by alchemizing their suffering into benevolent and constructive initiatives. This is tragic to magic in action.

Late last year my friend, Terumi did the same thing, if on a smaller scale. She was inconsolable at the sudden loss of her beloved dog, Almond. For someone who admits she keeps her feelings hidden, this opened the floodgates and she cried copious tears. Terumi had been practising hard for a dance competition at the end of the week. She channeled her emotions into her performance and won three awards.

In her words, 'Over the weekend I transformed the energy of grief and sorrow into love and gratitude. I have a renewed sense and vigour for life.'

Both of these friends experienced 'defining moments' which they did not let define them. They were able to create something positive out of their pain, which helped them to not only transcend it, but to inspire others.

Suffering is a crucible. As with everything that happens to us, how we react is our choice. What we focus on and engage with is critical. We can become victims and allow circumstances to drag us down or we can rise above them and help, not only ourselves but many more. This is how I have tried to deal with my daughter's illness and the Akashic Records have helped in innumerable ways.

From answering my questions and raising my vibration, to healing me and revealing my soul mission, they have given me hope and clarity. In her book, *Tears to Triumph*, Marianne Williamson wrote, 'the tiny crack of light you allow(ed) into your mind will expand into a miraculous blaze.' For me the Akashic Records have been that 'crack of light' and I know they are for others as well. We can't let our human pain define us because it is not who we are. We are so much more than that. We are souls in bodies with unlimited potential, especially at this time on Earth.

Information I have received in readings makes me excited for the future. On several occasions, when asking about a client's life purpose, I haven't been able to get a clear answer. Instead, I have received a sense of them doing something with advanced technology and knowledge, that I currently have no concept of. As we move into the Fifth Dimension it is becoming easier to reconnect with wisdom we had in other incarnations on Earth and elsewhere. We have all been through the process of ascension in other worlds, places and times. On some deep level, we remember this and we also remember and know about technology, inventions and practices that can alleviate suffering. This knowledge is innate and is stored in our cellular memory, which is getting easier to access as our vibration lifts, consciousness shifts and our non-coding DNA is activated. I believe there are lifeforms off planet that are also trying to help and that many of us are not only being reminded of what we already know, but are being impressed with new information that can help humanity.

When I opened Wendy's Akashic Record, I could see she was an Old Soul who was carrying the energy of trauma and deep feelings of self-blame and unworthiness. I saw that these feelings were closely connected to her immediate past life. She was a male nuclear physicist who helped to create the atom bombs which were dropped on Hiroshima and Nagasaki in 1945 and brought World War II to an end. The guilt and grief at what he had been part of, tainted the rest of this man's life. I saw him ending it in a mental health facility. Wendy's Akash revealed other lives of technological brilliance which included working in the Temples of Rejuvenation and Healing in Lemuria and Atlantis. In her last Atlantean lifetime, I saw that things had become unstuck when she had unwittingly shared her knowledge with those who then misused it and other technology, to destroy the civilisation.

In this life she has a passion for a new invention which has the potential to relieve the symptoms of anxiety and depression. She told me about new light technology that is currently in the experimental stage. With her past life experiences and credentials, she is the perfect person to introduce this more widely. That her mission has a redemptive aspect is perfect as well. On a soul level, having suffered through the last days of Atlantis and the destruction of two Japanese cities, as well as from depression at the end of her last lifetime, her life purpose resonated with us both. It was, I told her, 'to bring in the light (literally), in the form of a new technology which is life affirming, not life destroying.'

Margaret was one of my very first clients. Every year or two she has an email reading and in all of these she has asked about her life purpose which has been evolving over time. This is common as our thoughts create our reality and as a reflection of an elevating consciousness our life purpose can change. She has a rare soul lineage combining experience in **Alpha Centauri** with that of the Pleiades. In her first reading I told her:

You will develop and remember a technique which will help human beings to integrate and become whole by combining the heart and the head. You will combine the power of the mind of Alpha Centauri with the love and compassion of the Pleiades.

In the intervening years as I watched her go down different paths, a few doubts crept in. When asking about this I was told:

The timing has to be right. For many of us the vibration on the planet has to be ready for what we have to offer. Margaret is an advanced soul who has pioneering work to do.

The answers to her life purpose question, in the past, have been quite generalised so I was surprised and delighted in 2019, when I received more specific information:

There is the potential for you to develop a new way of holding the space for those who are here on Earth for the first time or whose souls originate in other parts of this galaxy and beyond. This involves consciously weaving strands of the energy you carry into their Merkabah, so they can feel stronger and become more resilient, balanced and integrated. You will thread your light into their field so it activates their own light and the truth of their soul. This process is one that you will eventually teach to others. It will help many people with 'labels' e.g. ADHD, ADD, Autism, Aspergers and also those suffering from anxiety and depression. You carry the same frequency as these souls. You have been preparing for this for a very long time. This work is now possible because of the vibration we have reached on Earth.

After giving Margaret some specific details of how she could work with her clients, I finished with:

The high frequency strands that you weave into them energetically will pull their bodies up to a higher vibration and instantly transmute anything that is discordant. In the final session you will be able to withdraw your energy from theirs as they will be fully activated.

Margaret's work is the work of the future. The time and the energy has to be right, not just for us personally, but for what we have to offer.

For years I joked that I didn't know what I wanted to be when I grew up. I worked as a mainstream teacher, with prison inmates and underprivileged teenagers and running my own parenting workshops. It was not until I reached the age of 53 that I began my current work. Looking back I can see that everything, up to that point and even those jobs that seemed to go nowhere, were preparing me for what I do now.

Our new Fifth Dimensional planet already exists energetically in what Patricia Cota-Robles calls 'the realms of cause.' This means it will soon be our reality. It is not a matter of if, but when, and will happen when our consciousness is high enough. In many ways Covid-19 has accelerated the process towards unity and cooperation. Every person on this planet has been affected. Governments have been forced to work together to share information about prevention, vaccine development and supply, and border and travel restrictions. Heart-based governments like that led by New Zealand's Jacinda Ardern, are forming. Consultative and humble, she is leading not in an old 'top down', hierarchical way but through a horizontal network of collective collaboration. Even though her party won a majority of votes in the 2020 election, she has given two members of the Green Party ministerial roles outside of Cabinet, because with their expertise in the areas of Climate Change, Biodiversity, and Family and Sexual Violence they are the best people for the job.

In the words of Ervin Laszlo and Kingsley Dennis in their book, *The Akashic Age*, 'there comes a time in a species development and growth when the necessity to collaborate, rather than compete, becomes not only an advantage, but an evolutionary imperative.' That time is now.

New energy structures are being created alongside the old. Many of these reflect the consciousness, creativity and problem-solving skills of the Millennials. This new economic model has been called 'the sharing economy.' Made possible by the internet it carries the energy of 'win win.' Uber, Airbnb and Fiverr are well-known examples. Initiatives like couchsurfing and crowdfunding have a similar vibe but have cut out the 'middle man.' In the area of finance, social lending sites are replacing banks. The ideas behind the 'Quantum Financial System', first mooted by Stephen Wiesner in the 1960s, are taking off. The pandemic has given new impetus to this trend. As Buckminster Fuller said, 'It is not about creating a new model, it is about making the old one obsolete.' These new energy enterprises are doing just that.

In the wake of Covid, businesses have had to adapt or die. Those that have survived, have responded to new needs and have repackaged what they offer to suit the altered social, economic and political circumstances. In my own case, after cancelling my in-person workshops, I was able to offer them online in a different format. This made my life easier and also meant that many people who couldn't attend them in person, now have access to the Akashic Records and some life-changing tools. I love working from home (my daily commute is down 14 stairs). The rest of the world has now discovered its joys. This and other forced changes are improving our quality of life and will make it easier to accept new innovations as we step fully into the Fifth Dimension. There is always a positive side to every crisis and the Covid situation is no exception.

On the threshold of a new world order everything is changing. Every business, organisation and human being, is literally being reconfigured. We are creating a new world through our collective intentions, one thought at a time. The higher our consciousness, the easier it will be to dismantle the structures that served us in the old energy, but have no place in the new.

❀

Victimhood is not attractive. It is an outdated construct. We can no longer abdicate responsibility or expect anyone else to rescue us. The Akashic Records are helping me to identify and to pull out the roots of the victimhood I have wallowed in during many of my incarnations. Like cars stuck in mud, in lifetime after lifetime we have returned to this default position. Our wheels have been spinning in self-pity for long enough. We no longer need to be sick and powerless. We can leave martyrdom behind forever. Our own miscreations have perpetuated the suffering we have experienced and come to expect. Now on the verge of an exciting new world it is time to raise our consciousness.

We are in the midst of a global reset and a new bandwidth of energy. Before we can embrace the future we must go to a place I call Zero Point. Quantum physicists and healers also use this term. (see Chapter 8). Zero Point is a place of unlimited potential and possibility. It is the moment of complete stillness where everything stops. It is what happens in the body before the profound healing of spontaneous remission can occur. It is the pause before the magic starts to happen. The Covid time has been called 'the great pause' and the pandemic has taken us to this place. It is a place of vulnerability, disempowerment and surrender – of no-time and of just being... of total peace and love... where everything has been stripped away and we can finally accept and understand our true nature.

The Akashic Records have helped me to make sense of our rapidly changing world. To get to Zero Point I had to take time out and the Akashic Records were my trusty companion. They helped me to ride the waves of fear, paranoia, self-righteousness and panic, to an island of calm and peace. As always, the Akashic Records have been a safe haven in a storm. We are all being taken to Zero Point in ways that are exclusive to us. What we feel and believe makes total sense in the light of our soul experiences on Earth (in this and other lifetimes). We all see the world through different lenses. My truth is different to your truth and that is okay. What's important is that we connect in with the truth of our soul. The energy of the Records has helped me to do this and has kept me positive and buoyant in these destabilising energies. For this I am truly grateful.

❉

Light has been pouring into the Earth in ever increasing quantities. It is affecting how we think, and this changed consciousness is creating a different world. Years ago I taught parents that our thoughts create our reality. Now I have scientific proof. Don't think you can't make a difference. What you think, feel, say and do affects every single person on Earth. Built on the bedrock of the collective consciousness of humanity, the world of the future will rise up from our thoughts and feelings. It is vitally important that what we express contains the signature energy of what we wish to experience.

Keeping our vibration high is a top priority. The energy we put out is returned to us. When we hurt somebody else, we are really hurting ourselves. The energetic imprint of every feeling of love or act of compassion goes into the matrix and affects the whole. What we are feeling in our hearts becomes part of the collective consciousness and alters the magnetic grids of the planet.

The more rapidly we can step out of fear, the sooner we will be able to create positive change. We are almost halfway through the twenty year transition phase, from 3D to 5D. It is intense. We are doing well but must keep our eyes on the prize. After thousands of years of suffering, it is finally within our grasp.

It was the arrival of high vibration energy at the precession of the equinoxes that kick-started our Ascension journey but it is our consciousness that will give it momentum. It has been a two-way process as the higher vibration has changed consciousness and vice versa. They work in tandem. The higher the vibration, the more quantum the energy becomes and the easier it is to shape our reality. We will get there. We are past the point of no return. We passed the crucial 21 December, 2012 marker and have successfully negotiated several more since. There is no precedent for where we are going. It is time to stop telling the same old story and to create a new one.

The Akashic Records have a foot in both camps. Like everything on this planet they are starting to reflect the new energy. As a conscientious record keeper of all that has gone before, they have charted the course of humanity through millennia of pain and suffering. They are also, however, a Fifth Dimensional repository of the new energy that is shaking up the planet and giving us a chance to create ourselves anew. They are a dynamic forcefield – a haven of 5D energy which we can utilise to uplift and bring us back into balance and wholeness. As the energy changes so will the potential and purposes of our Akash. It is vitally important as we move into uncharted waters that we hold the space for the rest of humanity – a place of unconditional love, compassion and non-judgement. The Akashic Records or Akashic Field can support us as we provide the greatest act of service, in the history of mankind to date.

❀

For years I waited for the 'right time' to write my first book. I told myself that when Mary left home, when Alice had fully recovered, when everything in my life was 'perfect' I would begin. One day I realised that was never going to happen, and I needed to make a start. Amidst the chaos that was my life at the time, I started to write. Immersed in the process, I began to heal. Eight years later, my life runs more smoothly, but there are different pressures. I am busier with work, giving readings, teaching and dealing with an avalanche of emails. It is difficult to make writing a priority as there is always something else to do.

Life will throw challenges our way and there will always be those with smaller dreams to drag us down. The energy, directly around us, from those we are closest to, is often the most turbulent. We can't let them deter us with their fear and negativity. My advice is to act like you are listening to their dreary portents, send them love and keep doing what your heart tells you to do. Tim Whild talks about the importance of 'rising above the storm zone.' Being in the energy of the Records helps keep me in the Fifth Dimension and above this maelstrom of fear and turmoil.

We are all initiates. For centuries the road of the lightworker has been littered with potholes and tests. There will be fewer to avoid in the future. We have to take the first step, believe in ourselves one hundred percent and keep on walking. As Adironnda, channelled by Marilyn Harper, a member of the Kryon team, has said 'Human beings would be horrified if they knew how close they came to fulfilling their dreams, when they gave up on them.'

Covid-19 has been a call to action for lightworkers. For all of you reading this book, the time is now! Don't let what you perceive as 'failure' in the past stop you from trying. Think of the lessons you learned and keep going.

When I was running my parenting courses between 1999 and 2013, I dreamed of training others to do this work. I had big plans that didn't come to fruition. The timing wasn't right. Now what I envisioned is coming to me in a form far better than I could have imagined. I am a teacher whose ideas and techniques are rippling out to many. It is the vision I have been holding, since 1998. This different version of my dream on a soul and human level suits me better. My dream has always been out there in the ethers. Once the energy is out there, it has to happen, and the way it manifests is often beyond our wildest imaginings.

I believe in magic. The quantum energy of the Records and of the New Earth will make our dreams come true even faster in the future. The light pouring into the planet is undeniable. It will take us way beyond any self-imposed limits into a miraculous new world that we are starting to sense. If we move forward with an open heart and mind the potentials for what we will be able to accomplish in the years ahead are huge.

❧

In the last few years Alice has come back to live with us on several occasions. She was with us for the seven weeks, in 2020, when our country shut down because of the coronavirus. Before that, she shared our home for short periods, in between living with others in rental accommodation, hospital and therapeutic communities.

In the early days of her illness this was stressful, as being at home was no barrier to self-harming attempts and may have on occasions precipitated them. We also had our younger daughter, Mary, to think of and as heart-breaking as it was, there were times we couldn't let Alice live with us. Having her at home and living close by in the last few years has been a gift. She left us at age eighteen and was admitted to adolescent and then to adult psychiatric wards. For the first four years of her illness she was mainly in mental health institutions or supported accommodation. She visited often and stayed some nights, but part of me never got over the sudden and dramatic way she disappeared from our home in 2007. Having her back as a grown woman, when after fourteen years she is showing positive signs of recovery, has been a blessing. I have nearly lost Alice so many times that seeing her as a mature and beautiful 32 year old is something for which I will always be grateful.

In 2018, Alice resumed the education that ended abruptly in her late teens. After a few false starts, she is working steadily towards a Bachelor of Arts degree and doing very well. She has started a blog and is devouring self-help books. The positive changes in the past two years cannot be put down to one thing. Alice's thirtieth birthday was a milestone and her university study has given her focus and structure. Regular sessions of EMDR therapy have helped with post-traumatic stress. She has started socialising more, sat and passed her driver's license and began a part-time job. At first it was two steps forward, one step back but since she met a beautiful man called Daniel at the end of 2019, the transformation has been miraculous. With Alice's permission I asked about their soul connection.

In her last life, I saw her as a sixteen year old girl, living happily in Czechoslovakia, until she was conscripted as a forced labourer by the Nazis. She eventually ended up in the brothel in Auschwitz, where she died. In that lifetime 'Daniel,' a friend of her fourteen year old brother, loved her from afar. In the years immediately after the war he went on a quest to find her. He eventually learned the truth and never recovered from the loss. Now they have been reunited. Both vegetarian, cat lovers, they laugh at the same jokes and even look alike. It is beautiful to see.

Of all the life choices, mental illness would be one of the most challenging. I have huge respect for Alice as a human being and as a soul. She has taught so much to so many. Because of Alice, permanent and lasting improvements have been made in the treatment of the mentally ill. She has been and still is my greatest teacher and inspiration. Her future looks bright. She has faced her demons and won. Every step she takes towards the light is helping others on this planet to move beyond fear and limitation. So far her life has symbolised the journey that all of humanity is taking… a journey from fear to love, from head to heart, from self-hatred to self-acceptance, from suffering to joy. In a very intense and concentrated way she is achieving what we are all doing on a collective level, leaving the trauma, pain and imprints of suffering gathered up during our many soul experiences on this planet, behind forever.

It has taken enormous courage and strength for Alice to turn her life around, especially given the heavy medication she is on. Recently with the support of Daniel and her psychiatrist she has begun to cut down on her nightly sleeping pills and other medications will follow.

Breaking news! As I was finishing this book Alice and Daniel became engaged. We now have a wedding to plan and I am wildly excited! Alice is getting married in 2022 when she will be 33. Thirty-three holds the golden christed energy of compassion and is a catalytic number for positive change, which is perfect. On a soul level of course, everything always is. Alice is no longer alone. She has the love of a decent, humble man and we are overjoyed. At the family engagement party that Marty and I hosted, the energy we all created (with Alice and Daniel at the centre), was magnetic. I invited all of our extended family and the turn-out was exceptional.

It was a night of explosive joy and family connection.

Alice is like a flower opening up to the sun. Her positive and uplifting social media posts are a blessing. She has fully embraced the totality of the human experience in one lifetime. Once in the grip of the darkness, she is now dancing in the light. Alice has experienced excruciating emotional pain in a way that no one deserves. Those close to her have felt that pain but now, at last, we can move out of the torture chamber and beyond suffering for ever. It is time for us all to embrace a grander vision of who we are. To leave the past behind, to see the good in everything and in everyone and to let the beautiful light of our soul selves and of a higher vibrational planet flow through our bodies and into our lives.

I have to pinch myself. I am in such a good place. Drama has gone from my life and I don't miss it. The Akashic Records have taught me that there is light at the end of the tunnel... that there are many gifts waiting for us when we wake up from our 'dark night' ... that in fact we have chosen our experiences to prepare us for our soul missions. I wouldn't be able to do my work without being the mother of a depressed and suicidal child, or my past life experiences that brought me into this one demoralised, defeated and desperate for redemption. I would not be able to do what I do without my family. I chose them and my life circumstances to give me the best chance of fulfilling my soul purpose.

My life is like a tapestry with many threads, each making its own contribution, all on some level consciously selected and interwoven to create the perfect image. No thread is there by chance, each has its place and has contributed to the overall picture. The Records have helped me to recognise and acknowledge the separate strands and to understand their significance. My life is by design, a conscious creation. It is an interactive process which I am choosing to participate in. I know, I have had many lifetimes where I have not taken this opportunity. I am proud of my creation so far.

We are all capable of producing our own masterpiece. We are 'masters' after all. The Akashic Records have helped me to remember that we are all divine sparks of the creative source and to accept and claim the mastery that is my birthright. They have helped me come to terms with the 'mixed bag' that can be our human existence, particularly, in these tumultuous times.

❧

The road to enlightenment has been paved with misery. The belief that suffering is a necessary part of the human condition has become part of our psyche. In many of our religious traditions, suffering and spiritual growth have been inextricably connected. Even those who have chosen to evolve rapidly, have usually believed the only way to do it is through crisis and pain. To Buddhists, experiencing the intensity of human heartache has been a necessary requirement for **nirvana**. When our human behaviours are not aligned with the wishes of our Higher Selves, the soul often stages an intervention to get us back on track. This 'wake-up call' has usually involved emotional and/or physical pain. As we become more closely connected to our soul this will happen less and less.

The soul doesn't feel our anguish. During our lifetimes of torment it has been a silent witness, a sentinel of hope. Whatever happens the integrity of the soul remains intact. In the words of Marianne Williamson, 'Your human self might be in hell right now, but your divine self is literally untouched by your suffering.'

It is time for us to invite the soul back into our lives. The incoming energy is making it easier for us to connect and the Akashic Records provide a direct link. Why should we have to suffer to come home to our true soul nature? Is it really necessary? I dream of a day when we won't need to be torn apart by grief to open up to the light. Can we become enlightened without pain? I believe this is possible and where humanity is heading. In his Kryon channels and his book of the same name, Lee Carroll has introduced us to 'The New Human' and some of the wondrous potentials for our future. In a Kryon class on the 'Twelve Layers of DNA,' in 2021, he said that our conscious awareness of what we are capable of is currently only 33% of what it could be. There is so much we don't know and so much more to learn. Our non-coding DNA holds the secret to life's mysteries and to a future that will be very different from our past.

As Christian teachings go, Jesus Christ came to Earth 2000 years ago and suffered for our sins. His behaviour and crucifixion introduced us to the concepts of redemption, repentance and forgiveness. He ushered in the Piscean age with his high frequency, golden vibration. As we move into the age of Aquarius, the 'second coming of Christ' is happening as many predicted. It is not, however, the arrival of another messiah, it is the 'be-coming' of a new human being. The human race in ascension status, here to activate its crystalline aspects and to anchor the Christ Consciousness vibration of love, hope and compassion on Earth. A new human, with enabled DNA, that is empowered and free and able to recognise and express the divinity within. A human being that has gone from tragic to magic and that no longer needs to suffer.

In the Records, we can connect with this golden christed energy and forge a close and enduring bond with our soul, so we can listen and respond to its voice and evolve, not in the brutal ways of the past, but through joy and grace.

As a species we have been busy integrating our shadow aspects. Now it is time to add our souls to the mix. If we are really serious about moving out of the darkness into the light, this transformation has to take place. Kryon talks of the 'meld' that happened for Lee Carroll after they had been working together for many years. There was such an exchange of energies that Kryon became Lee and vice versa. There was no difference. This 'meld' has made it easier for Lee to do his work.

I want my soul to become me and for me to become my soul. As I prepared for my first Level 3 workshop in 2020, I kept getting the message 'Get yourself out of the way.' With these words ringing in my ears and doing my best to keep my ego and fear at bay, I held the workshop and was amazed at what transpired for me and everyone present. With my soul in charge, everything was perfectly synchronised and coordinated.

Patricia Cota-Robles and other spiritual teachers refer to the soul as our 'I Am presence.' Others talk of our 'superconsciousness.' I have become aware of this part of us that is multidimensional and even grander than the human Higher Self. My inner knowing tells me that this is the piece we link in with when a soul merge takes place. This is what the Akashic Records have to say about it:

Our superconsciousness exists in the quantum field and consists of the Higher Selves of all of our soul aspects in all lifetimes, time frames and dimensions. It is like a bridge across time that pulls in the best of who we are. It is the sum total of the wisdom we have accrued in all of our soul experiences. We are just becoming aware of this magnificent version of ourselves and as the energy vibration lifts it will be easier to download its eternal wisdom.

The soul is the key to a future without suffering and the Akashic Records are a key to the soul. With the help of the Records we can live a soul-centred life. Working in partnership with our divine essence, it will be easier to live and express our truth and to trust and run with whatever life presents to us.

To quote Marianne Williamson, 'There is no room for darkness in a house that is filled with light' and 'A lamp must be plugged in to shed any light.' The Akashic Records and our soul selves can illuminate our path and provide the power source that will take us into the light.

The length of time it takes to move through the pandemic and other crises will depend on our level of consciousness. We can do it. According to one source it takes less than one half of 1% to reach critical mass and to turn things around. If our vibration and light quotients are high, we can vanquish the darkness and become midwives, birthing a new planet, where differences are accepted unconditionally – a place where all life forms are treated with respect, where love reigns supreme and we can fully express our divinity.

Atonement is defined in the dictionary as, 'making amends for a wrong or injury.' As we move into a new cycle of life on Earth the focus has been on cleaning up the mess and righting the wrongs of the past. Before we can become one, we have to become whole. The Akashic Records can help us to understand and integrate our subconscious selves from all of our lifetimes. Once this inner unity has been achieved, we will be able to welcome in our superconscious selves that are connected to all that is. This healing process of at-one-ment will usher in greater harmony and Unity Consciousness on this planet. According to Patricia Cota-Robles, in 2021, the template of Unity Consciousness is being anchored into the realms of cause.

Events on a global and local level, are bringing us together. Recently in a seaside town near my home, a situation occurred that has united and healed the hearts of many. A baby Orca whale became separated from his pod, was thrown onto rocks and found by a local teenager. He raised the alarm and for the next thirteen days the local community, supported by government agencies, Dr Ingrid Visser, a renowned whale expert, the people of New Zealand and many others, cared for him. The whole country held its breath, as Toa (the Māori word for strong), was nurtured and loved around the clock by volunteers. Other volunteers spent days scanning the coast for Toa's pod. The hope was that it would be found and he would be reunited with his mother. The winter weather was not cooperative and just as a pod had been spotted and the rain was clearing, Toa's condition deteriorated and he slipped quietly away. The daily reports and videos of Toa's antics melted the hearts of our nation. We were devastated at his death but much good has come out of it. He has been a force for unity, bringing together a diverse group of people. The local community, the **Tangata Whenua**, government conservation authorities and Dr Visser worked together tirelessly with the sole aim of keeping Toa alive. From the posts on Social Media, it is obvious that the shared experience with Toa, has been life changing for many. Ben, the sixteen year old who found him and hardly left his side, was completing a school assignment on Orcas when one landed (literally), at his feet. He now has plans to be a marine biologist and says the experience has shown him that 'humans are fundamentally good.' Dr Visser and her work have been in the spotlight (not before time) and people, the world over, now have a special heart connection. Toa is a gift that will carry us all forward.

From the 1820s, New Zealand participated in whaling operations that almost brought the species to extinction. The slaughter of these noble animals continued until 1964. Our coast line is littered with rusty pots that were used for boiling whale blubber. The treatment of Toa highlights the massive shift in consciousness in the last 150 years and gives me huge hope for the future.

We did not get the outcome we wanted but as a symbol of and catalyst for Unity Consciousness, Toa finished the job he came to do. Mission accomplished! Well done Toa. Well done.

The high vibration energy of the New Earth that exists in and around our bodies, in the magnetic grids of Earth, the cosmos and the Akashic Records is creating a soup of energy that is inter-dependent and magnanimous. Called the field or matrix, it is this loving and beneficent energy that will ultimately bring us together so there is no separation and we are one. The definition of the Sanskrit word Akasha is 'ether' and 'beyond matter.' The field is pure energy and so are we. With the help of the Akashic Records we can become one with the field. This oneness and unity is what we have to look forward to.

The Akashic Records are trending. Their time has come. It is my privilege to help get the word out. Having a soul perspective on life changes everything. Seeing our current lifetime, as a progression of many and knowing that there will always be another chance to get it right is comforting. The knowledge, that after this lifetime there will be more and that we can carry on our work if we choose, makes all the difference. Understanding, that our increasingly Fifth Dimensional world is connecting us more closely to source energy and the ability to be the creators of our own lives and to shape the future of this beautiful planet is also a game changer.

In a guided meditation I conducted for myself and a group of Level 3 students, we ventured into the future. A soul aspect of me living in 2250 appeared. He looked male but it was a bit hard to tell. His energy was beautiful and calming. I was thrilled when I saw that like me in this life, he was a History teacher. His curriculum was very different to the one I taught in the 1980s, however. He was teaching about the barbaric history of Planet Earth prior to 'The Shift.' We had a chat and he said he felt sorry for me and was concerned at how hard my life was. I feel like my life is fantastic now, but he was genuinely sympathetic. This loving exchange with my future self and the reassurance that things are going to get better, not just for me, but for all of us, made me very happy.

Knowing that the open-hearted and evolved souls who have incarnated in recent years, will soon be the stewards of Planet Earth also makes me happy. This story from my husband confirmed that the future of Earth is in good hands.

At our local park Marty watched a grandmother and her grand-daughter, who looked about three years old, walk up to a bridge. He heard the grandmother say to the little girl,

'A nasty old troll lives under that bridge.'

The child became fearful and scared and started to whimper. The grandmother laughed and smirked at her distress. The young girl went silent and paused... deep in thought. She looked her grandmother straight in the eye and said,

'There isn't a troll under that bridge. You're the troll.'

This gave me huge comfort. The new children of our planet won't let fear control and cripple them. They will stand their ground and speak their truth. They have too much light to let darkness defeat them.

❀

Earth is one of many sparks of light in the cosmos. Out there in the universe and multiverse, are other worlds seeded by the creative source, which also carry the light. Our planet is glowing more brightly by the day. We are all connected and contributing to the expanded radiance in the heavens. The ascension of Planet Earth will not only help all human beings but all forms of life in this galaxy and beyond.

The Akashic Records are being rewritten. Once a record of the pain from the past they now hold the glittering promise of a New Human, a New Earth and a human race that has moved beyond suffering. The Akashic Field holds the dazzling potential of our future as a species with an enhanced DNA capacity and reflects an upgraded consciousness which radiates out to the multiverse.

As we stand on the cusp of a new paradigm and a completely different world, I know that the human belief that we can only grow through suffering and pain can be extinguished forever. We have been through the fires of hell... have come from tragic... to magic. It is time to create heaven on Earth. We've got this!

Glossary

Agartha: A mythical land that is said to exist in the core of the Earth. It is sometimes called 'Hollow Earth.'

Akash: The term for the Akashic Records used by Kryon, who is channelled by Lee Carroll.

Akashic Template: The term Kryon gives to the energetic we hold in our bodies, on a cellular level, of our Akashic Record. (see Karmic Birth Template).

Alpha Centauri: One of the largest constellations in the Milky Way galaxy. It consists of three stars and is the closest star and planetary system to the sun.

Amygdala: Part of the limbic system in the temporal lobe of the brain. It is a repository of emotional memories and is often linked to fear and trauma.

Anatomically Modern Human: They appeared about 200,000 years ago and have a lighter skeleton than earlier human beings.

Ancestral Grid: An energetic magnetic grid that is part of the Gaia Grid (see below), that holds the wisdom and memories of our ancestors.

Aotearoa: The Māori name for New Zealand (translates as 'the land of the long, white cloud).

Arcturians: Benevolent beings from Arcturus who are supporting Earth's ascension process. They live on Arcturus, one of the brightest stars in the Milky Way and a part of the 'Bootes' constellation.

Ascended Masters: Souls who have lived human lives but who have reached enlightenment and no longer need to incarnate on this planet e.g. Jesus, The Buddha.

Ascension: A process currently occurring whereby Planet Earth and all of humanity are moving to a higher state of consciousness (From the Third Dimension to the Fifth).

Ashtar Command: An extra-terrestrial and intergalactic group responsible for the surveillance and protection of Planet Earth.

Atlantis: An ancient civilisation which allegedly existed in the Atlantic Ocean for a period spanning 240,000 years. According to Diana Cooper it was set up as a divine experiment to see if human beings in physical bodies could keep their connection to God/Source. Cooper says there were five Atlantean civilisations which were all destroyed when the balance of nature was upset. The final Atlantean civilisation ended between 11,000 and 9,600 BC, as a result of a cataclysm triggered by the human abuse of power (see Golden Atlantis).

Avatar: A divine teacher incarnated in a physical body on Earth.

Botafumeiro: A large metal container for burning incense.

Centromeres: Located in the central area of a chromosome.

Chromosome: A structure found inside the nucleus of a cell. Chromosomes are made up of proteins and DNA organised into genes. Each cell contains 23 pairs of chromosomes.

Climate Change: A long-term change in the weather patterns that have prevailed in the regional and global climates of Earth. This has resulted in global warming which is seriously impacting our biosphere (global ecosystem) and Earth's ability to sustain life.

Collective Consciousness: The beliefs, ideas, attitudes and know-ledge common to society at any given time. It is a direct reflection of human evolution and changes in response to it.

Consciousness Codes: A term used by US spiritual teacher, Patricia Cota-Robles to describe the cellular memories that the younger generation have of a higher level of consciousness. According to Patricia, these codes were activated in August 2018 and have reconnected many children and millennials with their purpose which is to assist in the creation of a more evolved human race.

Cortex: The part of the brain that is responsible for many higher-level processing functions such as perception, reasoning, conscious memory and thought.

Cro-magnon: The name given to the first early modern humans (Homo sapiens), to settle in Europe. They have continuously occupied the continent over the last 48,000 years and there is evidence of their existence from 210,000 years ago.

Crystal Children: Children who have been coming to Earth since the mid-1990s. They have soul origins in the stars but have lived some lifetimes on Earth. They are natural healers and have great wisdom and an easy-going and peace-loving temperament (see starseeds).

Darkness: The opposite of light. A blanket term given to human beings who have made the soul choice to learn lessons through power, control and ego and who are challenging the ascent of the human race into a higher vibration and consciousness.

Diamond Group: The name given by spiritual teacher, Judy Satori, to a diamond shaped cluster of twenty-two galaxies to which the Milky Way galaxy belongs. The beings that live in these galaxies are benevolent and are assisting Planet Earth with her ascension process.

Dis-ease: When our bodies are in a state of imbalance.

Dissociation: The process, where to protect ourselves following a traumatic event, we detach from our thoughts and feelings and let go of the memories from our conscious mind.

Dragons: Mythical beings from a higher vibration who are here to assist humanity to let go of the past and to prepare for the future. The increased vibration on Earth is enabling them to reconnect with and be of service to humanity.

Duality: Where there are two different but valid realities. Earth has been described as a place of 'duality.' Our freedom of choice has resulted in sharp contrasts such as darkness and light, good and evil, love and fear and our human potential to live as higher or less evolved versions of ourselves. Third Dimension Earth has been a place of duality and separation. The Fifth Dimension is a place of unity and oneness.

EFT (The emotional freedom technique): An alternative treatment for pain and emotional distress, which involves a combination of tapping the fingers lightly on meridians of the body while repeating a phrase e.g. For a fear of failure it could be, 'Although I have a fear of failure, I deeply and completely accept myself.' This restores an energetic balance to the body and relieves emotional distress.

Elementals: Mystical, multidimensional beings that are part of the Gaia Grid and are here to help humanity. They are called different things and in different places have been given names such fairies, pixies, elves, devas, leprechauns, gnomes and nature spirits.

Entanglement: (Sometimes called quantum entanglement). Where matter is connected to and influences the behaviour of other matter that is separated by distance and time.

Epigenetics: The study of how behaviours and environmental factors can influence the way our genes express.

Family of Origin: The family you grew up in. This includes parents, siblings and sometimes members of your extended family that lived with you during childhood.

Fifth Dimension: A dimension beyond time and space and

physical reality as we know it. It carries the high vibration energy that Earth is moving into during this time of Ascension or 'the shift of the ages.' The five dimensions are: height, length, width, time and quantum attributes connected to a higher consciousness.

Gaia: An alternative name for Mother Earth that comes from Greek mythology.

Gaia Grid: A magnetic grid that encircles the planet and holds the energetic memories of the Earth and all who have lived on her.

Golden Atlantis: The last civilization of Atlantis. It existed in approximately 10,000 BC and held a Fifth Dimensional spiritual vibration. This loving, heart-centred and technologically advanced society existed for 1500 years in the region of the Bahama, Azores and Canary Islands.

Gun Legislation: Immediately following the massacres at two Christchurch Mosques on March 15th, 2019, the New Zealand government banned military style, semi-automatic rifles. They gave the owners of these guns six months to hand them back in a government 'Buy Back' scheme. Later in 2019, a Gun Registry was set up to track the ownership of every legally owned firearm in the country.

Harmonic Concordance: The total lunar eclipse of November 8/9, 2003, where a rare alignment of six planets provided a portal for a rapid influx of high vibration energies. These contributed to the raising of consciousness and helped prepare Earth for the 2012 shift.

Harmonic Convergence: An extremely rare planetary alignment that occurred on the 16th and 17th of August, 1987. The sun, moon and six of the planets in our solar system formed a configuration which created a flow of positive energy from the stars. On these days thousands gathered globally, to meditate. It has been acknowledged as, not only a catalyst for many positive changes, but as the moment when the future ascension of human beings and of Planet Earth became likely.

HeartMath: A healing technique that brings people into a state of coherence and emotional balance which is helpful in dealing with stress and draining emotions such as anger and anxiety.

Indigo Children: The oldest generation of the 'New Children' who started coming to Earth in great numbers in the 1970s. They are sensitive, psychic and creative and are modern day 'warriors' with 'attitude.' They are here to expose and to break down old systems that are hypocritical and lack integrity (See starseeds).

Innate: Wisdom that exists in every cell of our body, is benevolent and knows what is best for us. It responds directly to our consciousness and instructions and has quantum attributes that make healing on all levels possible.

Inner Child: A subpersonality or part of us that represents our unmet childhood needs and which manifests as emotional intensity and child-like behaviour.

Junk: A Chinese sailboat of unknown ancient origin with up to six masts made of linen panels or bamboo matting.

Kahlil Gibran: 1883-1931. A Lebanese-American writer, philosopher and visual artist who wrote the best-selling book, *The Prophet*.

Karmic Birth Template: The term, given by Patricia Cota-Robles, to the energetic we bring into each lifetime from past lives and other soul experiences.

Khmer Rouge: The name given to the followers of the brutal, communist, military regime led by Pol Pot who ruled Cambodia between 1975-1979. They committed genocide and were responsible for an estimated 1.5-2 million deaths.

Kryon: A collective soul energy from the stars, which gives channelled messages of support and empowerment to humanity as we navigate the ascension process. There are several Kryon channels. Lee Carroll was the first to bring these messages through in 1989 (www.kryon.com).

Lemuria: A great southern continent that allegedly existed in the Southern Hemisphere before Atlantis (from 50,000 until 15,000 years ago). Lemuria was peopled by starseeds from the Pleiades (**Lemurians**), who arrived approximately 50,000 years ago and brought their wisdom and healing abilities with them. They taught these and their core truths to many generations who took them to different parts of the planet after Lemuria (modern day Hawaii), sank beneath the waves, 15,000 years ago. These (mainly), pleiadian teachings are now being remembered and drawn upon as we co-create a planet of higher consciousness.

Light Language: Multidimensional language from the stars. It is high vibrational and profoundly healing. It carries encodings of sound and light, responds to intention and works with the quantum DNA of the individual.

Lightworker: Those with a spiritual awareness who are working to heal and to raise the consciousness of humanity.

Manifestation: The idea that you can attract what you want in your life by focusing your thoughts and emotions on a personal desire or goal.

Māori: The indigenous people of New Zealand, who came from the eastern Polynesian islands, between approximately 1320 and 1350.

Masuru Emoto: A Japanese scientific researcher and writer who conducted experiments that proved that water can be affected/ programmed by consciousness. His book 'The Hidden Messages in Water,' was a NY Times bestseller. He died in 2014.

Matariki: The name the Māori, the indigenous people of New Zealand, gave to the star cluster of the Pleiades. It is also the name for the Māori New Year which is celebrated in mid-Winter when the stars are shining their brightest.

Mayans: The name given to a diverse group of indigenous people who lived from 2000 BC to 1519 in present day Mexico, Belize, Guatemala, El Salvador and Honduras. They created a sophisticated and complex civilisation.

Meridians: Energetic pathways in the body that allow for the circulation of the lifeforce throughout.

Merkabah: The energy field around our body. It is approximately eight metres wide and holds the energy of our feelings and beliefs as well as our non-coding DNA.

Millennials: The name given to those who were born (approximately), between 1981 and 1996.

New Children: (Rainbow and Crystal). Also called 'The Children'. The children that have been born since approximately 2000 AD. Many are new souls to this planet and are here to assist in the planetary ascension process (See starseeds).

New Scientists: Scientists who recognise the importance of the new (quantum) energy and whose research is dedicated to revealing its attributes and abilities e.g. Gregg Braden, Bruce Lipton, Lynne Mc Taggart, Dr Todd Overkaitys.

Nirvana: In Buddhist belief, a state of perfect happiness and peace where no human suffering exists.

Nodes and the Nulls: A system of twelve pairs of time capsules placed by the Pleiadians, within the crystalline grid at 24 power spots around the planet. The plan was that if, and when the consciousness of humanity reached the point where ascension was assured, they would be activated. Since the 21st of December, 2012 all of these have been recognised and are now active. The nodes release the lower vibrational energies of the past e.g. drama, fear, suffering. The nulls are bringing in the consciousness of the future and the wisdom and light from the stars which will help us to co-create a new ascended planet. Some of these matching pairs are: Mt Aoraki (NZ) and the Ural Mountains in Russia, Mt Shasta and Mt Ararat in Turkey, Uluru and Mt Logan in Canada, Glastonbury and Gunnbjorn Fjeld in Greenland.

Old Boys' Club: The name given by author, Chris Wilson to describe those who have possessed the power and wealth on this planet and to further their own ends have misused it, perpetuating the suffering of many.

Old Souls: Those who have had many lives over thousands of years on Earth. They came from the stars and agreed to take part in an experiment on this planet which gave their soul a rare opportunity to experience freedom of choice and the full range of emotions. Old Souls have retained a soul connection to elsewhere in the cosmos but have primarily been part of a process of reincarnation of birth and rebirth on Planet Earth. They have experienced both dark and light, been caught up in the energetic of karma and have returned to this planet repeatedly. They have accumulated much wisdom and many are the spiritual teachers and healers that have been at the forefront of the ascension process.

Partisan: The name given to a member of resistance groups formed in Europe during World War II, which actively opposed the rule of foreign armies occupying their countries.

Pleiadian: A being of extra-terrestrial origin from the star cluster, The Pleiades.

Precession of the Equinoxes: The name given to the 26,000 years it takes for the constellations to rotate around the Earth. The 21st of December, 2012 marked the end of a 26,000 year cycle. On that day Planet Earth lined up with the galactic core of the Milky Way.

Quantum Physics: Scientific discovery that explains the interaction between matter and energy. It has relevance not just to 'Physics' but to Biology and Chemistry as well.

Rainbow Children: Highly evolved souls who have been born on Earth since the year 2000. They are here to serve and to help change and upgrade our consciousness (See starseeds).

Reiki: A Japanese alternative healing method where practitioners, as conduits of healing energy and through non-invasive touch, work to relieve and cure the symptoms of physical and emotional imbalances in others.

Retrocausality: Going backwards in time before an event or experience to try to change the outcome.

Saint Germain (St Germain): An Ascended Master, the chohan (lord) of the Seventh Ray, who works with his violet flame of transmutation to free Earth and its inhabitants from limitation and fear.

Schumann Resonance: The name given to the level of electro-magnetic radiation in the Earth's ionosphere. These waves of electricity create a pulsation of energy that can be measured called the Schumann Resonance. Its variations are influenced by energy pouring in from off-planet and by the consciousness and thoughtforms of those living on the planet.

Sirians: Beings from the star system Sirius.

Spectrum: A name given to those who display cognitive and behavioural 'disorders' which have become more common in the last 30 years. 'On the spectrum' was first coined for autism but is now used to describe children with ADD (Attention Deficit Disorder), ADHD (Attention Deficit Hyperactivity Disorder), Asperger syndrome and other similar behaviours.

Star Nations: The name given to the other Christed civilisations (mostly in the Milky Way Galaxy), who have representatives on the Galactic Council and are assisting Earth with her ascension process. These include the Pleiades, Sirius B, Arcturus, Lyra, Mintaka Orion, Vega, Andromeda, Antares and Aldebaran.

Starseeds: The name given to those whose souls originated in other parts of our galaxy and in neighbouring galaxies, who agreed to be on Earth as we raise our consciousness. The first group of starseeds came to Earth approximately 100,000 years ago. There was a huge wave at the beginning of Lemuria and in the last 50 years many more have come to Earth to assist in the Ascension process – the so-called Indigo, Crystal and Rainbow Children. The Rainbow Children are the purest of modern starseeds, having never lived on Earth before.

Subpersonalities: Aspects of the human personality that split off as a result of trauma. These unintegrated aspects can sabotage our growth and progress.

Ta Moko: The permanent marking or tattoo as traditionally practised by the Māori, the indigenous people of New Zealand.

Tangata whenua: The Māori term for 'people of the land.' It can refer to the members of a local community or to the original inhabitants of New Zealand as a whole.

Telomere: The caps at the end of each strand of DNA that protect the end of a chromosome.

The Children: (see Rainbow Children).

The Pleiades: A star cluster in the Milky Way. Sometimes called 'The Seven Sisters,' it can be easily seen with the naked eye. The Pleiades was the last star system in the Milky Way to go through the ascension process (approximately two million years ago). The Pleiades is part of Greek mythology and is also a significant part of the creation story of many of the indigenous peoples of the world. The pleiadians are our star parents and are assisting Earth in the transition from a Third Dimensional to a Fifth Dimensional planet.

The Resistance: (see partisan). The collective name given to the secretive, 'underground' groups that sprang up in German occupied countries in World War II.

Theta Healing: The registered trademark for a healing method, developed by Vianna Stibal in 1995, where a client is taken into a meditative or 'theta' brainwave state and assisted to release limiting beliefs and programming.

Third eye: An energetic opening on our forehead. It is one of the chakras or energetic power points on our body. Those who have an activated third eye have a connection with the spiritual realms which can take them into other dimensions and connect them with esoteric information that is not accessible or obvious to most people.

Third Dimension: The reality humanity has lived in for thousands of years on Earth. It is the lowest vibration in the Milky Way galaxy and is characterised by ego, conflict and fear. The three dimensions are height, width and depth.

Toning: A form of vocal expression which utilises the natural voice to express a range of sounds that are unique to the individual and come from an intuitive, soul space. Toning is increasingly being used by musical therapists and sound healers.

Tui: A native bird of New Zealand that has a small tuft of white feathers at its neck and a small white wing patch.

Unicorns: A legendary creature that looks like a horse but which has a spiralling horn of light coming out from its forehead. In recent years, as the vibration has lifted on Earth, these etheric beings have returned to assist in transmuting the darkness and heavy energy of the Third Dimension. They spread joy and light to all and are particularly close to children.

Unity Consciousness: The idea that everything is connected and that we are all one. We are not separated by ideological, physical, gender or any other barriers but connected through our thoughts and feelings or consciousness. Underlying Unity Consciousness are high-minded ideals and heart-based emotions for the highest good of all. Unity Consciousness is diametrically opposed to the thoughtforms of lack and separation and of competition and greed which have characterised human life in the Third Dimension. Unity Consciousness espouses cooperation, collaboration, co-creation and compassion and the energetic of the Fifth and higher dimensions. It is what humanity is aspiring to and where we are heading in the ascension process on Earth.

Violet Flame: An ascension tool, gifted to humanity by St Germain, to assist us to free the planet and its inhabitants from the imprints of limitation and fear. It can be invoked to remove discordant and lower vibrational energy in people and places.

Websites of interest

- www.kryon.com
- www.lynnemctaggart.com
- www.greggbraden.com
- www.drtoddo.com
- www.unityfieldhealing.com
- www.terrimorehu.com
- www.brucelipton.com
- www.arohafamilyconstellations.co.nz
- www.judysatori.com
- www.goodvibrationssoundtherapy.co.nz
- www.adironndaspiritualhealer.com

Bibliography

Bartlett Richard, Matrix Energetics, Beyond Words, 2007

Bartlett Richard, The Physics of Miracles, Beyond Words, 2009

Braden Gregg, Human by Design, *From evolution by chance to transformation by choice*, Hay House, 2017

Braden Gregg, The Divine Matrix, *Bridging time, space, miracles and belief*, Hay House, 2007

Bradshaw John, Homecoming: *Reclaiming and Healing Your Inner Child*, Bantum, 1992

Chopra Deepak, Synchro Destiny, *Harnessing the Infinite Power of Coincidence to Create Miracles*, 2005

Chopra Deepak, Quantum Healing, *Exploring the Frontiers of Mind Body Medicine*, Bantam Books, 1989

Cooper Diana and Hutton Shaaron, Discover Atlantis, *A Guide to Reclaiming the Wisdom of the Ancients*, Findhorn Press, 2005

Covey Stephen, Sandra M Covey, The Seven Habits of Highly Effective Families, *Building a Beautiful Family Culture in a Turbulent World*, Griffin, 2007

Dyer Dr Wayne W, Living an Inspired Life, *Your Ultimate Calling*, Hay House Inc, 2006

Gordon Richard, Duffield Chris, Vickie Wickhorst, *Quantum Touch 2.0, The New Human*, North Atlantic Books, 2013

Guirdham Arthur, The Great Heresy, *The History and Beliefs of the Cathars*, Saffron Walden, The CW Daniel Company Limited, 1993

Guirdham Arthur, We Are One Another, *Astounding evidence of group reincarnation*, 1991 Saffron Walden, The CW Daniel Company Limited, 1991

Hay Louise, You Can Heal Your Life, Hay House, 1984.

Herman Judith, Trauma and Recovery, *The Aftermath of Violence – From Domestic Abuse to Political Terror*, Basic Books, 1992, 1997, 2015.

Howe Linda, Healing through the Akashic Records, *Using the Power of your Sacred Wounds to Discover your Soul's Perfection*, Sounds True Inc, 2016

Kehoe John, Quantum Warrior, *The Future of the Mind*, Zoetic Inc, 2011

Kryon, The New Human, *The Evolution of Humanity*, The Kryon Writings, Inc, 2017

Kryon, The Twelve Layers of DNA: *an esoteric study of the Mastery within*, Platinum Publishing House, 2010

Laszlo Ervin and Kingsley Dennis, Dawn of the Akashic Age, *New Consciousness, Quantum Resonance and the Future of the World*, Inner Traditions, 2013

Levine Peter, Healing Trauma, *A Pioneering Program for Restoring the Wisdom of Your Body*, Sounds True, 2008

Lipton Bruce, The Biology of Belief, *Unleashing the Power of Consciousness, Matter & Miracles*, Hay House, UK, Ltd, 2015

McTaggart Lynne, The Field, *The Quest for the Secret Force of the Universe*, Harper Collins, 2008

McTaggart Lynne, The Power of Eight, *Harnessing the Miraculous Energies of a Small Group to Heal Others, Your Life, and the World*, Atria Books 2017

Morehu Terri Lyn, The Only Way Out Is In, *From the Age of Unity Series*, Balboa Press, 2019

Muranyi Monika, The Human Akash, *A discovery of the blueprint within*, Ariane Books, 2014

Muranyi Monika, The Human Soul Revealed, *Unlocking the Mysteries from Beyond*, Ariane Books, 2015

Perry Bruce D, and Oprah Winfrey, What Happened To You, *Conversations on Trauma, Resilience and Healing*, Flatiron Books, 2021

Rothschild Babette, The Body Remembers, Volume 2, *Revolutionizing Trauma Treatment*, W.W Norton and Company, 2017

Van der Kolk, Bessel, The Body Keeps the Score, *Brain, mind and Body in the Healing of Trauma*, Penguin Press, 2015

Vowless Sylvia, QSM, The Miracle Effect, *Four Steps to Living Heaven on Earth Every Day*, Balboa Press, 2016

Williamson Marianne, Tears to Triumph, *The Spiritual Journey from Suffering to Enlightenment*, Harper One 2016

Wolynn Mark, It Didn't Start with You, *How Inherited Family Trauma shapes who we are and How to end the cycle*, Viking 2016

Chris Wilson

Chris Wilson lives in Wellington, New Zealand with her husband Martin. She has three adult children. Chris has a teaching diploma and coaching qualifications as well as a Master of Arts (Hons), degree in History. Her career has taken her from mainstream secondary schools to prisons, social work, alternative education, public speaking and running parenting and spiritual workshops.

Since 2011 she has been working in the Akashic Records, the energetic record of every experience we have ever had as souls on Earth. In one-on-one sessions she passes on soul information which:

- helps clients to see the bigger picture of their lives and to understand their soul mission and journey, **and**
- facilitates soul healing to remove energetic imprints and residue of past and current life trauma which is causing emotional and /or physical pain and holding her clients back.

In her Level 1, 2 and 3 workshops in New Zealand and Australia, Chris has taught many others her simple methods for accessing the Records and facilitating deep soul healing. For those unable to learn with Chris, in person, she offers an online Level 1 course and group Zoom classes.

A common thread in Chris's working life has been the empowerment of others by promoting self-awareness and acceptance and facilitating healing from within. Since she learned to access the Akashic Records she has been able to take her service work to a new level by helping others to understand their lives from a soul perspective.

Connect with Chris

- www.akashicreadingsnz.com.
  www.themagicoftheakashicrecords.com
- Facebook page: Chris Wilson-The Magic of the Akashic Records.
- Instagram: The Magic of the Akashic Records.
- chrisjwilson58@outlook.com

Lightning Source UK Ltd.
Milton Keynes UK
UKHW021228270922
409522UK00007B/1494